BASC
Guide to Shooting Game

Also by Michael Yardley and published by Quiller Publishing

Gunfitting 2nd Edn. (Swan Hill Press)
The Shotgun: A Shooting Instructor's Handbook. (The Sportsman's Press)

BASC
Guide to
Shooting Game

MICHAEL YARDLEY

SWAN·HILL
PRESS

DEDICATION

For my young guns – Harry and Jamie and possibly Elizabeth – not to mention Alexandra who has the strength of spirit to prefer tennis

Copyright © 2007 Michael Yardley

First published in the UK in 2007
by Swan Hill Press, an imprint of Quiller Publishing Ltd

British Library Cataloguing-in-Publication Data
   A catalogue record for this book
   is available from the British Library

ISBN 978 1 904057 97 0

Printed in Singapore by Stamford Press

Swan Hill Press

An imprint of Quiller Publishing Ltd
Wykey House, Wykey, Shrewsbury, SY4 1JA
Tel: 01939 261616 Fax: 01939 261606
E-mail: info@quillerbooks.com
Website: www.countrybooksdirect.com

ACKNOWLEDGEMENTS

The historical and technical sections of this book have grown from a series of articles (written with a larger volume in mind) that first appeared in the weekly magazine *Shooting Times* some years ago. Julian Murray-Evans, the former editor of that well-known periodical, was an early inspiration. There are others to whom I owe special thanks. James Marchington has helped greatly on the photographic front. Jack Montgomery, Dig Hadoke, Pat Farey, Paul Roberts, Alan Rhone, Vic Chapman, and Andy Riva are constant friends and reliable advisers (in this and many other projects). Wes Stanton has the power to motivate, amuse and analyse, and volunteered, most kindly, to edit an early draft of this work.

I would also like to thank all those with whom I have discussed the fine points of technique over the years – my knowledge has grown enormously through this interaction – and, most importantly, my students, young and old, many of whom have become friends and whose feedback has been invaluable in developing and improving the methods discussed here. My specific role of honour includes:

Jonathan Young
Will Hetherington
Charlie Jacobi
John Swift, Christopher Graffius, Jeffrey Olstead, Mike Eveleigh and Ian Danby of BASC
Roger Hurley, Brian Jackson and Peter Boden of Lyalvale (Express Cartridges)
Russell Wilkin, Steve Denny, Chris Bird, Andrew Perkins, Roland Wild, John Harding and Ken Davies (recently retired) of Holland & Holland
Richard Purdey, Nigel Beaumont, David Maynard, and the shop and factory staff of James Purdey
Steve Murray
Karl Waktare, Robert Frampton, Bob Bigwood, Emma Covington-Cross, Mark Course, Malcolm Grendon and Paul Lewry of GMK
David Becker
John Resteghini
Bernard Cole
Sally Traverse-Healey and Alastair Phillips of William Evans
Matt Hunt
Kerri Anne, 'Trigger' and all the team at E.J. Churchill
Roger Hancox and Bill Harding of the Birmingham Proof House
Andrew Litt
Bob Pitcher (now retired as Master of the London Proof House)
Michael White, Jeff Darbon and the Staff of the London Proof House
Chris Potter

Peter Croft
Sam Grice
Felix Appelbe
Mike Ladd
Mike Aldis
Phil and Will Beesley
Stuart Ogden
Ian Cawthorne
Mike Barnes
David Bontoft of Hull Cartridges
Andy Young, David Peel, and Rupert Haynes of BWM Arms
Alan, Michael and David Rose and Jonathan Irby of the West London Shooting
School
Bill Blacker
Nigel Teague
Chris Symonds
Tony Kennedy
Richard Kaminski and sons
Mike Hurney, Julie Comerford and Terry Blackman of Webley Ltd
Peter Jones
Roger Bryan
Andy Castle
Sgt Major (rtd) John Kenny
Robin Knowles
Fred Ward
Paddy Byrne
David Williams
John Egan
John Batley of the Gun Trade Association
Mike Meggison
David Hilton
Fred Robinson
Rebecca Hawtrey
Pam Dorrington
Dawn Essex-Dalton
Carolyn Longbottom

In the United States, Jack Montgomery as mentioned above is a close and generous friend and knowledgeable hunting companion. Others who have embarrassed me with their hospitality on the other side of the great pond include: Chuck Gomulka, Scott Blauvelt, Colonel Glen Baker, and, not least, Roy, Sally and Raz Sisler of 'Hunting Hills' in Western PA. In South Africa, Russell and Abigail Keeny, Jeff Smith, Bryn Thomas, Annette and Grenville Dunbar and Lilly and Bruce Wentzel have also been great hosts. Finally, there are my regular shooting companions at home: Peter Jackson, Paul Payne, Shirley Payne and Alec Birchall. Bless 'em all. These *are* our Golden Days boys (and girl) and don't forget it!

CONTENTS

FOREWORD

Whilst it could be argued that it would have been relevant for the BASC to endorse a book expounding all the fundamentals of shotguns and shooting for sport, at any time of the organisation's long history, it is certainly appropriate now. The interest in all forms of shotgun shooting has never been more popular with greater opportunity for so many to participate. Clay target clubs and grounds are within easy reach of any location and so not only is there every opportunity to practise or compete in competitions at any level but well trained, experienced instructors are able to introduce newcomers to the sport or offer good coaching to the more experienced whether as clay or game shot.

Game shooting is itself available to more people than ever before. A hundred years ago it was only those privileged to own estates where those invited were the friends of the owners or other landowners with whom shooting was reciprocated. Later syndicate shooting shared sport on an estate and only comparatively recently has the 'let day' become the norm for many farms and estates to welcome teams of guns who enjoy shooting together. Shooting is available to all from a modest walked-up day to a larger scale traditional double gun event. As with cars or restaurants you get what you can afford to choose to pay for. In addition there are more opportunities for people to enjoy pigeon shooting or wildfowling at no, or very little cost at all. This book is therefore well timed to bring together information, fact, both scientific and from experience, of all aspects of the shotgun and its safe use.

Michael Yardley is a great authority on every element of the shotgun and the technique of shooting. His qualifications and experience on weaponry and its use is second to none. However, these qualities alone could lead to a book of dry facts but the author has other very important attributes to share. Not only is he an excellent shot but he is also a brilliant coach and two of his earlier books – *Positive Shooting* and *The Shotgun: A Shooting Instructor's Handbook* cannot help but be of interest. Importantly, what lifts this book onto another plane is Michael Yardley's interest in the psychology of shooting and the part the mind has to play in producing a consistently good performance that connects this book to the reader. There is no shortcut to sound shooting technique but to lift the performance of an individual to the next level is where the mind comes in. After all why do we enjoy shooting at all if it is not related to the pleasure we get in using a gun. At its peak Michael Yardley refers to being in the 'flow'. This being in the 'zone' is a Zen-like state when mind, muscle, body and spirit are as one and a state at which one knows the next shot is going to be successful. On those occasions there is no doubt or question: natural coordination just makes it happen almost like an out of body experience. There is no recipe but this book has all the clues and advice to help you make it happen.

Michael Yardley has drawn together well-researched information on all topics of the shotgun and its use. He writes in a 'no nonsense' style to the point and without waffle. In fact as he titles his style 'Positive Shooting' so is his treatment of every chapter. He sees, thinks and writes clearly and succinctly, it is an authoritative tome.

Whilst of importance to anyone coming into the sport this book is really for the experienced shot: the backbone membership of the BASC as well as any regular shots who are not but should be members!

There is a fascinating history of shooting itself which briefly gives the background to all that has led to the sport, attitudes and enjoyment of shooting today.

There is a constant message throughout the book of the importance of SAFETY at all times. This point is comprehensively emphasised to a point the reader may find excessive. However this book could be seen as a day out with one's gun during which safety is a vital and constant vigil. The clay shooting world has a very good safety record because rules are quite rightly very strict. Game and other forms of shooting have not at times got such a clean bill of health. This is partly due to the fact that only loaded guns can cause accidents and clay shooters only have their guns actively with cartridges in the breech for a short time before shots are taken. At all other times their guns are unloaded, either open or in slips. The game, pigeon shot or wildfowler has his gun loaded for prolonged periods of the day in anticipation of a shot at an unknown moment. In 'rough' or 'walked-up' shooting the danger is compounded by a constant moving of position relative to others in the field. Therefore SAFETY is an issue at ALL times and rightly it is emphasised throughout this book.

Shooting technique though condensed to relevant chapters is expounded with great clarity. Michael Yardley has distilled all the elements that comprise a successful shot. These include a no nonsense gunfitting section, clear instruction on the importance of good footwork culminating in correct gun mounting. Emphasis on the movement of the whole body and importance of the left hand (in right-handed shooters) all being an integral part of a successful shot.

The mental attitude of the shooter links the significance of a personal shooting routine to concentration and focus which then builds confidence from success. Michael Yardley advocates practice to fine-tune points of technique and so enable the shooter to be disciplined whilst in his comfort zone; calm but alert, taking pleasure in style.

There is an extensive section on the shotgun, its history, development, design and most appropriate choice for the individual, and recommendation on how best to decide this. An interesting section follows on how to purchase, including the pros and cons of buying at auction.

The same good advice is given on modern cartridges, their capabilities and suitability for different guns and circumstances. Gun cleaning too is dealt with as a military procedure: a simple, clear explanation of how to maintain your gun in good working order.

My own passion for pigeon shooting meant I was particularly interested in the section on this subject. An important part of this sport is that successful reconnaissance and fieldcraft is more valuable than any amount of gizmos or car full of kit. The secret is to be in the right place at the right time.

Shooting is better managed today than at any time in history. Organisations representing our sport are rightly ensuring that self-regulation is the way to maintain our standards of gun safety and use, our ethics, attitude and respect for our quarry. At last it is being acknowledged that the shooting fraternity is contributing so much to conservation of all wildlife and the diversity of habitats that enrich the environment. Much of the beauty of our landscape is of woods, hedges, ponds and lakes created and maintained by those passionate about shooting. The sport contributes enormously to rural employment which helps maintain a living landscape. All involved in shooting have much to be proud of and every reason to hold our heads high as important guardians of the countryside, its wildlife and its beauty.

This book is a big rock in the solid foundation of shooting by its help to every boy, girl, man or woman who is the individual with an interest and passion for the sport without whose support there would be no BASC or any other organisation that can represent the shooting interest and voice its importance to media and politicians. Congratulations to Michael Yardley on this book and the BASC on this initiative.

Will Garfit

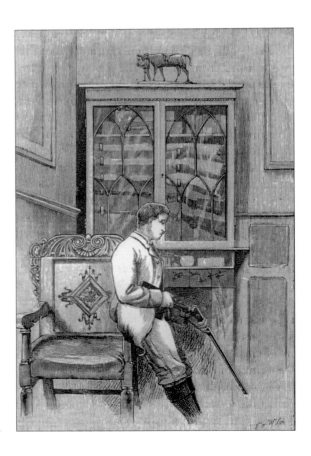

INTRODUCTION

Shooters come in two basic varieties in my experience – 'thinkers' and 'feelers'. The thinkers want to analyse and understand every aspect of their shooting (and can sometimes get themselves into a fearful muddle as a result). The feelers are not much bothered with theory or analysis and just want to get on with the job – good or bad results ensuing. Typically, thinkers need to be directed to think about *the right stuff*. They must also learn to feel more (i.e. to learn to trust themselves more and let the inner, unconscious, self take charge on some occasions). The feelers, on the other hand, with the exception of a few very gifted individuals, need to develop their *understanding* of what they do – without getting over-complicated – and not just trust to blind luck and natural prowess.

This book is intended for both groups. I suspect, however, it is destined to be bought by the thinkers and given to the feelers via Christmas stockings and similar. I hope that it will be put to good use by all those who acquire it. The intention, historical anecdote apart, is to encourage the naturally thoughtful to focus on the things that really matter and, in so doing, to prevent them from falling victim to, or extract them from, that classic, paralysing, shooting malady – *ballistic thrombosis*. This debilitating condition may be defined as the neurotic consideration of technical impedimenta and eccentric theory (such as the proposition that everyone should shoot with No. 3 shot, 14¾ bore guns or 25-inch barrels).

I hope a methodical consideration of the central sections of this book – those that relate to safety and shooting technique – will cause readers to ruminate upon what they do, don't do, and should do a little more than they might otherwise. The reward for this will be deeper understanding of their shooting technique (and that of others), and, with it, a remedy for seemingly inexplicable and frustrating events such as 'bad days'.

Once the subtleties are revealed – and no apologies are made for considering shooting in some detail in the pages that follow – shooting may become both science and art. The ultimate goal is to make the Perfect Shot. In it, everything comes together towards the same end. An observer can see it is *right* before the trigger is pulled. You can feel it is right without knowing the result. Nothing is out of place. You know it when it happens. It is not only efficient, elegant and apparently effortless, it is beautiful to watch and immensely satisfying to experience. You are *connected*.

If all this sounds a bit lofty or esoteric, let me state that good shooting is not just a question of whether you bag the bird or not, but *how* you do it. What used to be called 'shooting form' really is important. It implies self-respect, a respect for the quarry, and for our great sporting traditions. It also promotes consistency, and therefore more humane harvesting of game. If you shoot, why not determine to shoot well? This attitude will not only motivate you to improve your performance in the field, but it will lead you to a greater understanding of yourself and the environment in which you pursue your sport.

In a materialistic age, we seem too focused on crude result in the context of shooting: this becomes how many birds, rather than how many 'good birds', shot well. Some more pragmatic readers may relate better to a 'mission statement' than considerations of Zenish philosophy or old world sporting credo. For them, let me state simply that the aim of this work is to make you a better live quarry shot through improved understanding of precisely *what* you ought to be doing and precisely *when* you ought to be doing it. From this increased awareness, the goal is to create good muscular, mental and visual habits.

Consistent shooting requires that everything is in balance, that you are relaxed but alert, with all mental and physical focus on the bird and nothing but the bird.

Now, a little more background to this project; this is my fifth shooting work and as such crystallises some of the ideas that I have been developing over the last twenty or thirty years. There are, it might be noted, frequent references to clay pigeon shooting throughout this work, more than in most other books on game shooting, but the modern game shot must refine his technique on artificial birds first.

I am reminded of the comment by a French philosopher who once noted 'I have written you a long letter, because I did not have time to write a short one'. It would be good to say that this book is the equivalent of the harder-crafted, tightly argued, short letter. It is not that – too many byways have been explored – but effort has been made to ensure that the text on the methods of shooting is concise and the photographs and line drawings clear (they are as important as the words in any instructional work). An effort has also been made to distil the technical ideas presented here. All have been tested and re-tested in the field (often a pleasant alternative to staring at the computer screen). Not much of my thinking has radically changed in the last decade, but some points have certainly become clearer. For example, as a shooting friend recently observed: 'You know, when I look at the bird really hard, it seems to need less lead'. Perfectly put.

My teaching has also revealed how very different human beings are in the way they process information, hence my initial comments concerning thinkers and feelers – a gross simplification, of course. The specific problem in shooting instruction is that to bring about improvement in performance, one needs to get to that part of the psyche that can bring about a real change in behaviour. It is harder to reach in some than others. Intellectual understanding in itself is not usually enough to invoke change. It is not just about knowing that x number of feet of forward allowance is required on a particular bird (if you are one of those people who measure lead), it is about applying, seeing and *feeling* the appropriate lead as well. Shooting really well demands that you use your whole self – heart, head and hands.

Different approaches are required – via different channels of communication – with different people (psychologists might refer to right-brain and left-brain thinking in this context). Face-to-face instruction is, meanwhile, much easier than any attempt at instruction by print or picture. In the flesh, one can talk, one can demonstrate, one can remonstrate. You can modify the approach until a mental bridge is established. It is much harder to succeed as a virtual instructor and hence a special challenge. Repetition of words or phrases is not enough, nor graphic illustration (though both may help). You may write a dozen times that maintaining fine focus on the bird, or keeping the gun moving, are critically important. But, will the reader really understand? Will it break through from one side of the brain to the other?

Even at a shooting school, one may encounter a situation where the student does exactly the same thing no matter what he or she is told (typically because the client in question has no experience of what feels or looks right and therefore cannot correct effectively just on the basis of a spoken input – they need something extra). 'Go on, more lead!' you may say, but a miss two yards behind follows. 'Go on, risk it – twice as much!' The shot still flies behind. Then, realising a visual cue might be required, the increasingly desperate instructor may use a post, a fence or a barn as a reference of distance. 'Come on, give me two of those in front.' 'That much?' 'Yes.' 'Really?' 'Yup.' Result – on a good day – a broken target. 'Wow, did it really need that much?' The penny finally drops.

You may at this stage be saying that the 'Why' of the miss is as important as the 'Where'. This is, of course, true. If, for example, your feet are wrongly set without due consideration of where you want to kill the bird, you may inadvertently

A session at a professional shooting school is always a good investment. Even an experienced shot is well advised to go for an annual 'check-up'.

introduce tension into the swing (and hence tend to miss behind). If your 'point of insertion' of the muzzles is too far behind the bird, you may be encouraged to rush wildly through it only to stop as the trigger is pulled (and, again, tend to miss behind). Both the latter are very common problems. But, on some occasions, the 'where' – accurately diagnosed – is all the client needs or wants. The need for a more deliberate approach on some, harder, birds is also implied above. Generally, an instinctive, un-measured, technique is to be preferred. But, it is notable that for longer shots, and during the learning process, a more deliberate technique may be useful too. The subconscious approach is usually built on the foundation of conscious training.

Meanwhile, achieving breakthrough results by means of the written word is tough. Books and videos are not an especially effective teaching medium compared with live one-to-one interaction. In the context of teaching sporting skills, books and other media are best used to supplement conventional instruction. Their limitations must be realised. The problem is that there is no guarantee of communication, limited interaction with the student and no feedback from him or her, but books and videos do help towards a broader understanding and awareness. Only when no competent teacher is available should they be used as the sole source of instruction. *If you are really serious about your shooting, you must seek out help from a competent professional as well as reading this and similar works.*

It seems odd that so many shooters begrudge the price of a few lessons at an established school when they happily spend so much on their sport and equipment.

I suspect various culprits for this – simple stinginess, male ego (one of the most pernicious barriers to improvement, but also a potential motivator), and, not least, the sad fact that the quality of instruction available is variable (so make sure that your instructor has a qualification from a respected organisation like BASC (the British Association for Shooting and Conservation), APSI (Association of Professional Shooting Instructors) or the CPSA (Clay Pigeon Shooting Association). Some experienced shots, I suspect, also fear that instruction may require that they relearn the basics. They are concerned about stepping backwards as the necessary prerequisite of moving on. They shouldn't be, a bit of back-tracking may be neccessary, but a good instructor should build on what the client has rather than attempt to start 'from the ground up' according to some dogmatic plan.

As will be clear, this work is opinionated, but nowhere does it suggest that there is just one way to shoot. Certain universal principles of good shooting are laid down, and a number of different techniques are explored. An attempt has been made to construct a logical framework within which you can analyse your shooting as well. What is written here is, to a great extent, a record of my own journey in exploring the subject. I have been especially motivated to explain, in so far as it is possible, some of the contradictions in the literature and to separate opinion from fact. The intention is to be clear and to chart a steady course through the mist.

Some very good, but rather partisan, books have been written on shooting technique over the years; Churchill's *Game Shooting* (Michael Joseph, 1955) and Stanbury and Carlisle's *Shotgun Marksmanship* (Stanley Paul, 1986) immediately spring to mind (though both are classic works and worthy of study). The problem is that most books present one method of shooting to the reader as if it was the only one. I hope the approach here is less dogmatic and a little more objective. Different techniques are

Churchill's book Game Shooting *is partisan, but great nevertheless. Here he demonstrates his ugly but effective starting position for gun mounting. The muzzles do not have to be held this low to use this method. I'm not sure about the stockings either!*

discussed frankly. Strengths and weaknesses are considered. And, I do not shy away from admitting a certain bias in some cases (with suitably 'scientific' justification, of course).

Used carefully, this book can become part of a programme of self-improvement. It begins with history – we are all part of a tradition and should take pride in exploring and maintaining it – and moves on to safety, a fascinating subject when studied thoroughly, and one that deserves much more attention. Shooting vision – safety apart, the most important subject in any consideration of shooting technique – is considered in some detail too. Should we use one eye or two? How does one self-test for eye dominance? Can it change? These are the sort of practical questions that you will find answered in the pages that follow.

Subsequent chapters get down to the nitty gritty of shooting technique. Each section concentrates on a different component: stance, holding the gun, address to the target, forward allowance, shooting behind the line, double-gunning etc. You will also find information on mental attitude (to which I hope to devote a whole volume one day) and shooting 'style' (what it is and how to develop it). In the gun section, you will find more history, not to mention pragmatic advice on gun selection and fit. Does your gun shoot where you look? Does it control recoil effectively? Advice is given on choke and cartridge selection as well. What really works? Can anything give you an advantage?

The intention is to give the reader some interesting background, but to prevent him or her from becoming distracted or misinformed. KISS (Keep It Simple Stupid) is the guiding principle at all times when considering technique or modern equipment. For example, it is the experience of many shooting instructors that the over and under shotgun with its single, flat, sighting plane and improved recoil control is an easier gun with which to shoot consistently. I enjoy the challenge of a side by side, appreciate the convenience of its gape (the extent to which it opens for loading), and the inherent beauty of its lines (if well conceived). I also note that for those who have been brought up with the side by side, a change to another configuration may cause more harm than good. But, the over and under is, objectively speaking, easier to control and point, hence it has displaced the side by side as the dominant configuration.

The practical approach of my teaching is to sort out the eyes and gunfit first (and for fit read general suitability of the gun for the task). Next, one must identify and develop techniques suited to the individual with regard to such things as stance and forward allowance. If you are tall and lean, it is unlikely that you will want to stand in the same way as someone who is short and – how shall I put this delicately – stocky. Developing awareness of what is required to achieve consistent success is critical too. Instructors should not be in the business of creating clones, nor should the client become dependent on the teacher. The goal is for the shooter to become self-tutoring through improved awareness and understanding.

There has, not to put too fine a point upon it, been too much Bovine Scatology in instruction, too many people saying 'my way is best' and rubbishing everything else. In truth, each of us is different. Discount the opinions of those saloon bar experts that tell you everyone should shoot with both eyes open, with deliberate or subconscious forward allowance, no matter what, or with the weight always planted

Charles Lancaster (H.A. Thorn) demonstrates the mount in his famous work The Art of Shooting.

on one foot or another. It's not that simple. There are no absolute rules, just principles that hold true for most people, most of the time – maintaining balance, glueing one's eye or eyes to the bird, shooting with good timing, keeping the head down and the gun moving as the trigger is pulled. One stance does not suit all situations, nor does one system of forward allowance suit every bird. Reputations have been made by talking-up the differences. Here, I hope, you will find the common ground.

Each individual must develop a sound core technique but must also appreciate that in certain situations a different approach may need to be taken. You may prefer to stand like Mr Stanbury or (Mr Lancaster) on some occasions, and like Mr Churchill on others (or in any other manner that suits you better). You may rely on natural hand-to-eye coordination to apply lead subconsciously most of the time, but when facing a very high bird prefer a more deliberate approach. It is all about working out what works best for you in any given situation. You are the ultimate judge.

If you want to avoid bad days, start by learning the basics really well. Take pleasure in the process of shooting as much as in the result. Be disciplined. Be positive. Focus on those points that will help. Recognise distractions (such as worrying about pellet size or choke too much). Thoughts and actions are part of the same whole. The right thought process is just as important as correct foot and hand position. There is no mystical element. Concentration is no more than consistently applying the fundamentals. Confidence grows by applying proven techniques and noting good results. Psychology is all-important, but it is no great mystery.

Good shooting boils down to this. Attend to the basics. Cut the clutter. Make sure that you can achieve sustained visual contact, balance and good timing on every shot (this book will show you how). A well-fitted gun will help, as will the knowledge of how your eyes work and the awareness that stress or distraction may cause you to take your focus off the bird and stop moving smoothly. The aim here is to help you develop an individual style, based on increased awareness and experiment. Ultimately, though, what is presented here is about more than mere mechanics. My hope is that this book will help those sportsmen and women who see shooting not just as a means to an end, but who appreciate the form and beauty of it too – and the environment in which it takes place.

Michael Yardley
Witham, Essex 2007

To shoot well you must be in a state of relaxed concentration.

PART I

IN THE BEGINNING...

Birds have been shot in Britain with firearms for about five hundred years. It would be a good bet, though, that *wingshooting* first came to these shores during the Restoration with the courtiers of the newly enthroned Charles II. It is likely they brought the novel sport and the equipment for pursuing it – lightweight, single-barrel guns operating on the flint and steel principle – from their exile in France. Shooting flying was fairly new even in that country, the first dedicated guns appearing in the first half of the seventeenth century. The original 1674 edition of *The Gentleman's Recreation*, an English encyclopaedia of sport, makes no mention of the new style of bird hunting, but the 1686 edition not only mentions shooting flying as 'now the mode', but also includes illustrations of the strange new practice. These show ducks being shot on the wing and also partridges being engaged from horseback. The guns in use are distinct too: a long fowling piece with a barrel of about five feet in length for the duck; and a shorter and lighter style of gun for partridges.

Richard Blome's 1686 work The Gentleman's Recreation *was the first to illustrate shooting flying in England, it also illustrated the then more conventional practice of using a stalking horse to pot sitting birds.* See p.262.

Wingshooting appears to have become an increasingly popular recreation in Queen Anne's era, though its practice was still subject to severe restriction because of the harsh game laws (see box). Driving birds, as we know it, was unknown; they were walked up over dogs by the fashionable set, and still shot sitting or perching by pot hunters. G.M. Trevelyan presents a colourful picture of the developing sport in his famous work, *English Social History*:

> *Shooting in the eighteenth century was rapidly taking the place of the hawking, netting and liming [the use of a glutinous paste put on branches or twigs to entrap birds] of wild-fowl... The long, hand-cut stubble still made it easy for sportsmen to get near partridges, walking up to them behind the faithful setter. Pheasants were not driven out of covers high over the heads of the Guns, but were flushed out of the hedgerows and coppices by packs of yelping spaniels and shot as they rose. In northern moorlands, grouse were less numerous than today, but less wild. Blackgame and duck were very numerous on suitable land, and everywhere troops of hares did much injury to the farmer... Ruffs and reeves, bittern, plovers, wheaters, landrails and other wild birds were shot as freely as more regular game.*
>
> [page 407, English Social History, *G.M. Trevelyan, 2nd edition, Longmans, Green and Co., London 1946*].

A Brief History of Game Laws

William the Conqueror was responsible for introducing draconian game laws in England. This 'Forest Law' was developed by his successors and caused much popular resentment (with poaching remaining, meantime, something of a national sport amongst all classes despite the savage penalties that could be imposed).

Henry III's reign saw the introduction of the 'Forest Charter' – an expansion of certain sections of the Magna Carta concerning the royal forests (which accounted for about one-third of the country in his reign). It made the legislation protecting royal game more systematic and less despotic. Feudal barons, as frustrated by the Forest Law as more ordinary folk, created their own hunting enclosures and relied on the common law of trespass and theft to protect them. Henry VII first introduced the requirement for gun licences, Henry VIII introduced seasonal limits for wildfowl (and was also interested in the welfare of partridges and pheasants) and Edward VI placed prohibitions on the use of the wicked 'hayleshotte'. This is the old English for the multiple projectile shot charge being fired from a smooth bore, it was not necessarily spherical – the norm was cut up lead sheet, tumbled to remove the sharp edges.

The era of the Civil War saw the widespread destruction of game as armies went foraging and the old laws were forgotten. Disregard for game laws continued in the *interregnum*. The Restoration may have brought *wingshooting* to England, but, harsh game laws were once more put in place. These were especially detested because they limited the taking of game to all but the elite of large landowners whose power had risen at the expense of the independent peasantry and yeoman freeholders. The notorious Game Act of 1671 passed by a Cavalier Parliament under Charles II prevented any freeholders with an income of less than £100 a year killing game *even on their own land*. The only possible justification was that deforestion and enclosure was reducing the available cover and game was becoming less abundant. Deer, in particular, were becoming scarcer and, consequently, small game took on a greater significance.

During the eighteenth century enclosure continued to the benefit of large landowners and poaching took on a new, vicious, character. In a mood of some panic brought about by the murderous activities of the notorious Waltham Blacks gang (who operated in Waltham Forest in Hampshire), the Government made it a capital offence to go at night with a blackened face in pursuit of game. By 1823, it was reckoned that one-third of those imprisoned in English gaols were convicted under the game acts. The hated 'qualifications' of the 1671 Act were finally abolished by the Game Act of 1831. This restored the principle that the occupier of land had the right to kill the game upon it (unless the freeholder had retained the right in any tenancy agreement) and introduced the requirement to pay the Inland Revenue a duty on game shot. It also legalised the status of keepers (giving them powers of arrest) and makes clear that the preservation of game which the Act defined as hares, pheasants, partridges, grouse, black game and bustards. The English Poaching Prevention Act, 1862, went further, defining game as 'hares, pheasants, partridges, eggs of pheasants and partridges, woodcocks, snipes, rabbits, grouse, black or moor game, and the eggs of grouse, black or moor game'.

The honour of the most charming contemporary account of early eighteenth-century game shooting must go to George Markland, a fellow of Saint John's College, Oxford. It also has the advantage of being contemporary with the events and practices described. In his poetic but instructive little volume *Pteryphlegia: or the Art of Shooting Flying*, published in London and Dublin in 1727, Markland notes that English sportsmen of that era had not attained the same degree of skill as their French counterparts: '...it being as rare for a professed Marksman of that Nation to miss a bird as for one of ours to kill it'. (An exaggeration no doubt, nevertheless, a somewhat sad reflection on English shotgun marksmanship at the time.) Amongst much else, he gives instruction in forward allowance for a variety of situations:

Five general sorts of flying mark there are,
The lineals two, traverse and circular,
The fifth oblique-which I may vainly teach,
But practice only perfectly can reach.
When a bird comes directly in your face
Contain your fire awhile, and let her pass,
Unless some trees behind you change the case.
If so, a little space above her head
Advance the muzzle, and you strike her dead...

But when a bird flies from you in a line,
With little care I may pronounce her thine.
The unlucky cross-mark or the traverse shoot,
By some thought easy, yet admits dispute.
As the most common practice is to fire,
Before the bird, will nicest time require;
For too much space allow'd the shot will fly
All innocent, and pass too nimbly by:
Too little space, the partridge swift as wind,
Will dart athwart, and bilk her death behind.

And, the sportsman scholar is a stickler for safety. He wisely cautions against rushing or shooting too soon, emphasises the need to keep the muzzles of the gun pointing skywards at all times, and notes the importance of keeping the thumb under the hammer of the lock when walking:

Sometimes the Cock hammer may at half-bent half-cock go down,
True Sportsmen, therefore, always mount the Gun,
They walk with Flint by guardian Thumb restrained,
With Piece well handled, ready at command,
Nor need their jeopardised Companions dread
Their tripping Heels, or the strained Ankles tread.

There is no suggestion of driven shooting as now practised in Markland's book or any earlier English work (though the practice of driving larger game is ancient, with documentary references dating back at least to the Greeks). There is, however, much advice on using dogs in eighteenth century British sporting literature. Thomas Page, a Norfolk gunsmith, for example, went into considerable detail on 'the manner of beating a wood' with spaniels in another interesting little work, also called *The Art of Shooting Flying*. In the fourth edition, published in 1785, we find the following sage advice:

One, two or three brace of spaniels, well broken, may be used together; and they will find work enough in large wood or thick cover. If two persons intend hunting in a wood, it is best for one to go round it on the outside first, whilst the other goes opposite to him a little way into the wood, and afterwards to sink in deeper as you shall find the occasion, unless you know the most likely part to find game in; in which case you may hunt the interior part first. Some persons when they want to hunt a very large wood approve of taking a brace of high-mettled spaniels that have not been broken to hunt close, and turn them into the middle of the wood, whilst they with their well-broken spaniels hunt outwards. But I am of the opinion, that unless you have any extensive woods to hunt, that such dogs are more likely to hinder than add to your sport; that it will be better to hunt with patience with only such dogs as are under good command, let the woods or cover be ever so large.

On more open ground, however, pointers or setters – instinctive game finders – were to be preferred (and they can still offer wonderful sport where conditions suit). The use of dogs for shooting was clearly developed into a great art in this era (as is evident from the sporting art of the time as well as the literature). As is the case today, many seem to have taken as much pleasure in working their dogs as in the shooting itself.

Partridge shooting in the early nineteenth century. Note the wide stance, short front-hand position – to protect against barrel bursts – and flintlock gun.

The Origins of Driven Shooting

Driven shooting is, essentially, an import to Britain. Until about 1900, it was often referred to as 'battue' shooting (from the French *battre:* to hit or beat). This gives some clue to its Continental origins as well as its tactics. Many nineteenth century sporting writers were certainly prone to disparaging the battue as a nasty foreign practice. This was not just a case of xenophobia. The European driven shoot was, in most of its early forms, pretty despicable. Limited to the ruling elite, it was characterised by excess, wanton cruelty, and a very rigid code of etiquette.

Hunting pageants, or 'entertainments', some of the most surreal were those of the German princes in the seventeenth and early eighteenth centuries, might involve the slaughter of thousands of creatures over several days in bizarre circumstances. Often, there was a perverse theatrical element with costumes, masks, stages, painted backdrops, and even fireworks to add to the grim circus. Even the poor quarry animals – or more precisely the living targets – might be dressed up before being killed. Indeed, so extraordinary were these events that it is scarcely credible that civilised people could take part in them.

Typically, deer, boar, or whatever else that could be rounded up in quantity, would be driven into a central, canvas-fenced, killing area to be despatched in a frenzy of blood-letting by inexpert Guns placed in a gallery. Driving beasts into water features or ornamental lakes – the water hunt – achieved a special popularity. It was thought especially picturesque. Sometimes the whole degenerate show was brought to a palace courtyard where foxes might be tossed to death as a sideshow, or large cats or other beasts made to fight each other as in the Coliseum of ancient Rome. Musicians would play to drown out the cries and delight the jaded tastes of the audience. Of sport, there was none, but woe betide any guest who made the slightest slight mistake of etiquette. He, or she, might suffer a ritualised spanking with the blunt side of a sword or knife (the traditional Northern European punishment for transgressions in the field).

As the eighteenth century progressed, some of the worst degeneracy disappeared (much change was brought about by the French Revolution). Throughout Europe, meantime, a greater emphasis was being placed on shooting birds and smaller game with the rapidly evolving sporting shotgun. The numbers game continued. Record bags were a subtle form of propaganda for rulers who wanted to display their wealth and demonstrate their absolute power. Even the Edwardian 'Big Shots' would have been hard pressed to match the records for sheer excess achieved in Bohemia *circa* 1753 when a royal party from Vienna shot for twenty consecutive days, firing (allegedly) 116,231 shots and killing 47,950 head of game (including deer, boar, pheasants, partridges, quail, lark, foxes and hares).

This Ruritanian rhapsody, amongst other shoots of grand style and dubious sporting ethic, was reported in Volume II of *Rural Sports*, a major English work of the early nineteenth century. The author, the Rev. William Daniel, who was clearly concerned by a growing demand for bigger bags at home, wittily scolds such profligacy, noting elsewhere in his massive tome:

> *The lists of the Game that has been killed upon particular manors in England by parties, and even single gentlemen, exhibit such a wanton registry of slaughter, as no SPORTSMAN can read without regret, but to prove that* British *are rather more merciful than* French *Shooters, the account of the former Game Establishment at Chantilli [sic] is first presented.*

Daniel goes on to list the game shot on the estate between 1748 and 1779. It averages at about 30,000 a year (with a high of nearly 55,000 in the first year on record). He continues in splendidly jingoistic tone (and with more documentary evidence): 'The Germans too have a happy knack at massacre.'

An exceptionally detailed account of a grand, late eighteenth-century, Continental battue, comes from the diary of the second Earl of Malmesbury (see box). On 17 October 1799 near Vienna, Malmesbury took part in an event in which 3,000 or more shots were fired, and 1,008 head of game despatched. The Guns had more than 900 keepers and peasants to attend them. It is clear that he was rather shocked by the spectacle (though, it was comparatively mild compared with some of the Baroque extravaganzas). Other diary entries made by the young Englishman include a report of an outing to a large Bohemian 'pheasantry' near Trauenberg castle during which 540 pheasant were shot by 'six or seven' Guns, and a day in 'a *remise* where they had last year [1798] killed...1,200'. Interestingly, lady Guns were a feature of some of the continental shoots in which Malmesbury participated. It might be added as postscript that the earl – the keenest of shooting sportsmen – was never tempted to emulate continental practice on his own estates (nevertheless, he managed a lifetime bag of 38,475 head of game, including 10,744 partridges, 6,320 pheasants and 5,211 hares.

The Earl of Malmesbury's diary entry for 17 October 1799 (as published by Country life Books and quoted by Aymer Maxwell in *Pheasants and Cavert Shooting*):

Left Vienna early in the morning for Hinkenbrünn, a small hunting seat of Prince Esterhazy's. Reached the ground nearly an hour before the Prince. Many servants were, however, arrived, and a large breakfast was laid out. About eleven the whole party was assembled amounting to eighteen sportsmen, or rather shooters.

After taking coffee, we set out for the field of battle. The whole of a very extensive wood was surrounded by a net about four feet high, which was watched by women and children at every hundred yards. A vast number of gamekeepers and peasants had been employed all day and night in driving game within this net. Our scene of action was a piece of low, thick grassy cover about 900 yards long and 350 wide; this was surrounded on all sides by high copse wood.

The first measure adopted was to allot to every shooter his post. Eighteen stakes were numbered for the purpose, a ticket corresponding with that number having been previously given to us, and we had each of us the path pointed out that we were to pursue. Each man was at about 20 yards from his neighbour, and this intermediate space was filled up by peasants, so that the whole formed a complete and almost compact line, having its flanks on the high wood, and sweeping the Remise or low cover from side to side.

Each shooter had three people to attend him for the purpose of loading guns, of which he had a relay of six, carried on a stand behind by a peasant. Some of us had for loaders grenadiers from the Prince's bodyguards, the finest men I ever saw.

We walked six times backwards and forwards the length of this Remise. Whenever the line reached the extremities, it faced outwards from the centre, and filed off by wings into the corners, where it remained till the peasants had gone beyond the high wood, and driven the game back again into the low cover, so that but little could escape us. The whole lasted until about 3pm.

In advancing, no one was allowed to step out and pick up the slain, but this was done by peasants as they stepped over them. The Remise had here and there higher clumps of brushwood interspersed with it, where I have seen the pheasants rise by fifties together. They have also rows of twisted stakes placed at intervals to prevent their running. In these spots, I have fired my seven guns, one a double barrel, as fast as they could hand them to me. I killed one hundred and nine head myself, being well placed, 60 of which fell to my double barrell'd Manton. I conjecture that I could have not fired less than 220 shots, and should certainly have been more successful had my borrowed guns been equally good. But the difference of their locks and make rendered it extraordinary that I killed anything with them - and, what is more so, that the Grand Maîtres des Chasses or Grand Veneur (who always presents an official report to the Prince after dinner), should have stated what my modesty ought to prevent my relating, that the 'Young Englishman shot the best'. As nearly as I could make out, I killed 25 hares, 2 woodcocks, 2 partridges and about 80 pheasants. I calculated at least 3,000 shots were fired by the whole party. Nine hundred and thirty peasants and keepers were employed in this chasse, allowed to be the finest thing of the sort given in Germany. The signals for beginning, for notifying the arrival of the Princess, and for dinner, were all made by a field piece brought for that purpose. Wagons were posted in our rear to carry off the game, which I understand was sold at market.

Upon the whole, it was for novelty and magnificence one of the finest sights that I ever beheld, though in point of sport it was little inferior to butchery.

A New Style of Sport

Britain was changing rapidly in the eighteenth and early nineteenth centuries. Six million acres of land were enclosed in England and Wales (and a proportionate amount in lowland Scotland). Although this improved farming efficiency, one of the many less than happy consequences for the general populace was that the squire typically took over the village woods as part of his allocation. Coverts could then be stocked with game and 'preserved' for his own, and his friends', sport – but not without considerable tension ensuing as noted in the box on game laws, see pages 20 and 21.

The clearance of woodland and drainage of marsh, meanwhile, boosted the populations of hare, rabbit and partridge, but had the opposite effect on the pheasant. The problem was soon recognised and remedial action taken: pheasants began to be reared in quantity by artificial means with new species' being introduced. The Chinese ringneck was imported in 1768, and the Japanese southern green around 1840 (by Lord Derby). The rearing of birds developed into a considerable science on the great estates, so much so that by the late nineteenth century, the use of incubators for gamebird hatching was well known, though hatching under broody hens was more common.

The mechanisation of agriculture – land was increasingly seen as an economic resource – and the proliferation of 'dark satanic mills' also had effects. A fetish for game preservation developed – not least amongst the mercantile and industrially empowered *nouveau riche* who had the inclination to build Paladian mansions in the country rather than town houses in Grosvenor Square. The early nineteenth

These Michigan Blue Back pheasant were shot over pointers in the USA. Blue Backs and more commonly, Blue Back crosses have also been bred with success in the UK.

century world view, as prevalent amongst aristocrats as mill owners, saw nature as something to be both exploited and enjoyed. It led, however, to richer sportsmen developing a more artificial relationship with the natural world under ever more controlled conditions.

Mechanical reaping, meanwhile, first introduced in the 1820s, deprived birds of much of their cover, as did the practice of sowing crops in rows or 'drills' rather than 'broadcast', hence making the traditional walk-up, less productive of game. The increasing number of industrial blots on the landscape, motivated those who could afford it to create ever more splendid rural retreats as noted, complete with landscaped gardens, and newly planted coverts. Quantum leaps were being made in gun development as well (see pages 177-80). All of these factors, plus an increasing expectation for larger bags on established estates – evident from the late eighteenth century in England, though not striven for obsessively until the second half of the nineteenth century – made it almost inevitable that new forms of shooting sport would develop.

Origins of Driving in Britain

It would be misleading to present the history of British shooting sport as splitting conveniently into the eras before and after the introduction of driving. In studying the records of the great estates, one sees a steady increase in game bags in the early nineteenth century. Shooting, generally, was becoming more popular. A competitive element seemed to be creeping in too (wagers involving famous shots such as Coke of Norfolk and the plucky Squire Osbaldeston drew much attention). The heroic, frequently solitary, expeditions of Colonel Hawker were giving way to a more social, more regimented, more competitive, style of sport.

Grouse shooting, for example, is first mentioned in sporting literature of the late eighteenth century, but it did not become fashionable until the opening decades of the nineteenth. Osbaldeston was a particular fan, and was a member of an early syndicate in Yorkshire paying £20 a year (*circa* 1828) for the privilege of shooting on the moors of the Earl of Strathmore. He describes a day's sport in a letter written to his friend Edward Budd (reproduced in 1867 in *Sportascrapiana*). The contents make clear that grouse shooting in those days was not for the faint-hearted.

Having spent a sleepless night in a rowdy pub, the legendary sporting squire rides nine miles to Bowes Moor, arriving at his 'post' at half-past-three in the morning.

> *There were several parties lying near us watching for the light, and we nearly all started together. It put me in mind of what one reads of a storming party springing from the trenches... I ended the day with bagging 22 brace, no other man that I could hear of killing above 12½ brace... it was quite a scramble; birds flying in all directions, men swearing, and dogs howling from the whip... I walked from half-past-three until six at night, when we gave up – not a bird to be found.*

So, we may note a transitional phase before the general introduction of driving, in which bags increased significantly and the pace of sport too. Shooting, evidently, was becoming something of a numbers game *before the widespread introduction of driving or the breech-loader.*

Grouse

Grouse appear to be the first birds shot routinely by the driven method in Britain sometime in the first half of the nineteenth century. Lord Walsingham quotes a letter from W. Spencer Stanhope to William Lipscomb in the Badminton Library volume *Shooting: Moor and Marsh.*

> *My Dear Lipscomb... As to grouse driving, it was first commenced here by my grandfather's keeper, George Fisher, who told me he used to drive the low moor at Rayner Stones for my uncles when they were boys...this would be about the year 1805... I began to shoot grouse in 1841; we had our regular drives then, but without butts.*

The Reminiscences of Colonel R.F. Meysey-Thompson (published in 1898) note, however, that a moor once leased by his father in County Durham had had butts since 1803 and had been driven until 1854 when, apparently, there was a lapse for some years. Sir Ralph Payne-Gallwey, however, writes in *Shooting: Field and Covert* (a companion volume in the Badminton series to the one mentioned above), that Sir Henry Edwards was one of the first to introduce the driven system on his Yorkshire moors 'somewhere about thirty years ago' (i.e. during the 1850s). The Marquis of Granby writing at the dawn of the twentieth century in *English Sport*, is of similar opinion, citing the game books for the Longhshaw Moors in Derbyshire, which begin in 1826, and include no record of driving until 1849.

The Famous Grouse

According to the Rev. H.A. Macpherson, the word grouse may come from the old French *griesche* meaning grey or speckled. From this came *grice*, a plural word used to describe the moor-henne, the female of the moor-fowl, muir-fowl or moor-game. This later evolved into grouss or grouse as we write and say today. A second school of thought suggests a Celtic derivation from the words for heather *grug*, and hen, *iar*. Gor-cock is yet another old word (gor can mean red in Northern English dialect). The scientific name for the red grouse is *Lagopus lagopus scoticus*, to be distinguished from *Lyrus tetrix britannicus* (the black grouse), *Lagopus mutus millaisi* (ptarmigan) and *Tetrao urgallus* (capercaillie). The latter is no longer a legal quarry species in Scotland, though it remains one in England and Wales (where, to my knowledge, there are no capercaillie populations).

Although it is impossible to put a precise date on the introduction of grouse driving in Britain, we can state that it first became *fashionable* on English moors in

Early season grouse shot on a Scottish moor – note how beautifully camouflaged these native birds are.

the third quarter of the nineteenth century (the season of 1872 causing particular comment because of a great abundance of birds related to new methods of moorland management). It is significant that the breech-loading gun was already well established at this time (pin-fire guns having been introduced commercially in Britain in the 1850s, and centre-fires in the early 1860s). It is also evident from contemporary writing that driving was introduced to Scotland later than in England. Shooting over dogs remained the favoured method north of the border for many years.

What about the driving of other quarry? In *Shooting: Field and Covert*, Walsingham and Payne-Gallwey quote an extract of the *Norfolk Gazette* of 1823 as indication that at that date 'it was already recognised that shooting over dogs was not the most profitable method of pursuing partridges'. Referring to Mr, later Lord, Coke, the Norfolk estate owner and his bags of 80½ and 82 brace in September and October 1823, the Norfolk paper reports that he: 'was attended by several gamekeepers, and by one dog only to pick up the game. Several respectable neighbouring yeoman volunteered their services to beat for game, and rendered essential services thoughout the day.' This is not quite a driven shoot as we know it, but certainly appears to be a step towards it.

Walsingham and Payne-Gallwey also inform their readers that 'the system of driving partridges' appears to have been introduced on Lord Huntingfield's estate at Heveningham in Suffolk in 1845. Granby, however, notes in regard to Cheveley

Park near Newmarket, that the first record of driving partridges is in November 1850 with another in 1859 'this leaves a gap of nine years to be filled in – presumably, driving became more usual during that period'. And, J.J. Manley MA writes in *Notes on Game and Game Shooting* (published in 1880): '…of late, much more than was the case formerly, recourse has been made to "driving".' He also records that 'bitter things' had been said against it and worse against the practice of 'kiting' (shooting partridges under kites, which appeared like hawks to the confused quarry).

Having considered grouse and partridge, we may now turn to the more decorous, if alien, pheasant, a bird becoming ever more popular in the nineteenth century among those of a preserving disposition. In its earliest, most primitive, form, the pheasant battue involved nothing more than a line of Guns and beaters walking through a covert *together* like a line of soldiers advancing with fixed bayonets. A scathing account may be found in 'Martingale's' (James White's) book *Sporting Scenes and Country Characters* (published in 1840):

> *The battue is that description of wood shooting in which are assembled a large number of sportsmen; and, in addition to the keepers, many beaters. The whole party form a line in the well-preserved woods and plantations, and drive everything before them. All – whether bad or good shots – fire away - bang, bang, bang – right, centre, left – at pheasants, woodcocks, hares or rabbits. This sport, <u>however, fashionable</u> [author's emphasis], is not relished by the true sportsman, who is desirous of preserving as well as killing game.*

White tells us that the rule was to shoot immediately in front 'and to take crossing shots only when crossing before the ground occupied by the shooter'. He

Careless John 1821 (taken from Robin Shute).

states that many fatal accidents had occurred in battues, despises the rivalry 'as to who shall kill the most' that they engendered, and notes the particular danger from foppish younger Guns 'ornamented with kid gloves and perfumed like milliners'. Such sentiments, evidently, have long been with us. Some of the 'old guard' today might be scathing of 'city boys'. Post World War II country squires were similarly rude about 'syndicates' – by means of which those not to the manor born might buy their shooting. (It seems silly now, but more recently, there was a silly prejudice against the over and under shotgun in some reactionary quarters.)

In more complex form, the battue required a party of Guns and servants to advance through a prepared covert in which the sides and back were blocked by nets in Continental fashion. There would be some shooting as the line progressed, the correct form was for the entire line to stop whenever a shot was fired to allow for reloading, but the 'best' shooting was at the end when the pheasants – which as a species, far prefer *terra firma* to the wild blue yonder – tried (vainly), to push their way through obstructions and were eventually forced to take flight. To quote *The Dead Shot*, a work of 1866:

> On reaching the net, after attempting to get through, they run back in the direction of the beaters and are then compelled to fly. The best shooting always takes place at the end of the covert: where being driven into close quarters, the birds are at last obliged to take to their wings. Without nets, few shots only could be had; but immense slaughter may be made by preventing the pheasants running out of the covert.

Happily for the future of the sport, someone came up with the thoroughly British idea of splitting shooters and beaters into opposing teams and pushing the birds towards and over the Guns instead of away from them towards artificial obstructions. In a few early driven shoots, it appears that birds were sent over the Guns with the latter keeping their *backs* to the drive. This had some safety advantage, but was soon changed to the modern system of putting the Guns forward of the advancing beaters and *facing* the ground to be beaten.

The battue continued to be seen by many as 'a regrettable foreign aberration' mid-nineteenth century – something associated with foreign royalty and the *nouveau riche*. It led to the most heated debate in the sporting press. Many older sportsmen disparaged the new style of shooting and contrasted it with the manly exercise of traditional walked-up sport. Typically, the champions of the modern method argued that it offered more sporting shots than the short-range going-away birds of the walk-up.

The diarist Charles Greville condemned Queen Victoria's consort, Albert, for shooting 300 roe in a single drive by the Continental method, and expressed shock that the Queen herself watched. *Punch*, a radical journal in its early days, launched a particular campaign against the battue and lampooned the Prince Consort mercilessly on the subject. The battue became a political issue. One memorable cartoon *circa* 1845 shows Albert seated in an armchair shooting a pheasant with a double gun attended by a servant holding two more. Dead, ruffled, and plainly scared creatures are all about. Even *The Times* reported upon royal shoots with

A Punch cartoon of 1845 lampooning Prince Albert and the curious foreign battue shoot.

something less than reverence in this era. It is perhaps most bitingly summed up by Albert's modern biographer David Duff: 'Albert was a battue man… he regarded the killing operation as one to be conducted with the maximum efficiency in the shortest possible time, without interference with his hot lunch.'

From about 1870, the rapid growth and gradual acceptance of driven shooting in England is, however, evident. The quarry might be grouse, partridge, hare or rabbit (ground game generally was considered more important in this era than today) or the increasingly popular pheasant. The controversy about the ethics of driving continued, however. As late as 1886 – by which time driving to Guns was a regular practice on many great estates – the famous sporting writer 'Stonehenge' (aka Dr J.H. Walsh, editor of *The Field*) could still be scathing in his criticism of battue pheasants and the whole concept of big bag shooting.

Albert's son, Edward, Prince of Wales (later Edward VII), following his father's example, took much interest in introducing the new style of sport to his recently-purchased estate at Sandringham, Norfolk, in the 1860s and 70s. Edward's involvement as leader of fashion was highly significant but a host of other factors played a part in promoting driven shooting and the improved battue: enclosure, the development of game preservation and changes in agricultural practice as noted, the sheer excitement of the new sport, the perfection of the centre-fire, hammerless, breech-loader, perfectly suited to driven sport, and, not least, the mobility made possible by the expanding railway system, which allowed the wealthy easy access to one another's estates.

For those who had the funds for artificial rearing, more birds than ever before became available and the new quick-loading and firing guns and the driven method of presentation made it possible to shoot them without great physical effort (though the need for skilled marksmanship was as great or greater than before). Plutocrats who would not have considered walking up game, now had a sport well suited to their anaerobic lifestyle. The less than strenuous nature of the new sport did not go unnoticed or uncriticised at the time as discussed. There was also some ill-feeling between shooters and fox-hunters developing in this era as the historian J. P. Watson notes:

> *In landowning circles, in lowland Britain, pheasant (and to a lesser extent, partridge) shooting soon became the close rival and competitor of foxhunting... A host of sportsmen were foxhunters and game-shot too, but many of the really dedicated riders to hounds regarded the battue shot... who took little exercise... as no real countrymen. [p. 69* Victorian and Edwardian Fieldsports.*]*

Arguements between riders to hounds and battue men notwithstanding, prowess at driven shooting in the late Victorian and Edwardian eras became a considerable social asset. It was certainly seen by some as a means of social advancement. The rigid, complex, and hard-learned etiquette that developed around the sport – reminiscent of the old Continental hunting codes in some respects – not only promoted safety but limited the social access to what had by then evolved, once again, into a very elitist and expensive game.

During the game season, the 'Big Shots' – the likes of Lord Walsingham, Earl de Grey (later the 2nd Marquis of Ripon), and the Maharaja Duleep Singh – supported by a corps of dedicated retainers, led a congenial life wandering from one great estate to another to shoot driven game and live in the most conspicuous luxury. As one might expect, in an era of bloated excess, bags were enormous. Estates competed with each other (sometimes bankrupting their owners in the process) in a numbers game that would be rightly condemned today.

In 1883, six Guns at Croxted Park, Lord

Lord Walsingham, arguably the greatest game shot of all time.

Perhaps the biggest of Big Shots – Edward VII. His muzzles look a bit low though! It's good to be the king – provided you're not a beater.

Sefton's estate, bagged 2,373 pheasants, but, perhaps more grimly impressive, was the achievement of Lord Walsingham who shot 1,070 grouse to his own guns (four, 30-inch barrelled, cylinder-bored, Purdeys) on 30 August 1888. On 26 November 1895, a party of six Guns including the Princes V.D. and F.D. Singh and Earl de Grey despatched 1,160 pheasants, five partridges, forty-two hares, 2,362 rabbits, and seven various (driven ground game was much more popular in the late Victorian era than it is today).

Some 2,310 birds were shot by a party including the Prince of Wales on a day at Elvedon, Norfolk, in 1900. On 7 December 1905, at another great Norfolk estate, Holkham, Lord Leicester's Guns shot 1,671 partridges. On 12 August 1915, Lord Sefton and eight Guns shot 2,939 grouse at Littledale, Lancashire. Perhaps all this is best summed up by George V who, keen shot though he was, is reputed to have said in 1913, after a day in which nearly 4,000 birds were killed: 'Aren't we overdoing it a bit.'

Peter Hawker had only managed 17,753 head of game in his fifty-one years of sport, but the Marquis of Ripon 1852-1923 had shot more than half a million head of game by his death in 1923 (having accounted for more than 300,00 before 1900) including 229,976 pheasant between 1867 and 1895 alone. The circumstances of Ripon's passing may be of some interest to fellow sportsman. He dropped dead in the heather of a grouse moor at 3.15 p.m. having shot fifty-one birds during the drive. Not a bad way to go for a shooting man.

The modern shooter participates in a sport which is much evolved and beautifully in harmony with the environment.

MODERN SHOOTING

The picture that has been painted of the origins of driven shooting has not been an altogether positive one thus far. It is important, however, that we should confront our past honestly, if only to avoid making similar mistakes in the future and to be in the strongest possible position to justify our sport today. Driven shooting, though still recognisable in its basic form, has developed considerably and much for the better in the last half century or so. There were some notable excesses in the 1980s concerning excessive bags and poor quality birds – which led the major British shooting organisations to create a Code of Good Shooting Practice – and some have arisen more recently (and, frankly, require prompt action again). Generally speaking though, quality has become more important than quantity. Shooting has evolved as an important part of the wider conservation process. As such it is not only defensible, but an evident benefit to the broader society in which it takes place.

The woodcock is one of the most fascinating and elusive of all quarry species. This was one was shot on the West Coast of Ireland.

Beautiful dogs – two black and one yellow Lab.

Responsible, well-managed, sport helps to preserve the moors, marshes, woods, and hedgerows of the British Isles. It provides jobs directly and indirectly for many thousands and is a check to prairie farming methods. Modern shooting is, in most cases, beautifully in balance with its environment. The many benefits of shooting can appear paradoxical to those who have no first-hand experience (and who may have an entirely false image of 'chinless wonders' blasting poultry out of the sky). Without shooting, the countryside would be a much poorer and more barren place.

Every concerned modern Gun needs to be able to justify his (or her) sport. There are three essential aspects to our case: hunting tradition (which, of course, concerns far more than driven shooting), conservation, and, not least, individual liberty. We have an obligation to try to explain to the non-shooting and sceptical public that what we do is positive. It is sometimes infuriatingly hard to get over the fact that shooting, conducted well and with sensible controls and imaginative use and reclamation of ground, is not only a 'green' activity with regard to conservation, but an excellent means of harvesting healthy game in a humane manner.

Happily, there have been a number of cases in recent years where those expressing hostility have been invited to shoots, or onto the marshes, only to become converts when they saw what was really going on. They have picked up a gun, joined the beating line or become involved in dog work. Shooters, and the less rabid 'antis', actually have much in common: we all love animals and the beauty of the natural world. I think much more might be made of this common interest. There seems to be too much conflict in modern Britain. It is often less apparent abroad. I went to Denmark some years back and happened to ask a group of students what they thought of the national hunting association: 'Oh, they do some very good conservation work.' Would that be the first response of their British peers? In the United States organisations like Ducks Unlimited and Pheasants Forever are widely honoured.

The point should also be made that driven game shooting in Britain, though far from cheap, is no longer the sport of a social elite; people from all walks of life come together to enjoy it. In my shooting life I have, literally, shot with carpenters and kings. This levelling aspect is one of the sport's greatest charms. In the field all that matters is whether or not one is a 'safe and jolly shot' (an excellent expression for which I thank my shooting friend, David Hilton). Character, kindness and competence are things that you will be judged upon, not – amongst the sensible, at least – the registration letter of your new 4x4 or the maker's name upon your gun.

COMMON FORMS OF LIVE QUARRY SHOOTING

In Britain today we see, principally, four types of shooting: driven, rough, pigeon shooting/pest control and wildfowling (although each may, of course, be subdivided into specialities). One might also include the old, but delightful, practice of shooting, over pointing dogs – the art of which is still kept alive on the grouse moors of Scotland and Northern England and also, with great expertise, in the United States – where it is the dominant form of hunting for quail, grouse, and pheasant – not to mention Scandinavia, Continental Europe and Southern Africa.

Driven Shooting

The most popular forms of driven shooting in Britain today involve pheasant, partridge and grouse. Other species, such as rabbit, hare, duck, woodcock and snipe, are sometimes shot by the driven method, but will, most commonly, be added to the bag when the primary quarry is something else. The high pheasant of the West Country, Hampshire and Wales are famous, as are the partridge of East Anglia, but in the public imagination and in the minds of many sportsmen, the grouse of Scotland, though increasingly scarce, are probably pre-eminent. (The author's birthday falls on 12 August – 'the Glorious Twelfth' – the start of the season for grouse; evidently his fate was sealed long ago!)

Shooting over pointers for grouse in Scotland is a great sport with plenty of effort required as you traipse through the heather.

These birds look high, but are well presented and shootable by a competent shot who is properly equipped.

English partridge (*Perdix perdix*), red grouse (*Lagopus lagopus scoticus*), black grouse (*Lyrus tetrix britannicus*), ptarmigan (*Lagopus mutus millaisi*), capercaillie (*Tetrao urgallus*)*, the common snipe (*Capella gallinago*) and the woodcock (*Scolpax rusticola*) are native species. Pheasant (genus *Phasianus*), originate from Asia and were probably introduced into Britain by the Romans (for culinary and/or decorative purposes) and reintroduced by the Normans. French partridge (*Alectoris rufa*), or, as they are also known, 'red legs' (which may be a rude English epithet related to the alleged running tendencies of French troops who once wore red leggings), were first introduced into England in the seventeenth century by the gamekeeper of Charles II; they did not thrive, however, and were re-introduced in the mid-eighteenth century. Now they are the most commonly encountered partridge in Britain, though many valiant efforts are being made to try to ensure that our native partridges thrive as well (at the time of writing they do not appear to be succeeding as well as might be hoped).

Organisation

In driven shooting, whatever the specific quarry, a line of beaters (their number will depend on the resources of the shoot and/or volunteers on the day) walk towards a line of Guns, typically six to a dozen strong and spaced 40 yards or so apart at 'stands' or 'pegs'. Beaters may be sent ahead on the flanks to prevent birds swinging away and stops may be positioned with flags to achieve a similar end. The art of driving is to keep the birds coming at regular intervals on each drive rather than in one great rush. This requires considerable planning and preparation, great knowlege of the ground, and on the day, good communication and coordination between the keeper and his team of beaters. In all cases the aim is to produce sporting birds that will challenge the Guns.

Conduct in the field

It is perhaps worth pausing at this point to define this much misused word – sporting. Most experienced shots would probably agree it means relatively fast-flying birds presented to the Guns at interesting angles at ranges between 20 and 45 yards. One regrettable modern trend is to offer so called 'extreme' birds on some self-conciously 'exclusive' shoots. There is no glory in shooting pheasants at 60 or 70 yards when the odds of connecting with one's quarry and *cleanly* killing it may be 1 in 10 or less. The practice of shooting extreme birds is in truth no more sporting than that of shooting tame or low ones. The latter practices are rightly condemned, the former deserves to be.

One of the joys of book writing, is that one may get such things off one's chest. So, where angels fear to tread, the author shall continue to go in with galoshes. Many have criticised big bag days recently. I have shot more than 500 birds on only two occasions in my life. As far as the last was concerned, at one of our most

*The capercaillie is no longer a legal quarry species in Scotland, though, theoretically, remains one on the other side of the border where there are no populations as far as the author is aware.

More high birds – but not too high for a good team of Guns. Who wouldn't want to be on this day? (Picture courtesy David Williams, Nantclywd Shoot)

My youngest son, Harry, with Peter Jones (father of Vinnie) after his first day's driven shooting on Peter's shoot in Hertfordshire.

famous estates, it was at least 100 too many for the day in question (though several of the Guns present complained that they had shot 900 plus on the same estate the week before).

I hesitate, however, to suggest that any *absolute limit* should be imposed (because quality is everything and any arbitrary number will be used against us by those who want to see nothing less than complete prohibition). What is required is the exercise of commonsense. One of my favourite shoots, run by Peter Jones (father to Vinnie) is a walk-and-stand event with a typical bag under 100. I enjoy shooting more birds on occasion, but, a large bag – more than 100 birds – should always be considered a treat. There is no right number. It all depends on the effort put into presentation and the attitude of those taking part.

Apart from misconduct by some greedy Guns at home – a few of whom seem to believe self-indulgence with regard to numbers has no consequence – there is a new and specific danger from certain very wealthy foreign shooters organising huge days in Britain echoing some of the despicable practices of the past. They may not be familiar with our evolving sporting culture nor care much about local sentiments. If their excesses cause serious consequences, they can leave and shoot in Spain or South America – we are left to carry the can. Our sport is not yet doomed, but it may easily be damaged by such selfish or silly behaviour. There have been many rumours in recent years of birds from Big Bad Days being buried. None of these have yet stood up to scrutiny, but I have, on too many occasions, seen dead birds being treated with insufficient respect by those who should know better.

Part of the problem is the pathetically low prices now paid for game (there is also the problem of food processing bureaucracy becoming so complex that few want to get involved). Nevertheless, the sale of game meat has risen in recent years, and may well be boosted now that the game licence has been abolished and the sale of game will be allowed throughout the year. The old legislation was passed in an era before refrigeration was commonplace.

The improved marketing and use of harvested game (as for example, demonstrated by BASC's 'Game's on campaign') is a project that must not be abandoned. It is notable, meantime, that Continental sportsmen are much less wasteful than we are. It would be inconceivable in France, Spain or Italy that something might be shot and not eaten. British shooters also have much to learn from continental shooters with regard to their attitude to the fallen quarry. No-one who has attended an end of shoot ceremony where a horn is blown after the animals have been laid out and a period of respectful silence has passed, can fail but to be moved by it. There is a feeling of connection with nature and with an ancient past. One is reminded by the ritual of the privilege of taking part. Could we not develop a ritual of our own? Something that makes clear that a shooting day, and the game harvested from it, is something special and to be cherished.

Finding a shoot

Assuming that one does not have one's own shoot, or an invitation to someone else's, driven shooting may be bought by the day or one may buy a share in a

In many European countries there is a ceremony after a shoot to honour the fallen game.

syndicate, that is, a group of Guns who pool financial resources to maintain a shoot (this became a common practice – though not without its critics – after many family estates were ruined by death duties after World War I). At the time of writing, driven pheasant shooting prices might vary from £100 to £2,000 or more a day, with £250 to £750 being the norm. However, modern driven shooting is not necessarily a rich man's sport. Many shoots are run on minimal funds as co-operative ventures, with daily costs brought down to £50 per Gun or less. Although bags were typically higher on estate shoots during the Victorian and Edwardian era, the overall number of birds shot has risen because there are so many of these small shoots today (more than 30 million pheasant are now bred each year).

> An interesting variation on the normal, increasingly commercialised, pheasant and partridge shooting theme is demonstrated in those smaller shoots where Guns and beaters exchange roles between drives. This is an idea with great potential: more people get to enjoy the sport at less cost. Moreover, it increases the Guns' involvement in the shoot and in the process of habitat and wildlife management. Whether or not shooting on the day is involved, it might be added that all keen Guns, young or old, should seek out experience in the beating line. All four of my children have acted as beaters and greatly enjoyed it. Beating is an excellent introduction to driven shooting, as well as great fun in its own right and good exercise. One notes more and more beaters who have come to the beating line late in life, perhaps after busy professional careers.
>
> It can also be great fun to share a gun on a driven or walk-and-stand day, provided one's host has no objections (if these are raised, bear in mind that an extra gun creates extra hassles most notably with regard to transport and food). With permission, the role of active Gun may be swapped on alternate drives, or one may change roles after a specified number of shots. I have often enjoyed doing this with old friends and also with my sons. The enjoyment is no less than when one has a full gun to oneself. The situation may also be used for instructional or supervisory purposes (inexperienced Guns should always be provided with a minder/loader for their first few shoots, of course).

Finding a driven shoot is not always easy, especially in the early days of one's sporting career. First one must distinguish between purely commercial shoots, syndicate shoots and private shoots. As far as the first two are concerned, classified advertisements in the back of magazines may be consulted and sporting agents may be approached as well. There is an interesting new publication called the *Good Shoot Guide* (produced by William Evans in association with Tony Jackson former editor of *Shooting Times*). It lists more than 200 shoots, and, commendably, concentrates on the quality offered rather than the bag size. The internet may also provide leads as individual shoots may have a website and there is at least one web business: (shooting4all), operating as an online brokerage service for shooting lets. Further advice on obtaining shooting may be sought from the BASC at its Marford Mill headquarters (see appendix) or by visiting their excellent new website www.goshooting.com which offers a comprehensive shoot-finding service.

Adventurous Guns may also consider travelling abroad. The partridge shooting in Spain is excellent (but pricey). France and Scandinavia offer some good wingshooting too, as does eastern Europe. Sport may be had in the United States for the cost of a hunting licence on millions of acres of State game lands (as well as on private properties). Southern Africa has fantastic bird shooting potential with quarry such as guinea fowl, francolin partridge, and rock pigeon, not to mention world-class wildfowling.

Sport abroad is always interesting, in this case guinea fowl in Africa – large pellets and a bit of choke are required to bring these tough, wild, birds down effectively in my experience.

Shooting with your own dog doubles the pleasure of the day – for both of you.

Rough Shooting

In rough shooting, a Gun or Guns walks up quarry in a field or wood in the time-proven manner as described by Markland, Page, Hawker and so many others. Most of us brought up in the country were introduced to shooting via rough shooting of one sort or another. It requires more fieldcraft and energy than driven shooting and the bag at the end of the day is likely to be small but well-earned. Although it is increasingly difficult to find, anyone interested in learning the art and craft of shooting would be well advised to spend time rough shooting. It will do a lot to make you more comfortable handling a gun in the field and teach you much about the habits and habitat of game.

Quarry on a rough shoot might include game birds when they are in season (assuming you have permission to shoot them), rabbits, hares, wildfowl and pigeon. It might also include the odd grey squirrel, jay, magpie or crow, if the Gun is interested in pest control (which, of course, he should be). Rough shooting can be a really satisfying end in itself, a supplement to formal driven shooting (and an especially attractive one for those on limited funds), or a halfway house between the shooting school and the formal driven day for anyone trying to learn the true nature of the sport. I am especially fond of rough shooting with a smaller bore gun – it is lighter to carry and a challenge to use well.

Some Guns – the present writer may be one – prefer rough shooting since it involves more walking, is less formal and the bag is so unpredictable. One learns simple stuff. For example, if you bag a hare early – remember you have to carry all seven pounds or so of it. A statement of the obvious? Wait till you have to carry one for a few hours! A few sporting hotels in western England and in Scotland still offer rough shooting as part of a package deal. A more traditional route to obtaining such sport is to develop a relationship with a local farmer or landowner. Rough shooting is not as easily available or, consequently, as popular as it once was: shooting of all sorts has been so commodified. But, if you can get it, rough shooting has a real charm, all the more with your own dog in attendance.

Pigeon Shooting

'There is no kind of sport which tries more severely the nerve and skill of those who delight to handle the shotgun' observed the legendary game shot Lord Walsingham on the subject of pigeon shooting. George VI was another famous enthusiast. The king's sporting biographer, Aubrey Buxton, observed: 'Like every good shot, the king thoroughly enjoyed a pigeon flight.' His best day – a surprisingly modest one – was in 1930 at Massingham, near Sandringham, when he managed forty to his own gun. The king's game books, include many references to pigeon shooting. For example, on 8 February 1951 His Majesty and five other Guns shot fifty-one birds; a week later, eight Guns accounted for more than ninety birds. So keen was his late Majesty, that he spent his final days at Sandringham shooting at hares and pigeon. One account even suggests that the last shot he fired was at 'an incredibly high pigeon' (though another account suggests it was a hare). More recently, the Duke of Edinburgh has been a keen pigeon shot and no doubt he has passed on his fondness for the sport to his sons and grandsons.

This was a fantastic day's shooting with over 300 birds shot – a big bag, but the farmer who owned the fields was delighted. You don't have to shoot so many birds to have a great day.

When British shooters refer to pigeon shooting, they do not mean shooting at captive pigeon released from traps as was once popular in this country and abroad, but to the art and (increasingly) the science of shooting at wild pigeons. The pursuit of the wood pigeon or 'woodie' (*Columba palumbus*) has always ranked high on any serious list of shotgun pursuits. In winter, there are opportunities for roost shooting. Few experiences can be more thrilling on a windy evening. Spring drilling heralds the start of serious decoying. Pigeon offer supremely challenging but relaxed shooting*. The dress code is informal; the quarry is wild and wily and reacts instantly to the sight of man or gun (pigeons are gifted with exceptional eyesight and a 340-degree field of vision).

---

*Pigeon Shooting
Strictly speaking Pigeon shooting is not a sport. It is conducted as a form of pest control and although the law admits that there may be a sporting element you can be prosecuted if you fail to shoot within the terms of the general licences. (see Appendix 5)

These licences are issued under a derogation from the EU Birds Directive and are renewed every year by the UK government. You do not need to apply for your own individual licence – they are general and cover everyone who is shooting legally, with the landowner's consent. In practical terms this means that you must be shooting the pigeons to protect crops or public health and safety. This does not need to take place in the immediate vicinity of crops that are being damaged but, if challenged, that must be given as your reason for shooting.

It would be absurd to pretend that there is not a sporting component, but the law is explicit: your justification for shooting must be to control a major agricultural pest.

Modern professionals, men like Archie Coats and John Batley, have turned pigeon shooting into a distinct shooting discipline, with its own literature. Volumes on the subject are now published on a more or less annual basis. Few will beat Coats' concise 1963 classic, *Pigeon Shooting* or Batley's *The Pigeon Shooter*. John Humphries, another talented author on this and many other shooting subjects, makes the good point that unlike other sorts of shooting, pigeon shooting methods evolve quickly as the birds themselves adapt in order to outsmart their pursuers.

Broadly speaking, there are three types of pigeon shooting: flight lining (simply getting under a known or suspected flight path); roost shooting (shooting birds approaching the woods or copse where they are going to sleep, at dusk, or rest, in daytime); and field decoying (which involves setting out a pattern of decoys in imitation of feeding). Roost shooting tends to be a winter activity (December to March, with the best results in January and February), but flight lining and decoying may be pursued all year round. In all cases, it is essential to know your ground and to invest time in studying the feeding and resting habits of your local pigeon populations.

The wood pigeon is an extremely wily adversary. It has excellent vision and reacts instantly to the gun. Woodies fly fast too, typically about 50 mph in level flight but they may reach 70 mph or more on occasion. Coming into decoys they may be much slower.

Those who have no experience of serious pigeon shooting are well advised to find someone who has (there may be a local pigeon shooting club near you; if not, ask local gamekeepers, beaters and wildfowlers). At the least, buy Major Coats' little book or John Batley's, and armed with a pair of binoculars, get out and look at the quarry. Gathering intelligence about these extraordinary birds is a vital prerequisite to shooting them. One needs to know on what they are likely to feed – for example, when are the beans or peas being drilled or breaking though – and where the birds are holding up for the night. No less important, one needs to learn to distinguish between different types of pigeon. No great harm is done if a feral is accidentally shot, but a racing bird is another matter (racing birds tend to fly in straight lines and flap their wings more constantly than woodpigeon).

The protected stock dove (*Columba oenas*) is descended from the caged birds once kept by monks for food. It must not be shot, but it is quite easily confused with the wood pigeon, not least because it often flies with them, however, it has no white wing bars or collar. The rock dove (*Columba livia*), mainly seen on the western coasts of Ireland and Scotland and distinguished by its light grey body, black wing bars and white rump, is also protected, as is the attractive little turtle dove (*Streptopelia turtur*). The collared dove (*Streptopelia decaocto*), a small bird of similar size to the turtle dove, with a fawn-coloured body, long tail and black half-collars at the neck, may be shot. Unlike some of its larger cousins, it does not move about much and is typically found around farm houses, barns and grain silos.

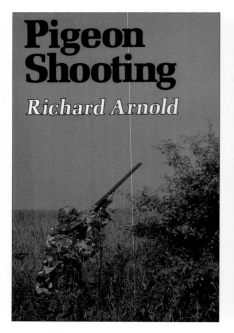

Pigeon shooting books have become a distinct genre of British sporting literature and have helped the modern discipline to evolve. A second revised edition of John Batley's book has just been released.

Pigeon professional, Will Beesley, putting a dead bird out as a decoy.

Feral pigeons which, as visitors to Trafalgar Square will be well aware, present themselves in a variety of colours and sizes (how many, though, realise that some of the birds are the ancestors of escapees from Victorian pigeon shooting matches, many of which took place in and around London?). Ferals may be shot, but one must be careful not to confuse them with racing pigeons as noted. The latter tend to fly in flocks, but not always. During spring and summer, pigeon racing is in progress and many valuable birds are in the air. All things considered, the best and simplest advice to the novice is only to shoot birds with white wing bars (i.e. wood pigeon).

Archie Coats once wrote that, 'pigeon shooting is a simple business really'. There is certainly a danger in overcomplicating it. Provided the aspiring pigeon shooter identifies the 'menu of the month' and learns to think like a pigeon when setting out his decoys and placing his hide ('What does it look like from the air?' should always be in mind), he should have some success. Experiment with no more than a dozen decoys initially placed a yard or so apart. Make sure that their heads are facing more-or-less into wind and leave a space in the middle of your pattern (a diamond or broad arrow head is a good one to start with) which will encourage passing birds to 'drop in'. Forget the space and they may think the 'parking lot' is full.

Real birds make better decoys than plastic ones (in particular, wet, shining decoys will scare off birds). So, as you shoot replace the decoys with the real thing, wings outstretched to show their distinctive markings. Another recommended route – sometimes so effective that it may almost be considered cheating – is to acquire a 'Pigeon Magnet'. This is a device with a motor (run from a battery) and two long arms, each with a cradle at its end into which a dead pigeon or, in some models, a decoy may be fitted.

Sometimes pigeons seem magically attracted to these mesmerising machines (on occasion, though, magnets can act as a deterrent). They see an image of two birds circling and about to land. It can be so realistic that you may find your eyes being confused when sitting in a hide. I use one quite frequently – especially with guests and with beginners when there is a need to ensure some shooting – but I usually prefer traditional decoys for my own slow-paced outings. It is more visually relaxing to look out over still birds contemplating creation and one's flask and sandwiches. One does not have to make a vast bag to have a good day.

Pigeon shooting presents a great challenge and one that was underrated for years (but no longer). Still cheaper than driven shooting, it offers a challenge to the Guns every bit as great as a formal pheasant or partridge day. It is also a valuable service to farmers. Pigeons have legendary appetites and are crop destroyers of the first order. As a prescription for improving the performance of any wingshot, pigeon shooting cannot be bettered. Many of the greatest modern game (and clay) shots started as pigeon shooters.

Wildfowling

In wildfowling, the quarry is likely to be duck or geese although the odd wader such as a golden plover or snipe might creep into the bag. It is an ancient practice and long pre-dates firearms. The ancient Egyptians were keen wildfowlers and used decoys to attract the birds and bows or throwing sticks to kill them. It was also popular among the Greeks and Romans as a method of food gathering, but was not considered a sport. Plato, who praises hunting, mentions the practice disapprovingly; clearly, the use of snares and nets, which became common, was not considered very courageous. Henry VIII introduced seasonal limits on the taking of wildfowl. The first reference to 'hayleshotte' (lead sheet cut into small pieces, the precursor of modern round shot) concerns its use in guns for wildfowling. His son by Jane Seymour, Edward VI, legislated against it in 1548, evidently with limited success, considering our subsequent history:

> *Ys growen sythen to the maintenance of much ydleness and to such libertye as not onlye dwellinge houses, dovecotes, and Churches are daylye damaged by the abuse thereof by men of light conversacion but that also there ys growen a customable manner of shoting of halyeshotte, thereby and infynite sorte of fowle ys killed and much Game thereby destroyed to benefytt of no man.*
> [An Acte against the shooting of Hayle Shotte, *1548*]

As well as the wicked hayleshotte, early, gun-toting, wildfowlers made use of stalking horses to get close to their quarry. John Nigel George in his *English Guns and Rifles* refers to drawings by Stradanus, *circa* 1570, in which: 'parties of countrymen are seen shooting wild duck upon ponds and rivers, creeping up under cover to within gunshot of the game and firing with their long fowling pieces as the ducks take off from the water' [p.22]. The sport of wildfowling, rather than mere pothunting, developed considerably in the late eighteenth (the era when truly massive guns began to be constructed) and nineteenth century (when wildfowling

Neither Brent geese nor swan (or for that matter, curlew) are on the quarry list today. This engraving is from the 1838 edition of Hawker's Instructions to Young Sportsmen.

developed into a considerable science). Colonel Peter Hawker's famous book, *Instructions to Young Sportsmen in all that Relates to Guns and Shooting* (first printing, 1816) not only provides a lucid description of early nineteenth century wildfowling, but also helped in its many subsequent editions to promote wildfowling as a sport in which large numbers participated. The Wildfowlers' Association of Great Britain and Ireland (WAGBI) was formed in 1908 and thrives to this day as BASC (the British Association for Shooting and Conservation).

Wildfowling Today

Wildfowl may be shot below the high water mark on salt marshes and estuaries, or inland over rivers, reservoirs, ponds and freshwater marshes. Some would argue that only the former is real wildfowling; it certainly requires more skills and can be most uncomfortable – every bird shot is well earned when one is lying in mud on a January dawn. Most modern wildfowlers access the marsh on foot, but some use small boats or specialist punts (a tradition that has happily survived into the twenty-first century). The skills required are considerable. One must be able to shoot under difficult conditions (see page 156), one must be able to identify all quarry and protected species in poor light (no mean feat) and one must learn to read the tides and weather if one is to survive on the foreshore.

This shooter's face tells the whole story. This Canada goose was part of a mixed bag on a walk-and-stand day in Hertfordshire.

Duck shooting, like pigeon shooting, is about discovering where ducks rest and where they feed. Generally speaking, they rest on water and may come inland to feed. The evening flight usually takes place an hour before sunset and the morning flight normally begins shortly before dawn. Wildfowling is the most physically demanding of shooting sports. For anyone who is interested, by far the best place to start is at a wildfowling club. Many of our marshes are wardened by club wildfowlers and their efforts deserve far more praise than they get. Who else would do the work just for the satisfaction?

With regard to shooting practice: duck and geese are sometimes shot at longer ranges, but the wise fowler using non-lead shot in a conventional 12 bore gun will stick to 40 yards or so as an absolute maximum. Shots beyond that distance are more likely to cripple than to kill cleanly. Anyone interested in taking up wildfowling would also be well advised to shoot over flight ponds or fleets (drainage ditches, also called delphs in some parts of the country) if the opportunity arises. Ducks may also be driven as noted earlier (not my favourite sport). They may be shot over stubble early in the season (ducks are especially fond of barley). Creating ponds for flighting has also become much more common in recent years. The advantage of this sort of shooting to the novice is that it provides the opportunity to identify and shoot wildfowl without worrying about tides and navigation. Nothing, however, compares with a crisp, bright dawn on the foreshore.

The art and science of puntgunning is still kept alive by some diehard enthusiasts. (Picture courtesy Alan Myers)

PART II

SAFETY: NEVER, NEVER, LET YOUR GUN…

Those who shoot game are expected to adhere to a rigid and quite complex code of conduct. This has some interesting origins as we have explored, but, beyond tradition and etiquette, it is a means of promoting safety. Never has it been better summed up than in the memorable poem '*A Father's Advice*' (written by the late Commander Mark Beaufoy MP for his son on reaching his thirteenth birthday in 1908).

If a sportsman true you'd be
Listen carefully to me.
Never, never let your gun
Pointed be at anyone;
That it may unloaded be
Matters not the least to me.
When a hedge or fence you cross
Though of time it cause a loss,
From your gun the cartridges take
For the greater safety sake.
If 'twixt you and neighbouring gun
Bird may fly or beast may run,
Let this maxim e'er be thine;
'Follow not across the line.'
Stops and beaters, oft unseen,
Lurk behind some leafy screen;
Calm and steady always be;
'Never shoot where you can't see.'
Don't be greedy, better spared
Is a pheasant, than one shared.
You may kill, or you may miss,
But at all times think of this –
'All the pheasants ever bred
Won't repay one man dead.'

I wonder if Commander Beaufoy ever imagined that his words would enter the minds of so many. Few writers can claim to have had such a positive effect on human affairs. His remarkable poem, without doubt, has saved lives and prevented countless injuries.

Let us now cut straight to the chase. Most who are experienced shots like to think that they are safe. In truth, most of us are not safe enough because we are not sufficiently aware of our actions. In some, ego, or pride, prevent them from accepting fallibility. In others, it is a case of plain ignorance or lack of training. Most shooters know that they must not point guns at others, but few are truly 'muzzle aware' at all times.

You may be thinking that some of the comments above are a bit harsh, but my work as a shooting instructor and specialist witness, not only leads me to have a healthy respect for guns at all times, but has made me much more aware of safety (or lack of it) in others. Looking at pictures of people who have been shot, or reading reports on such incidents, will have that effect. Once you become really aware of safety issues, you will frequently note breaches of basic rules by those who should know better and who remain, typically, unaware that they are doing anything wrong. Watch people getting guns out of cars at shoots, for example, and you will note that about one in three has suspect gun handling. It is, moreover, rare to attend a driven shoot without seeing someone do something potentially dangerous.

Safer gun handling requires that you *accept personal fallibility* and learn some basic rules. It is not just about rules, though, it is primarily about attitude of mind. 'It can happen to me,' that is the modest thought that will partially protect you. Here is the really bad news: *there is an accident out there waiting to creep up on you.* You must be active in preventing it. As one of my army instructors used to say: 'guns grow cartridges.' Whatever precautions you take, no matter how aware you become, it is still possible, indeed, it is likely, that one day you will have an accidental – or, as they now say in the services, negligent – discharge. When it happens, let us hope that you have acquired the habit of disciplined muzzle control and the gun is pointing in a safe direction.

As will be clear by now, I have a very specific philosophy concerning safety. One must recognise the danger in oneself, and in others, of familiarity breeding contempt. I have tried to make myself much more aware of safety and to integrate safety into all my published systems of shooting. Having emphasised the importance of mental attitude – to which it might be added that the same discipline and control that makes you a safer shot will also make you a better shotgun marksman – I will now present Twelve Commandments. They are certainly not as memorable as Mark Beaufoy's poem, but they should be considered carefully. Perhaps you can improve upon them.

1)   TREAT ALL GUNS AS LOADED
2)   NEVER POINT A GUN AT ANYTHING UNLESS YOU INTEND TO SHOOT IT
3)   CHECK THE CHAMBERS ARE EMPTY AND THE BARRELS UNOBSTRUCTED EVERY TIME YOU PICK UP A GUN OR PASS IT ON
4)   KEEP YOUR FINGER OFF THE TRIGGER AND KEEP THE SAFETY CATCH ON UNTIL YOU HAVE DECIDED TO MAKE A CONSIDERED SHOT

5)   ALWAYS BREAK A GUN BEFORE REMOVING IT FROM A SLIP
6)   NEVER PULL A GUN FROM A VEHICLE MUZZLES FIRST
7)   NEVER SHOOT WHERE YOU CANNOT SEE
8)   DO NOT SHOOT GROUND GAME ON DRIVEN SHOOTS UNLESS GIVEN EXPRESS PERMISSION TO DO SO
9)   DO NOT CROSS A FENCE WITH A LOADED OR CLOSED GUN
10)   KEEP YOUR MUZZLES UP; DO NOT SHOOT WITHIN 45 DEGREES OF A HUMAN BEING
11)   CHECK THAT YOUR GUN IS IN GOOD CONDITION AND IN PROOF
12)   BEWARE THE INVISIBLE MAN

<u>Treat all Guns as Loaded.</u>
Never Point a Gun at Anything Unless You Intend to Shoot it.

Commandment 1 and 2 amount to the same thing, but I have stated them separately above. They support each other and create a deeper memory trace. These Golden Rules need constant thought. For example, if you are at home, cleaning a gun (the scenario for many accidents) consider if the wall towards which you are pointing it would stop a shot charge. The rules also apply in gun shops (not that you would think so if you ever visit one: guns are typically handled without thought and pointed at all and sundry).

The only, and very rare, exception to Commandment 2 – and one about which there has been some argument – is when a professional instructor is fitting a client and needs to look at the relationship between eye and rib by looking down the barrels. In this very special circumstance, both client and instructor must be aware of the potential risk. They should have checked the gun is empty and unloaded to their mutual satisfaction. The checking protocol should include both visual and physical elements (a finger, if possible, should be inserted into each empty chamber). The safety should be applied and the finger should not be placed on the trigger when the gun is mounted.

Commandments 1 and 2 also dictate that one should never horseplay with guns. This, of course, is common sense to those who use firearms routinely and know their lethal potential. But, tragically, many people have been shot in such circumstances, (often because guns have been poorly secured and fallen into hands other than of those of the owner).

Always check for barrel obstructions before loading or when you pick a gun up or pass it on to someone else.

Check the Chambers are Empty and The Barrels Unobstructed Every Time You Pick Up a Gun or Pass it On

Checking the chambers and making sure that the barrels are free of obstructions should become an habitual action every time you pick a gun up, put it down, or pass it to someone else. This Commandment supports the first two and helps to develop *multi-layer* safety. I am also in the Army habit of saying 'clear' aloud (even in my own company) every time I check a gun unloaded. It is a verbal support to a physical action. With others present, it shows that you have made an effort and encourages them to adopt good practice.

You should routinely check for barrel obstructions *every time* you load a gun too. The muzzles might have become blocked with mud or snow, a wad might be stuck in the barrels, or a smaller-bore cartridge could have slipped into the chamber creating a potentially explosive obstruction. Because of the latter danger, always keep 12 and 20 bore cartridges separately. If you are using a small-bore gun occasionally, check your pockets and cartridge bags carefully after each shooting session. To use 28 bore cartridges is just as dangerous to a 20 or 16 bore as 20 bore cartridges are to a 12. A .410 may also block a 28.

I have a 'black museum' in my gun room of half a dozen guns burst in various ways. Happily, I have never been present when a gun has blown up, but I have prevented the classic 20/12 confusion leading to disaster on one occasion. Having noted a 12 bore shell accidentally loaded on top of a 20 on a simulated game day, I was able to rush to the confused individual concerned just before he pulled the trigger. Don't confuse your cartridges.

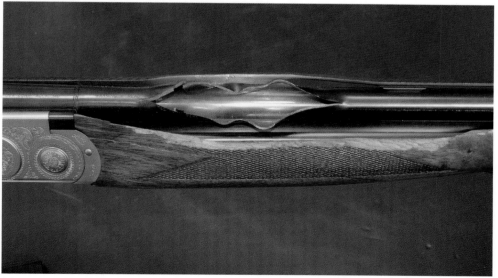

It is well known that 20 bore cartridges can be dangerous if inadvertently loaded in a 12. This accident, however, was created by a 28 bore cartridge accidently inserted in a 20 bore gun. Note the barrels have split forward of the monobloc proving the inherent strength of this type of manufacture. (Picture courtesy of K.D. Radcliffe Ltd)

Keep Your Finger Off the Trigger and Keep the Safety Catch On Until You Have Decided to Make a Considered Shot

Keeping the finger off the trigger *and the safety catch* on is another means of building up multi-layer safety (if you make a mistake at an earlier level, disaster may yet be averted by good gun handling protocol). I prefer to see the trigger finger extended along the trigger guard, but some like to extend it along the head of the stock. Either is acceptable. The safety should be removed *just before* mounting the gun at an <u>identified target</u>. *It should not be removed as the gun comes up to face and shoulder.* The trigger finger should only come onto the trigger at the last moment. It might be added that this is the technique for game shooting; competitive clay shooting demands that the safety is removed before calling for the bird. The use of the safety will be considered in more detail later.

I always keep my finger extended on the trigger guard when I am handling guns or waiting to shoot.

Break a Gun Before Removing it From a Slip

Removing guns from slips, like taking them from racks or cabinets, is something that must always be done with care and control. The right way to remove a gun from a slip is to:

1) grip the barrels through the material of the slip and control them safely downwards
2) place one's hand on the grip of the stock with the trigger finger extended forward (off the trigger)
3) break the gun and check the chambers are unloaded as soon as the action clears the slip *before the barrels are removed*
4) check the barrels are unobstructed as soon as they clear the slip

Too often guns are removed from slips in sloppy fashion, with the muzzles sweeping bystanders before the gun is opened. It is remarkable how many people remove guns from slips with their finger on the trigger.

Learning to take a gun out of a slip properly is an essential skill to acquire. Note that the action is opened with the trigger extended on trigger guard before the gun is removed from the slip.

The slip should be carried with the fastener and flap to the top – if you forget to fasten the flap, or if it fails, the gun does not fall out. Nevertheless, one sees many walking with guns in slips muzzle-up, sometimes because the slip itself is poorly designed.

Use of slip

When driven game shooting the gun should be slipped between drives. The use of a slip promotes safety – there is no temptation to take pot shots between drives – and it protects the gun (padded, lined or leather slips are preferable to plain canvas ones for this reason). Slips should always be carried with the fastening at the top. If one forgets to close it, or it fails, the gun will not fall out and be damaged. Again, it is amazing how many do not carry slipped guns in this prudent fashion.

It might be added that the use of snap caps should be discouraged. One often sees them in the chambers of guns being removed from slips (on many occasions, moreover, one notes them subsequently bouncing on the floor or ground because the owner has forgotten they are in the gun). Though gun shops love to sell them, snap caps are an unnecessary accessory for most modern, coil-spring powered, guns. If you are putting the gun away for an extended period, the main springs may be eased by dry firing provided the gun is proven empty and pointing in a safe direction (although I prefer the use of a nylon block or coin held against the face of the action of the disessembled gun to take the impact of the striker/firing pin). The use of snap caps removes a level of safety and creates a potential confusion with live ammunition.

This method is also acceptable in my opinion – open on the shoulder, barrels forward and secured with one hand.

The best way to carry an unslipped gun – open, on the forearm, trigger guard behind the arm.

WRONG. This is a bad way to carry a gun as you may inadvertently bang the barrels against someone or something else.

WRONG. This is another poor way to carry the gun. If the trigger guard is forward of the forearm the gun is less secure and it is much less comfortable.

I only suggest carrying a gun like this in your own company.

This is another debatable position. I do admit to using it on occasion. The trigger guard must point upwards and the muzzles must be kept well up. I also like to see the trigger finger extended on the guard.

Keep guns slipped wherever possible and never pull a gun from a car muzzle first.

Never Pull a Gun from a Vehicle Muzzles First

The Commandment concerning the prohibition on pulling the muzzles of a gun towards you when the gun is in a vehicle is the direct result of a number of fatalities that have occurred in this manner. A gun is put into a vehicle loaded by accident or folly and the trigger is caught by some projection as the muzzles are pulled forward. BANG! The centre of your chest or your head no longer exist. You may think that description excessive, but I hope you never share my experience of seeing someone who has been shot. A shotgun is one of the worst weapons with which to be blasted at close quarters. It creates a terrible wound. One has a much better chance of surviving a shot from a pistol.

One much-experienced shooting friend, Jack Montgomery, never leaves a gun in a vehicle in a slip of any sort. He prefers to disassemble the gun and place it in a hard case. His rationale, a wise one, is that by this means a loaded gun cannot be put into a vehicle accidentally (or taken into the house). Many years ago, Jack had been on a shoot when one his companions suffered a suspected heart attack. The concern about this and the disturbance of normal routine it created had a significant consequence. Jack discovered later, in his gun room, after the crisis had passed, that the friend's gun with which he had been entrusted had been brought in loaded. This event – which happened to someone who takes great pride and care in his gun handling – led him to change his habits and make more use of hard gun cases. The story is also interesting, and inspiring, because it shows Jack had the right attitude to safety. He accepted the mistake and determined to do something about it. It also demonstrates how an unexpected eventuality can break normal safety routines and, potentially, kill you or someone else.

Never Shoot Where You Cannot See

This Commandment has all sorts of implications. Do not shoot into hedgerows, for example. What you thought was a rabbit, might turn out to be a berry picker. When I was very young, I nearly shot an old lady in such circumstances and was only saved from disaster by the keen eyes of a friend. You should always remain aware that an ambiguous visual stimulus may be misinterpreted by your brain. Human perception does not work like a camera as many might assume. An ambiguous image may be 'completed' by the brain based on previous experience and consequent expectation. Reality may be momentarily distorted with dreadful consequences.

It is often said that one should not shoot low birds. The danger is that in the heat of the moment you shoot at a low bird, having failed to note a person in cover behind, i.e. you are shooting where you cannot see. The prohibition on low birds is absolute in the case of all birds being driven *towards you*. You would be well advised, moreover, to keep your muzzles well up at all times when waiting for, or walking up, birds. The old – and excellent – advice is that one should always see sky before pulling the trigger when driven shooting.

On most driven shoots, one will see birds being taken lower than they should. I have been involved in several legal cases (one involving a settlement of more than £300,000) where individuals have been blinded in such circumstances. Apart from the very serious safety issues, low birds shot at close range are often spoilt because they are excessively damaged by a tight pattern of shot.

Low birds may, on occasion, however, be shot to one's rear on open ground *provided one can see where one is shooting* and there is no breach of local custom or etiquette. The no low birds rule remains a good one for beginners in all situations (on driven days, it may be combined with a 'no birds behind the line' injunction). Even when all safety criteria have been met, shooting low birds and shooting birds behind the line has an increased potential for danger and warrants significant caution.

Do Not Shoot Ground Game on Driven Shoots Unless Given Express Permission

Ground game may be shot within the shoot rules on occasion. Experience leads me to caution against it, though, unless one is in a position far away from other guns.

You may on occasion be put under considerable pressure to shoot foxes (even on those shoots – now the majority – where ground game is prohibited). Foxes are best and most humanely shot with a .22 centre-fire rifle or similar, in my opinion, though others may argue they may be properly despatched with a shotgun provided a suitable load of shot is employed. The strong emotions their appearance creates on a driven shoot are a cause for potential danger. The problem with unexpected 'targets of opportunity' is that they may encourage Guns to take shots without

The best tool to shoot foxes is a .22 centre-fire rifle in the author's opinion. They may be shot with a shotgun provided an appropriate load is used – No. 1 or No. 3. (With lighter loads there is a serious risk of wounding).

sufficient analysis in difficult, unfamiliar, conditions. Taking a bird at a safe angle in mid-air has fewer potential pitfalls. I like to keep life simple, so I usually avoid ground game when shooting driven birds (going out to shoot rabbits with a shotgun is an entirely different matter).

Do Not Cross a Fence With a Loaded or Closed Gun

Most shooters now realise that they should not cross an obstacle with a loaded gun. BASC and other organisations have issued a lot of positive advice on this subject. It is always good practice to lay the unloaded, open-actioned, gun on the other side of the fence before crossing. If two people are out shooting together, one should cross first without guns, and then the other should pass both, open, unloaded guns, butt first to the man on the other side. Crossing streams or ditches alone presents something of a conundrum. Here, my routine is to unload and close the gun before negotiating the obstacle. My rationale is that an open gun might close and cause injury in a fall. When one gets to the other side, check the barrels for obstructions immediately.

*If two shooters have to cross a fence, one should climb over first and the other should pass the **open** proven empty guns butt first to his companion.*

Keep Your Muzzles Up: Do Not Shoot – or Let Your Muzzles Pass – Within 45 Degrees of a Human Being

This is a more sophisticated version of 'do not shoot low birds'. It is based on the concept of an absolute safety angle and applies in both vertical and horizontal planes. When driven shooting, one should be especially aware that braking effort with the hands may be required in some circumstances to prevent the barrels of your gun carrying through into a danger zone (i.e. within 45 degrees of someone else). This makes the point once again that safety is always an *active process*.

The 45-degree rule may also require considerable thought in some circumstances. If you are below other Guns or beaters your safety angles may change. This was brought home to me on a shoot in Gloucestershire recently, where the beaters advanced down a steep bank towards the Guns. It took the greatest care on that drive to maintain one's safety angles. The setting was glorious, but many of the birds driven over my peg had to be left. In such circumstances, young or inexperienced Guns need to be advised accordingly and watched carefully.

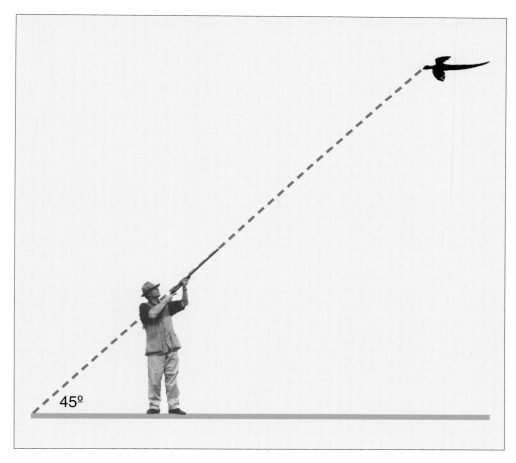

Proof marks on an older Purdey – note the imperial bore size .729"; NP indicating nitro-proof; the nominal bore size 12 in a diamond; the chamber size, 2½"; and the proof pressure, 3 tons.

Check That Your Gun is in Good Condition and in Proof

That one should only shoot with a gun in good mechanical condition is no more than common sense, but, that said, many do not know how to assess the condition of their gun beyond its superficial finish (see Appendix 2 for more information). Buying and using old guns has all the same pitfalls of buying and using old cars. Things are not always what they seem. Proof is an even more complicated subject. *If you have any doubts whatsoever about the proof status or safety of your gun consult a professional gunsmith or one of the proof houses.* The latter institutions have been set up to promote public safety and will always be happy to advise.

One significant danger for game shooters using older guns is forgetting to check the chamber length. Most older English guns are proofed for 2½-inch (65-mm) shells; most modern cartridges are intended for 2¾-inch (70-mm) chambers. Happily, there are still plenty of 2½-inch cartridges on the market. Meantime, using an excessively long cartridge in a short chamber can not only damage your gun but may also damage you. Steel shot is another area for care. In some cases it is unsuitable for classic guns (see the section on cartridges and choke and also note the proof information in Appendix 1). It may also be noted that *some* interchangeable chokes should not be used with steel shot.

Beware the Invisible Man

Just as guns 'grow' cartridges, woods and fields 'grow' people. They appear mysteriously in places where they should not be, places where common sense suggests that they cannot be. Always be on the look out for the invisible man, child or courting couple. Keep checking on the position of companions, beaters, flankers, girlfriends, wives, children and dog men. Keep the barrels up. Never take risky shots. Consider the consequences of risk taking. You must identify your target *positively* every time before you shoot. If in the slightest doubt leave it. I take pride in leaving more shots than many. Frankly I do not think that we are strict enough about dangerous shooting. Anyone who takes a suspect shot more than once, or is greedy after warning, for example, shooting more birds than their given limit on a walk-and-stand day, should be sent off the field.

Having stated the Twelve Commandments. There are some other points of safety that must also be considered:

The traditional 'wood-to-metal' method for closing guns – not advised for beginners or over and under users.

Closing Guns

Do not slam guns shut, they may go off. The old practice of always bringing 'wood to metal' is a sensible precaution – it ensures that your barrels are pointing at the ground as you close the gun (see pictures above). The critical point, however, is this: *always close guns with control and with the muzzles pointing in a safe direction (about 45 degrees down).* Should the gun go off by accident, it will discharge harmlessly into the ground.

There can, sometimes, be problems bringing 'wood to metal' in the traditional manner. If the gun is a little stiff to close – as many mass-made over and unders are when new – it may rotate about the axis of the front hand as you attempt to close it. The muzzles may end up pointing at your feet. Bringing wood to metal may also result in cracked stocks if performed with too much self-righteous gusto: it increases the vibration going through the grip.

I prefer an alternative technique (note the picture sequence on next page), first secure the butt against the side of your body, gently squeezed between rib cage and inner forearm. A right-hander should then cant the still open gun slightly clockwise, a left-hander slightly anti-clockwise. Canting the gun makes it easier to close. As the gun is canted the bottom edge of the butt remains in physical contact with the body. Now the weight may be brought onto the front foot, and the barrels may be lifted smoothly up with the front hand, while downwards pressure is exerted with the rear hand holding the grip. The method of closure described requires the minimum effort and provides the maximum control. All through the process, the muzzles are kept pointing down towards the ground at about 45 degrees.

When Should a Gun be Loaded and Closed?

A gun should only be loaded and closed when one is in the process of walking up game, standing at a peg or other position expecting game, or when one is in a hide waiting for game (and it is one's turn to shoot in cases of double occupancy). In all these circumstances, of course, the muzzles should be controlled forward and skywards, and the safety catch should be applied.

On a driven day, the gun should only be loaded and closed at the beginning of the drive as instructed. On occasion however, one may be told to load – and shoot – as soon as one gets to the peg. There are other occasions, for example when 'blanking in', when one may be told to walk to one's position with a loaded gun and 'take any birds you see breaking back'. Such special circumstances require special care.

The preferred modern method of closing a gun – controlled between rib cage and forearm and pointing safely down at about 45 degrees.

You must never put down a loaded gun when game shooting. If any interruption occurs, break the gun and unload. As soon as the final horn or whistle blows, the gun should be unloaded immediately, checked for obstructions, and slipped.

Always a good way to carry an unslipped gun: unloaded, action open, trigger guard behind the forearm.

Standing with Guns

When one is standing in a line on a driven day, or when one is rough shooting with a companion, great care is required not to inadvertently point a gun at one's neighbour at any time. On driven days, one faces forward with muzzles up with the safety applied. The trigger finger should be extended along the trigger guard or along the head of the stock, and is only brought to the trigger as a shot is taken. A relaxed ready position may have the muzzles pointing near the vertical. An alert ready position will have the muzzles pointing something just above 45 degrees (depending on the situation), with the eyes scanning the 'zone of engagement' to one's front. In this situation two hands should be holding the gun (always good practice).

Some wait for birds with the muzzles pointing down, either with the gun held in the hands or resting on the forearm. You will get told off at some shoots for doing this. This lazy method has the great disadvantage that at some stage the muzzles must be brought through the horizon (unless one turns to the rear to raise the gun).

Wrong. The gun is unslipped, the dogs might step on the trigger, and – worst of all – it is being pulled out muzzles first and pointing at someone whose attention has been distracted.

Sitting With Guns

Some sit with guns on driven days making use of a shooting stick. Sitting is also a common ready or shooting position when pigeon shooting or wildfowling. The trouble with sitting is that it can encourage lazy gun-handling. There is a greater temptation – because more muscular effort is required to prevent it – to bring the barrels back across the body so that they may stray potentially into a danger zone. Shooting sticks have the added risk that perching on them can be rather precarious. If one is likely to shoot sitting, it is sensible to practise the technique. The big problem, and a potential safety as well as shotgun marksmanship issue, is that the upper body movement is restricted (Will Garfit gets round this by using an old office swivel chair when he is pigeon shooting).

Walking With Guns

Great care is required when walking with a gun. Always walk with the muzzles up, with two hands on the gun, and with the safety applied. If you are in any way unsure of your ground – break the gun and unload. The trigger finger should be extended forward, and if you are walking with others, you must keep an eye on the line to make sure that you are not falling behind or moving excessively forward (this can be very hard work when one is the last Gun in line on a walked-up grouse day). Keep an eye on the other members of the party at all times, and consider your shots with care. Walking in cover is an especially dangerous situation and requires that you remain alert and thoughtful at all times. Clothing is an issue to be considered when you walk. Do not overdress – wear layers rather than bulk – and make sure that you are sensibly shod with boots or shoes with good soles that grip well. I also think it makes sense to wear an American style orange cap or hat band if walking in or near cover.

When walking up game, the muzzles should be raised, the trigger finger extended on the guard, and both hands should be on the gun.

When to Shoot

Rough shooting

First, the target must be a legal quarry species and it must be a safe shot. You must always pick a specific target. Shooting or 'browning' in the direction of a covey or flock is almost sure to result in a miss and is extremely poor sportsmanship as well. Particular dangers while rough shooting are moving companions and cover (which may conceal a human being or a dog). Novices need to be taught to wait a moment before firing when they flush a bird at close range. This allows the bird to rise, thus giving one a little more time to assess the safety of the shot. It also prevents the spoiling of the meat by an excessively tight pattern at close range.

Driven shooting

First, one must be in position on one's peg. One must have noted the positions of neighbouring Guns and others who may be in the vicinity. The horn or whistle must have sounded (unless one has been given instructions to the contrary). The target must not be prohibited and any shot at it must satisfy the basic requirements of safety and conform to the rules of shooting etiquette.

Arcs of Fire

As a general guide, as discussed, a shot should never be taken (and the muzzles of a closed gun should never point) horizontally or vertically, within 45 degrees of any human being. On driven shoots, one must also consider which birds one may

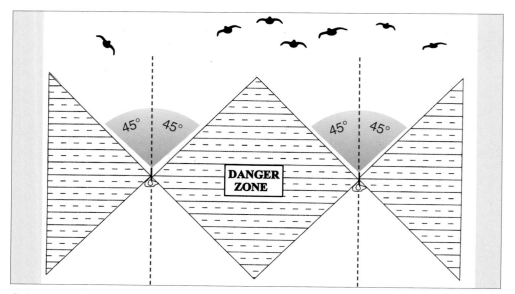

Safety zones for game sharing (after Churchill).

properly shoot and which are best left for neighbouring Guns. A typical arc of fire when you are placed in a *straight line* might be about 90 degrees to front and rear (assuming no prohibition on birds behind the line). This approximate 90-degree arc – you must be the judge on the day – is most easily understood as 45 degrees to either side of an imaginary centre line charting the flight of a bird driven straight towards you (see diagram). Much will depend on the ground and the positioning of the pegs.

It is impossible to lay down a general rule when the distance between Guns and ground varies and the shooting line itself may not be straight. If one is positioned on the flanks of the line, a much wider arc may be safe. If one is in a staggered line (something to avoid when planning a driven shoot if at all possible), one might have a much reduced arc of fire on one side. Rather than get into complex geometry, I prefer to show novices a diagram of typical safe zones, and reinforce the really important rule: that no shot should be taken within 45 degrees of any person. Other rules of engagement relate to etiquette more than to safety.

Shooting 'down the line'

As far as driven shooting is concerned, novice shots must fully understand the dangers of shooting or swinging 'down the line'. There is a particular danger of swinging into a danger zone when taking a second shot at a bird that was missed on the quarter with the first shot. The momentum of the gun combined with adrenalin induced over-eagerness can carry the muzzles towards one's shooting companions, unless the movement is *deliberately checked*. Shooting at fast, unpredictable, targets, like woodcock, grouse, quail or snipe, is especially dangerous because of this.

Use and Function of the Safety Catch

In most circumtances, as we have already noted, the safety should only be disengaged once the target has been identified as safe (and legal) a moment before

Remove the safety, a moment before mounting the gun at an identified and legitimate target.

The thumb should immediately move to its proper gripping postion and not ride the safety during the mount.

The combined safety catch and barrel selector on a Beretta Silver pigeon.

the gun is raised to the face and shoulder. <u>The index finger must not be resting on the trigger as the safety is removed</u>. It is best placed extended along the trigger guard. If no shot is taken, the safety should be reapplied at once when the gun comes down. It is a bad habit to remove the safety as the gun is mounted or to fiddle with it while waiting for birds.

The 'safety catch' on some shotguns may be no more than a trigger block. Even intercepting safety sears can fail (as Robert Churchill used to enjoy demonstrating). Though its action must not be relied upon, the safety does have an important function when game shooting. When properly used, it makes accidental discharge less likely. To fire a gun with the safety applied, two distinct actions are required: pushing off the safety and pressing the trigger. The possibility of nervous compression of the trigger is thus reduced. The safety should be applied at all times when the gun is closed, unless one is in the act of shooting.

Tradition and common sense dictate that drop or break-action game guns should be equipped with an automatic safety catch. Its application cannot be forgotten under pressure. However, automatic safety catches are not foolproof. Although they may be applied automatically, they can be removed prudently or imprudently any time thereafter. Nor should it be forgotten that safety is primarily concerned with attitude of mind and, most particularly, where one points the muzzles – not the function of any mechanical 'safety' device.

Use of the safety catch: clay shooters new to game shooting game

When you watch them game shooting, you will notice that many clay shots do not use the safety catch properly. This may occur because they have not been taught how to use it correctly in a game shooting context, or because they are under pressure in an unfamiliar environment. It is not because they are generally unsafe shots – on the contrary, the average clay shooter is probably more disciplined with regard to safety than the average game shot. It is, however, a general principle of firearms training that individuals, when stressed, tend to revert to what is most familiar to them, Clay shots finding themselves shooting game may thus remove their safety catch too early – whether or not they know better – simply because they are used to removing the safety catch well before pulling the trigger in clay shooting (or keep it permanently in the 'fire' position). Clay shooters may also forget to reapply the safety catch (especially if they are using a non-automatic safe clay gun). If you are moving from clays to game, you should be aware of this tendency, and condition yourself into a new, safer, habit.

Shooting From Hides

The first thing to note is that there are important safety considerations in hide construction. A hide that is too small will be awkward and increase both the likelihood of accidents and the temptation to handle the guns improperly. In particular, there must be sufficient room to the front to allow for safe loading and handling. Guns must never be loaded and propped up whilst waiting for a bird; if the gun is loaded, it must be controlled by the user.

Shooting from hides always warrants special care. My preference is for hides that are not too restrictive.

The problems of shooting from hides are compounded when more than one person is shooting. Many experienced pigeon shots now consider it bad practice for two guns to be simultaneously in use in a hide. They believe that during double occupancy, one person should shoot and the other should act as observer and spotter. Roles may change periodically. When they do, the observer/spotter's gun should be proven clear and placed in a slip. My own feeling is that two guns may be used simultaneously when one is shooting with a regular, proven, partner, but not otherwise.

Position in the hide is an important consideration in double occupancy. When two Guns sit side by side, there is always the danger, in the heat of the moment, of one person pointing a gun at the other. Loading is dangerous too. The best position for the non-shooting person is always to the rear. Moreover, the non-shooter should be positioned to one side (the right rear when behind a right-handed shot; and the left rear when behind a left-hander).

Lofting poles

A specific danger when decoying for pigeon is the use of aluminium lofting poles which, like carbon fibre fishing rods, can conduct electricity from high tension cables. The pole does not actually need to touch the cables either; the very powerful currents in pylon wires can jump to a nearby conductor.

Pigeon shooting – other safety considerations

One should be very careful about other people straying into your area when out pigeon shooting. Many shots are taken at low elevation and one must be absolutely sure of one's ground. I know of one case where a pigeon shooter built his hide so well that a courting couple decided to lie down immediately in front of it. He dined out on that one for a few years (he did not reveal his position), but the serious problem is that hides not only fool pigeons, they can fool anyone who is walking in the vicinity.

Ricochets

I have known at least one case of someone blinded by a pellet deflected by a power cable. Ice, water and trees all present a potential ricochet danger as well. Pellets may also occasionally deflect off birds. The counsel of perfection would be to wear protective glasses at all times when shooting – they would also prevent 95 per cent of eye accidents in the field.

Misfires

If you get a misfire do not open the gun instantly. Wait a few seconds in case a hang fire is in progress. The old rule was to wait thirty seconds. This may be excessive in an age of nitro-cellulose propellants; but counting to ten is a wise precaution (with black powder weapons stick to the old thirty second rule). It should also be mentioned that very cold conditions can affect the mechanisms of some (over-oiled) guns and may cause a delay in the hammer falling.

Field/Hotel Security

Make sure that your guns are well secured when they are not with you (and indeed in your home). Consider separating barrels from action or removing the forend when storage conditions are less than ideal. However you secure your guns, make sure that you could justify it to a judge in open court – do not leave gun cases visible in cars; lock them in a secure boot in a disabled state. You may want to consider equipping your vehicle with a gun-safe. *Never leave guns unattended in the field.*

Protect Your Ears and Eyes

Too many shooters have lost their high-frequency hearing. You will too if you do not use effective protection. High-frequency loss is not the only issue; as I write this my ears are ringing with tinnitus. I have worn plugs all my shooting life, but the latest research suggests that damage to the inner ear may be caused by vibration though the skull and, notably, the bone around the ear. If I had my time again, I would wear muffs on all occasions.

Your eyes are an even more precious asset. The best advice is to wear protective specs in the field. The most common accident when shooting live birds is someone else's pellet in your eye. Safety glasses, especially those with side protection, will offer you significant extra safety. Different tints may also help shooting in strong sunlight or twilight (polarised brown or bronze may help in the former case and gold or yellow for the latter). Make sure the lenses are made from toughened glass, polycarbonate, or CR-39 plastic. You should choose shooting glasses with care. Do not just consider the looks, but also the lens and frame size (not so small that you are forced to look into the very top of the frame when the head is in a normal

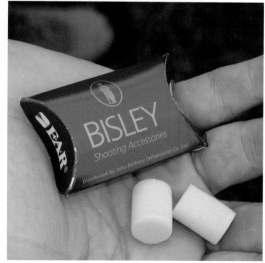

Ear protection must ALWAYS be worn when shooting.

shooting position). Frames should not slip on the nose and their arms should locate securely behind the ears. The wrap-around ear-pieces of some aviator style frames are ideal for game shooting.

> Hearing damage is caused by prolonged exposure to high, constant, levels of sound or to sudden peaks of sound. In the former case, as used to be encountered in some industries (and may still be experienced at pop concerts or in the home) sound over 85 decibels is known to be harmful. In the latter case, exposure that goes beyond 140 decibels may be hazardous. Shotguns generate about 150 decibels and full-bore rifles in the range of 160–170. There are two components to the noise: the muzzle blast (increased in short-barrelled guns or guns firing magnum loads) and the sonic boom or crack when the shotcharge or bullet exceeds the sound barrier. One must protect one's hearing or one will suffer irreversible damage to the cochlea – the spiral cavity in the inner ear that converts vibrations into nerve impulses. It is likely that you will lose your high-frequency hearing first. This is also affected by age, but it is important and helps, in particular, to clarify speech. Even occasional shooting without muffs or plugs can lead to damage (which may not become apparent for many years). Don't take the risk.

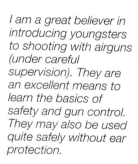

I am a great believer in introducing youngsters to shooting with airguns (under careful supervision). They are an excellent means to learn the basics of safety and gun control. They may also be used quite safely without ear protection.

THE ETIQUETTE OF SHOOTING

In formal shooting, the line that separates safety and etiquette is not easily drawn. Much shooting etiquette is connected with safety. I am often asked by beginners for definite rules concerning shooting field etiquette and, as far as possible, attempt to comply with the request. By far the best advice one can give – apart from suggesting formal instruction on the field – is to tell students to find an experienced game shot who will stand behind them on their first few outings. Such a 'minder' will also explain the customs and terms of game shooting, things that are best learnt in the field. Shoot captains should insist that any new gun should be accompanied by a suitably experienced individual.

Nevertheless, there are some basic points of etiquette with which the novice must be familiar with before he or she reaches the field. For, example, one should not shoot at birds that are too close (although they may satisfy the requirements of safety), nor birds that are too distant and likely to be wounded. It is bad form to shoot a bird, even if it is within one's arc, if it is flying toward a neighbouring Gun or would make a better shot for a neighbour than you. If you are walking with the beaters do not shoot birds going towards the Guns, but only those birds that come back. If a neighbour on the line misses a bird, do not shoot until he has fired a second barrel or until it is apparent that he is not going to fire a second time. Never be greedy.

My eldest boy, Jamie, on his first day's driven shooting. He's just picked his birds after an excellent drive and I don't think he can believe his luck!

When positioned on a peg, keep still and keep quiet. If you miss a bird shoot again if you can – rather than look for the next bird. If you wound a bird and it flies on, note carefully where it comes down if you can. If you shoot a bird well, do not brag about it. Do not forget the peg number you draw and remember that it is normal to move up two positions between drives – but listen carefully for exceptions when briefed by the shoot captain. When you shoot a bird, note where it falls as precisely as you can, the eyes should be kept on the bird for a moment after the shot is taken, so that you may give instructions to pickers-up or retrieve it yourself at the end of the drive. Following the bird after the shot is taken also promotes a good follow-through.

Count your birds. Do not leave the field until all your birds have been retrieved (unless directed otherwise by shoot captain or pickers-up). Do not retrieve your neighbour's birds without asking. While shooting is in progress, do not be tempted to leave your shooting position to retrieve a bird, even if it is wounded, but do allow the bird to be picked by a dog. Do not shoot pest species on a driven shoot unless you have been told it is permissible. Similarly, do not assume that you can shoot pigeon (many shoot captains prefer Guns to avoid pigeon in the early stages of a drive). A useful general principle on any game shoot is: 'If in doubt, don't'. This obviously applies to safety, but it is also a good principle as far as etiquette is concerned.

If someone has been kind enough to invite you to a shoot, write a thank-you letter the evening after the shoot and post it as soon as possible. Never retract an acceptance of an invitation because a 'better' opportunity is subsequently offered. On the subject of tipping, the best advice to anyone who goes to a new shoot is to ask the other Guns what they usually give. Do not be stingy; tips are an important part of most gamekeepers' income, which at best is modest considering the skills and responsibilities of the job. Also remember to thank the beaters and pickers-ups individually after the shoot; their hard work is too often taken for granted.

Despatching Game

All game shots have a duty to despatch their quarry as humanely as possible. Not all birds will be dead when they hit the ground (although the number of wounded birds will be reduced if one restricts oneself to birds within sensible range, one's equipment is appropriate, and one has a responsible attitude toward improving and maintaining one's marksmanship skills). Some novices will attempt to pick up birds by their feet rather than their necks. How to pick up a bird may seem obvious to someone who has done it all their life, but it is precisely the sort of point that needs explaining to a new Gun.

A good way to kill wounded game is by a swift blow to the back of the head. This may be done with a stout stick or a 'priest' – a metal, horn, or wooden truncheon made especially for the purpose. There are also pincer-style humane despatchers. Birds should not be held by the head or neck and swung in an attempt to break their necks. This technique is used by some experienced countrymen, but there is a knack to it. It is easy to get it wrong and not kill the game cleanly. The novice is far better advised to buy or make a priest. Rabbits may be despatched with a karate-like chop to the back of the neck, or similarly with a priest, or by

Never forget the effort put in by beaters and pickers-up on a shoot day.

holding the neck with one hand and pulling the rear legs sharply with the other until the neck vertebrae are dislocated.

In discussing this, I am reminded of an incident some years ago that happened to me on the East Coast. I was driving out of the ancient Cinque Port of Brightlingsea – where I was living at the time – when the car in front collided with a large cock pheasant and drove on. I stopped to despatch the poor creature, which was flapping on the road. As I was performing the necessary rites, a police car with blue flashing light pulled up behind me. I faced a burly sergeant with the bird's neck in my hand, caught, quite literally, red-handed. 'Suicide was it, Sir?' 'Well in all honesty, yes.' After a pregnant pause in which my fate was evidently being considered, came the reply: 'Well give it a decent burial.' There is a postscript. Somewhat enervated, I returned to the car and placed the booty on the passenger seat. About a hundred yards down the road, it came back to life..

Basic Points of Etiquette

1. Stay safe – keep your muzzles up and don't shoot low birds. Always see sky before shooting.
2. Don't shoot down the line – control your muzzles at all times.
3. Don't poach – only shoot birds within your legitimate Arc of Fire.
4. Keep still and quiet.
5. Don't shoot at a neighbour's bird until he has fired twice or left it.
6. Don't forget your peg number and how many places you need to move up.
7. Mark where your birds fall and make sure they are picked up.
8. Don't boast about your marksmanship.
9. If walking with the beaters only shoot those birds going back.
10. If in doubt – don't.
11. Thank the beaters and pickers-up as well as the host and keeper.
12. If invited, write to thank your host as soon as you get home.

SHOOTING VISION

The eyes are everything to shooting. If you cannot see the bird you cannot shoot it. Practically speaking, every shooter must ensure that his or her eyes are capable of sustained focus at distance and that they suffer from no abnormalities such as astigmatism (usually caused by an irregularly shaped cornea). Regular eye checks are a must, and with middle age they become even more important (after forty, it makes sense for any keen shot to have an annual eye test).

As well as going to a specialist to see whether there might be a need for glasses or a change to an existing prescription, it is sensible to seek out the services of a professional instructor-gunfitter periodically to check eye dominance. If you have a problem in this regard – and many shooters do without realising it – you may not be pointing the gun where you think. Eye dominance, moreover, may not be constant (see below).

Your eye dominance determines the method by which you should shoot – right or left shoulder, one eye or two – and can affect your equipment choice. I am always surprised by the number of shooters who assume that they are right-eye dominant. Only about half turn out to be absolutely right dominant when thoroughly tested. Many of the remainder are predominantly dominant in the right eye (which is best considered a separate category because it may necessitate different actions), or have a left eye that cuts in on some occasions. Cross-dominance (e.g. right-handed/left-eyed) is common too, but true central vision – where neither eye is dominant – is much rarer.

Right-eye dominance.

Left-eye dominance.

Eye dominance can change temporarily: when we are tired; when we are ill; when we have been staring at a computer screen for too long, or after long-distance driving. Bringing the focus back to the gun instead of keeping it locked onto the target – a very frequent mistake even amongst experienced shots – can also cause mysterious shifts. Eye dominance is subject (with much individual variation) to age related change as well. Before puberty most boys do not have clearly established dominance in either eye. Post puberty, most men develop absolute or predominant

Testing for eye dominance using the simple pointing method. This shows right-eye dominance.

This shows the rarest form of eye dominance – true central vision where neither eye is dominant.

This appears to show, left eye dominance. Eye dominance should always be checked at the pattern plates and on clay targets as well. People do not always shoot as tested.

eye dominance in the eye corresponding to their 'handedness'. To what extent this relates to genetic or learned factors is not well understood. But, it is interesting to note that the distribution of eye dominance amongst sportsmen seems to differ with the players of different sports.

With the onset of middle age those men who were clearly dominant in one eye may find the other begins to have a significant effect (the usual prescription for which is a bit more cast or, if this does not have sufficient effect, squinting the eye opposite the rib). There are very significant sex differences too. With women, as with pre-pubescent boys,

This circle method can show up subtle differences. Note that the eye is not centred – there is some 'pull' from the left eye.

absolute eye dominance in either eye is the exception. Many have what might best be described as indeterminate eye dominance with both eyes fighting for control. This is different to central vision where the effect is equally balanced. Because of the subtle individual variations, testing for eye dominance must always be done with the greatest care. It is all too easy to misdiagnose.

My favoured testing method is to ask the client to create a circle by bringing the tip of the thumb and forefinger of the weak hand together. The tester then indicates one of his own eyes as an aiming point and the client – standing about 10-15 feet away and keeping both eyes open – extends the arm forward as far as is comfortable and brings the circle up into his or her line of sight whilst looking at the tester's finger tip. With the circle method, which I usually repeat with both the client's hands, left- or right-eye dominance will be immediately apparent (because the eye will be in centre of the circle) but so will more subtle differences where the eye will appear to be off to one side (which can be missed by other methods such as 'finger pointing' or the use of a card with a hole pierced in its centre).

I cannot emphasise too strongly that there is more to eye dominance than a simple right/left decision. Testing methods that result in an either/or, right/left, diagnosis are inadequate. 'Dry' testing is never enough either. The diagnosis must always be confirmed at the pattern plates and after that, by watching the individual shoot a variety of clay targets actually in flight. A simple going away or straight driven bird is useful to check for gross right/left errors, as are mid-range crossers (if

Squinting is a simple remedy for eye dominance issues, but some people (including many women) cannot squint or wink one eye, they are candidates for this remedy. Careful positioning of the block to vision is critical – what counts is where it will be when the head is on the stock.

Sights like the Easy Hit and Hi-Viz Magni Optic (both of which can only be seen by the eye looking down the rib) can be a useful aid for those with eye-dominance issues. The Magni Optic is shown here.

the right-hander continually misses the right to left bird in front suspect that the left eye is taking over). Sometimes, only one target will cause a problem (for example, a slow bird, crossing the field of vision).

If you are right-handed and absolutely right-eye dominant you can and should shoot with both eyes open (gaining the full perceptual advantages of binocular vision). Similarly if you are left-handed with left-eye dominance. If you are predominantly right- or left-eye dominant, a little extra cast (or offset) to the comb may solve the problem (and still allow you to keep both eyes open), or, you may choose to close or dim the offending eye as mount and swing progress (by keeping both eyes open at the start of the shooting process, you benefit from a wider field of view).

Those who are cross-dominant or suffer from visual confusion can shut or dim one eye, block its vision by some other method (such as raising the thumb of the forward hand as Robert Churchill used to do, putting a small well-placed patch on their shooting glasses or, on a side by side, using a dedicated 'blinder' incorporated into a handguard). They may also consider one of the new

A sophisticated cross-over stock from an old Churchill gun. Note the swept face and extension piece.

generation of foresights – such as those made by the HiViz and Easy Hit companies that are only visible to the eye looking down the rib – or shooting off the opposite shoulder. The latter course is not one to be taken lightly. Its prerequisite is usually that you are absolutely dominant in the opposite eye (otherwise a change may only add to visual confusion). I have come across many people who have been told to swap shoulders, but who would have been much better advised to dim or wink an eye as the mount and swing progressed while shooting off their strong shoulder.

Another option for cross-dominance, and one that used to be encouraged by gunmakers far more than it is today, is to use a specially constructed gun with a so-called cross-over stock. This usually has a very evident dog leg in it. It allows for a gun to be mounted on the right shoulder, but it brings the rib in line with the left eye. Such guns have serious disadvantages. They are ungainly, and they may be prone to cracking through the grip because of the increased stresses in this area. Nevertheless, one cannot help but be amazed by the ingenuity and craftsmanship that went into some of these contraptions. If found in the racks of gun dealers or in auction, they may not achieve the prices of more normal models (but don't buy one just because they appear to offer relatively good value). Semi-cross-over stocks also seem occasionally intended for those with central vision.

Yet another option for dealing with cross-dominance – not an especially practical one in the field – is the use of an extra rib parallel to the main one attached by clips or out-riggers. There is also the possibility of using supplementary front and rear sights similarly attached as in the 'Monopaeian' sighting system (as illustrated in W.W. Greener's book The Gun and Its Development). This was actually invented by the Reverend E. Elmhurst (though Greener, characteristically, does not mention it). I have experimented, quite successfully, with a simple out-rigger foresight made from brass or steel (and designed simply to replace the original bead). Although vulnerable to knocks, this seemed to work surprisingly well without any rear aid to sight alignment.

Having mentioned all the exotic alternatives, I am of the opinion, that simply squinting the eye is usually the best advice for those afflicted with cross-dominance or central vision. It can also be a simple cure for those who are predominantly but not absolutely dominant in the eye looking down the rib. Dimming an eye can make the straight driven shot more difficult, but even this can be mastered at closer ranges with practice (the technique is to shoot the bird as one loses sight of it under the barrels). In the case of longer birds, the David Olive system of taking them side on as a high-crosser is to be advised. Those with indeterminate eye dominance (which is easily misdiagnosed as full cross-dominance) are best advised to close an eye or block the vision to it by one means or another as well. They should never change shoulders.

Low-stocked guns and short-barrelled guns tend to aggravate eye dominance problems in my experience. And, be warned that testing does not always give definitive results. Some test absolutely right- or left-eye dominant, but do not shoot accordingly. If you have any doubts, if you suffer from persistent visual confusion, it is imperative that you seek out the help of a professional instructor. At the very least enlist the help of a friend and check your eye dominance as described above without too many preconceived notions. You may be surprised at the result.

Eye Dominance: Simple Advice

The options once your eye dominance is determined are as follows.

1) Absolute dominance in the eye looking down the rib: shoot both eyes open and get the full benefits of binocular vision.

2) Predominant dominance in the eye looking down the rib: keep both eyes open with extra cast, or dim the eye as the shot is taken.

3) Full cross-dominance: close an eye, use a 'blinder', eye patch or modified shooting spectacles. Consider a parallel rib, use a cross-over stock or change shoulders.

4) Predominant dominance in the eye opposite the rib: shoot from the 'strong' shoulder closing eye, or otherwise blocking vision to opposite eye. If eye dominance in opposite eye is nearly absolute, changing shoulders may be considered with a suitably cast gun under professional guidance.

5) Central vision: close an eye, use a 'blinder', eye patch or modified shooting spectacles, or consider the use a semi-cross-over stock.

6) Indeterminate dominance: close an eye, wear an eyepatch, modified shooting spectacles, or use a 'blinder'. Don't change shoulders!

GUNFIT

Once one has determined one's eye dominance precisely, gunfit should be considered. A well-fitted gun – one that points naturally to where the eye or eyes are looking and controls recoil effectively – will make anyone shoot better. Gunfit is not rocket science yet it has been shrouded in considerable mystery over the years. Whilst there is room for individual interpretation, and the 'prescriptions' of different gunfitters are not always the same, the basics of gunfit are straightforward.

Essentially there are five basic sets of variables of gunfit: drop (sometimes called bend), length, cast, pitch and grip. Drop is, in my opinion, the most important. It controls the elevation of the shotgun in much the same manner as the backsight of a rifle (the shotgun usually has no rear sight, one is entirely reliant upon the relationship of head to stock for the control of elevation). It is difficult to make consistent allowance for unsuitable drop dimensions, whereas small variations in length or cast do not make that much difference unless one is looking for excuses.

Too high a stock may make you, unknowingly, shoot high. Too low a stock can

A try gun used by an expert is a good tool for determining gunfit provided it is of similar pattern to the gun to be made or fitted. I would not, for example, advise fitting someone for a new over and under with a side by side try gun. Some makers have try guns dedicated to their products.

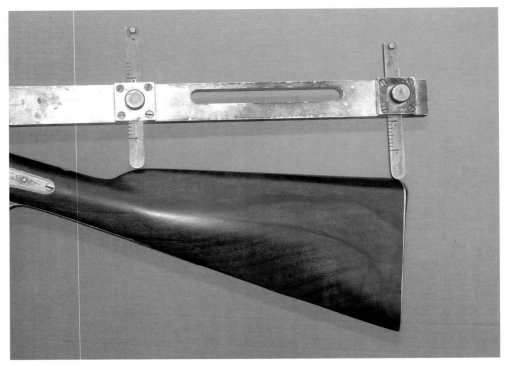

Drop, measured at the nose of the comb and also at the heel is the most critical of all the gun-fitting variables. It establishes the critical vertical relationship between the eye and the rib axis.

cause low shooting, but it can also cause inconsistent high-low shooting because of head lifting in compensation for the poor fit. Another problem with a low stock is that it can encourage the wrong eye to take over (because the view to the true master eye is blocked by the breech when the head is held on the stock). All things considered, a stock a little too high is far better than one a little too low.

What is usually required for live quarry shooting is a drop measurement that will result in about 60 per cent of the pattern being placed high and 40 per cent low of the point of aim when the head is comfortably positioned with normal cheek pressure. This results in a natural shooting gun and allows for the fact that game birds are usually rising and hence missed low. Some may prefer a 50:50 split, but they are a minority.

Drop is usually measured 'at comb' and 'at heel'. Sometimes a more central 'drop at face' measurement is also made. Holland & Holland, who have specialised for many years in guns with swept and/or offset combs, always take this measurement. It may also be useful when considering custom-made stocks. Drop, by the way, is the distance between the top of the stock comb and the axis of the top surface of the rib as measured at the front and rear of the comb. Typical dimensions would be 1½-inches and 2-inches for a side by side and 1⅜-inches and 2⅛-inches for a recently made over and under (in the United States guns may have more drop at heel).

There is some argument about what is best with regard to eye position in the vertical plane, but the intention here is to avoid complication as much as possible. When I fit a side by side for game shooting, I am usually looking for the first picture as a starting point:

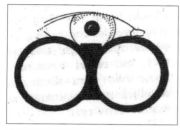

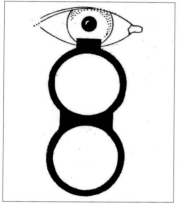

The bulk of the iris, the coloured part of the eye, should appear to be sitting on the breech when the Gun's head is in a normal position on the stock. When fitting an over and under for game shooting, I usually like to see the pupil sitting just above the breech/rib*, as in the second picture:

Side by sides tend to shoot a little lower than over and unders – all other things being equal – and may, sometimes, need to be fitted slightly higher. It has been suggested that this flat shooting is because the barrels and grip are more flexible than those on over and unders and therefore subject to more downward flex in recoil. (Recent experiments support this: guns with thin grips will shoot significantly lower when used with heavy cartridges. In a 20 bore side by side, for example, the difference in point of impact in the vertical plane might vary by 12-inches at 40 yards depending on the cartridge type. Low-velocity cartridges will not only make some guns seem to shoot higher. They may make a significant difference to apparent lead as well.)

A high fit can be useful in any game gun because it helps one to keep up on the line of birds and also equates to a little more lead on driven targets. In particular, a higher than average fit for the 'one-eyed' game shot may be advocated, because it will allow for more visibility on driven shots before sight of the bird is lost as the swinging gun passes through the target (unavoidable for Monopaeians unless they take driven birds as crossers).

Now we must add a complication: drop not only locates the position of the eye over the breech, it also affects the positioning of the butt sole at the shoulder. Generally speaking, the top line of the stock of the mounted gun should be more or less in line with the top of the shoulder (exceptions occur because some people prefer to mount the gun stock lower). One certainly does not want to see any significant amount of the butt sole projecting above the shoulder line. (If it does, do not automatically assume it is a fit issue; it could be caused by poor mounting. Try the Churchill mounting technique – see page 123-4 – and see what happens.)

Some people – notably those with long necks, sloping shoulders or small heads – may be well served with a 'Monte-Carlo' stock. This can also be useful for young shots and women. Anyone with a head smaller than the average adult male norm is likely to need a higher stock than average to get their eye properly in line with the rib. Monte-carlo stocks keep the top of the comb parallel, or more or less parallel, with the axis of the rib and have added benefits because of this.

---

*For sporting clay shooting, however, I usually prefer to see the pupil sitting on the breech.

My daughter Lizzie shooting a Beretta 20 bore with a much modified stock. It has a Monte Carlo comb created by inletting wood onto the top of the stock – most young people need a higher than average stock as well as a shorter one, yet many struggle with stocks intended for adults.

In any stock, if the comb is excessively sloped, felt recoil will be increased. This is a failing of many older guns and one that sometimes may be rectified to some extent by raising the heel. If the comb is parallel or nearly parallel with the rib axis (and if the comb itself is well shaped), it will glide back under the cheekbone as the gun is fired and felt recoil will be reduced.

This highlights quite an important principle when fitting for drop: a stock which is inclined significantly – in which there is a great difference between drop at comb and drop at heel – will increase felt recoil. It is a good principle to keep the difference between drop at comb and drop at heel as small as possible on any stock. My preference is to keep the difference in dimensions to no more than ¾-inch. In other words, a stock that measures 1½-inches and 2-inches at comb and heel respectively is well within my arbitrary limits, but one that measures 1½-inches and 2½-inches is not and may cause discomfort.

Length

The length of the gunstock (also called the LOP 'Length Of Pull') is the distance from the middle of the trigger to the middle of the butt sole. Sticking to the KISS philosophy: use as long a stock as you can comfortably mount. This is most easily determined on a high overhead shot – a tower bird or something similar. Too short a stock will increase the felt recoil; too long a stock will check your swing. More experienced shots tend to prefer a longer stock. Once they have perfected their mount, it allows for more control. A typical length measurement for an adult male would be something in the range 14 to 15½-inches (stocks in the UK tend to be a bit longer than those in the USA). The norm these days is 14¾-inches (at least as far as the UK is concerned).

Do not assume all your guns should have the same length of stock. For ease of mounting, very heavy guns should be shorter and very light ones (such as small-bores) slightly longer, all other things being equal. You must also consider the clothes that you will be wearing. Grouse shooting in shirt sleeves in August, may call for a longer stock than shooting pheasants in January wearing a heavy jacket.

As a rough guide for 12 and 20 bore game guns, look for between one and two finger-widths of gap between the base of the thumb and the tip of the nose when the gun is properly mounted. The popular method of holding the gun at the grip and seeing if the butt sole makes contact with the lower bicep when the arm and gun are held up is imprecise and should be used only as a very rough guide (it can be useful occasionally when assessing beginners for rough fit). In conclusion, never start with any 'ideal' measurements in mind for drop or length, what is right is what suits you as assessed by trial and observation. Let me conclude this section by noting that you cannot transfer the dimensions from one gun to another and automatically assume the two will shoot the same.

ABOVE:
Length looks about right – one to two finger-widths of gap from the tip of the nose to the base of the thumb. It looks as if there could be more contact between the shoulder and the top of the butt sole – a more concave shape may be required.

RIGHT:
Measuring the Length of Pull (LOP) of a gun in the E.J. Churchill gunroom.

Cast

Cast is the extent to which the stock is angled to right (cast-off) or the left (cast-on) and is an especially important variable of gunfit to those who have less than absolute eye dominance or have a body shape that does not conform to the 'Mr

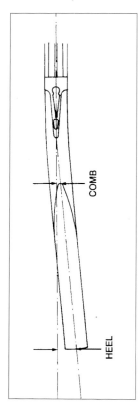

Average' norm. Cast is measured at heel and toe (and by some gunmakers at the action and 'at face' – the mid-point of the comb. Typical dimensions for cast at comb and heel would be ⅛-inch and ³⁄₁₆-inch or ¼-inch and ⅜-inch. The difference in the heel and toe dimensions is explained by human anatomy; the bulk of the breast and the pectoral muscle calls for the sole of the stock to be slightly offset to achieve firm and comfortable support in well-developed males.

Usually a right-handed shot has a cast-off stock and a left-hander, one that is cast-on. Those with especially broad chests may want more cast than average, and it can also be used to accommodate differences in facial width and type (a right-hander with a very broad face and wide-spaced eyes may occasionally be accommodated by a cast-on normally reserved for southpaws).

In fitting for cast it must be understood that it is not simply a question of getting the eye precisely aligned with the rib in the horizontal plane, though this is often used as a starting point for fitting. Some people will need very considerable cast because of eye-dominance anomalies; the extreme being those who need a stock with a distinct dog-leg in it to compensate for the effects of cross-dominance or central vision. In these cases the eye will be nowhere near the centre line of the rib. Many more may need ⅛-inch or ¼-inch extra at heel to compensate for a left eye that is having the effect of pulling the aim off target slightly.

This overhead view shows how cast is typically applied on mass-made guns – from the rear of the action tang. On bespoke guns, cast may begin in the action itself.

Cast, which may be tested at the pattern plates and on straight driven and outgoing targets, should always be kept to the minimum, however. It can increase felt recoil; it puts more strain on a potentially weak area of the stock, and, in its extremes, will hinder natural gun pointing. Extremes of cast should, especially, be avoided on over and unders. An alternative or supplement to cast in some circumstances is to offset the comb. One often sees the combination of an offset comb with cast on bespoke guns. This means the cast at heel can be substantially reduced.

Another point worth making is that very thick combs, as seen on many over and unders of Continental origin, may unintentionally push the eye to the left of the rib (a simple cure for this is to get a stocker to thin taper the comb or to fit an adjustable comb and offset it slightly). On older English guns the face of the comb

The beautiful form of the butt on a Holland & Holland 'Royal' over and under 20 bore. Note the wide-radius semi-pistol grip, an ideal form for a single trigger game gun.

was often 'swept', or, 'scooped' (post manufacture), as a means of altering the eye-rib relationship. Both thinning/reprofiling and scooping (a cruder process) can be a useful means of modifying an excessively thick stock (before you consider either, though, check that the butt has not been hollowed to any great extent).

As with drop, cast also affects the positioning of the gun at the shoulder. It is often said that the butt sole should sit in the so-called 'shoulder pocket' between the shoulder joint and collarbone. I do not accept this as an absolute rule. For some (perhaps the majority) it is the right place, but many first class shots do mount the gun on the shoulder joint and would be uncomfortable doing otherwise. What is absolutely wrong (and indicative of absolute error) is to mount the gun on the upper arm. This results in the butt being insufficiently and inconsistently supported and typically leads to bruising.

So far we have not said much about pitch – also called 'stand'. The length of the stock from the middle of the trigger to the heel and from the middle of the trigger to the toe determine the pitch of a gun. Typical measurements are plus ⅛-inch (length to heel) and plus ⅜-inch (length to toe). Older guns may have more toe. Pitch is the angle of the vertical 'line' through the toe and heel of the butt sole relative to the axis of the rib and may be approximately measured by standing the gun against a wall, with the top of the action touching (but like cast, is better measured in a specialist jig). Typically it is about 2-inches 'pitch down', but may be less on guns intended for some forms of clay pigeon shooting. The pitch measurement – which may also be stated in degrees – is especially important on a game gun, where the gun needs to keep well up on the line of the bird as the swing progresses: the vast majority of shots are taken at high elevation.

Returning to KISS, the simple rule for pitch is to create a stock in which the butt sole is in comfortable contact with the shoulder throughout its length. The curve of the butt sole should also match the shoulder and mounting technique of the user. Someone who mounts the gun on the shoulder joint wants a curved pad to match. Someone who mounts in the 'shoulder pocket' or lower, on the chest, wants a different shape to achieve consistent support. If the toe or heel of the butt sole are not in firm contact with the shoulder, or if the pitch measurements cause the mount to be impeded, something is wrong. <u>Watch to see if the heel or toe are coming to the shoulder first</u>. Temporary adjustments to pitch can easily be made to guns with butt plates or recoil-pads by loosening off the screws and introducing shims. Women and men with large chests may want a reduced toe measurement and, often, a rounded toe as well.

Grip shape and size are other important variables. The grip must be so formed that the wrist is not obliged to be excessively cocked down or up (some tightly radiused pistol grips can, notably, increase wrist strain in a game gun, the muzzles of which must often be held up to maintain safety). The grip must be wide and deep enough to achieve good purchase, and not excessively rounded in cross section. The most ergonomically efficient designs are usually oval or diamond-shaped: good grip shapes promote good purchase and hence good muzzle control.

Grips must not be too short (a common problem) or too long. They must complement the width of the palm and the length of fingers (it is the former that primarily dictates grip length). The position of the nose of the comb is important too; if it is too far forward (a common failing of mass-produced guns) it is easily modified. The flutes either side beneath the nose of the comb (often exaggerated in cheaper, machine-profiled, stocks) may benefit from a little hand-shaping by a good stocker too (see below).

Stock Alterations

Alterations for cast and drop are usually made by placing the stock in a jig, heating the grip area by means of hot oil, steam or infrared light and applying pressure in the desired direction. The wood is pushed a little further than required as there is a tendency for it to spring back when it cools. Changes to cast and drop may also be affected by alterations at the 'head' of the stock. These involve cutting small amounts of wood from the stock in the area where it meets the back of the action. Combs can be lowered by removing wood from their top and side surfaces – a job best left to an expert if the shape of the comb is to be properly preserved. Combs may be raised (and changed in angle) by inletting wood. Temporary adjustments to drop can be made by use of a comb raiser or simply by card strips and vinyl electrician's tape (which, unlike other types, is usually kind to stock finish).

Many mass-produced stocks benefit from having their combs reshaped by an experienced craftsman. Although this will necessitate re-finishing, it is often well worth doing. Some mass-produced guns have club-like stocks with combs that are

A simple rubber comb raiser (with nose cut off) fixed with vinyl tape. Also note the rubber butt extender. (These can be useful but the leather type is less prone to snagging).

far too thick and lacking in taper to their front. An excessively thick comb has the same effect as cast as noted and may push the eye to one side of the rib. Such stocks can also increase felt recoil. Some old guns, on the other hand, have very thin, acutely angled, combs, which can have similar effects.

The butt sole, the part of the stock that meets the shoulder, may also benefit from subtle modification by a good craftsman. I always like to see a distinct 'bump' at the heel (a protrusion, the high point of which is an inch or so below the extremity of the heel). For many it is an aid to positive location and recoil control. Frequently, stocks are encountered on Continental game guns that have excessively flat butt soles. Mounting technique is an issue as noted – but a classic, concave butt sole profile is usually to be preferred. This not only looks better but, in most cases, is more efficient, beds well against the shoulder, and prevents slipping in recoil when classic shooting syles are employed.

Other Issues

Trigger pulls must also suit the user as must the weight of the gun. A first pull of 3½ or 4 pounds and a second pull ½ pound heavier is about right for the average 12 bore (excessively light or heavy or inconsistent pulls are evidently a handicap; very light pulls also create safety issues). A gun must be well balanced as well. This subject is covered in more detail on page 193). The phrase covers all sorts of imponderables but let's keep it simple. If the gun is grossly barrel; or stock-heavy, as measured using the near-hinge-pin balance as a simple index, you are unlikely to shoot as well as you might.

The single triggers on most modern mass-made over and under guns are extremely reliable – the majority are recoil activated, but a mechanical trigger can be a useful feature on a game gun – especially if light loads are being used. Some inertia triggers are easily converted to mechanical operation.

This pattern placement looks ideal for live quarry shooting – just a fraction high and left of the point of aim.
Note by the wad holes that this is the result of a test involving a number of shots. This establishes a mean point of impact.

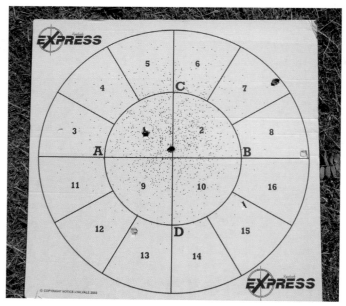

When does high become extreme? Never shoot beyond your ability level. If you take up the high bird challenge you must ensure that both your marksmanship and your equipment are up to the mark. Gunfit and cartridge choice are critical.

Weight may be taken from a stock by hollowing it and introduced into it by means of lead or lead shot and putty (or, of course, by adding an extension or recoil pad if required). For game shooting, I generally prefer a gun that is fairly light in the barrels. Most modern, multi-choke guns tend to be fairly barrel heavy, however. At the least ensure that back and front balance out more or less (I have no objection to a slightly front-heavy gun). A heavy, well-balanced gun is vastly superior to a light ill-balanced one. The comment is often made that sidelocks may balance better than boxlocks because there is more weight between the hands. There is some truth to this, one certainly notes in mass-produced guns that a more even weight distribution can to result in an apparently 'lifeless' gun.

Gunfit: Simple Advice

Pick up your <u>proven empty</u> gun and stand in a normal shooting position. Mount the gun without rushing. Dismount. Now, mount the gun again, but as you complete the action shut both eyes. Maintaining normal cheek pressure, open the eyes. What can you see? Is the bead visible? Does the rib look like a ski jump before your eye? Are you looking along the rib or to one side of it? Each of these results has a remedy. The stock may need to be raised, lowered or cast appropriately. This is only a rough guide, however. Pattern plate testing and professional advice will give more reliable results.

PART III

We have considered something of the history of our sport, we have looked at the modern forms of shooting, and we have explored the important subject of safety (not least, the Golden Rules: treat all guns as loaded: *never* point a gun at anything unless you want to shoot it). We have also looked at the subjects of shooting vision and gunfit. Now it is time to consider the business of how to shoot well. Each of the sections that follows is quite detailed – so you may develop your understanding of the subject – but within each there is, again, a box entitled 'Simple Advice' to which beginners, or anyone wanting straightforward guidance is directed.

SOUND FOUNDATIONS: FOOT POSITIONS

A good stance provides the platform for a consistent, unimpeded swing. In particular, a good stance provides good *balance* throughout the swing, mount and follow-through – something rarely achieved with wide-spaced feet, an excessively bent front knee or a protruding bottom. Watch people shooting and you will see that many are out of balance at the moment the shot is taken. They run out of swing through poor technique or poor preparation and are forced to compensate with the most ungainly body positions. We can all get wrong-footed, but a little understanding and a bit of practice and experiment can keep those occasions to a minimum. How should we stand? Let us look at the classic styles first.

A classic Stanbury style stance.

Percy Stanbury famously advised a stance where the weight was kept on the front (left) foot throughout the shooting process (this applied whether the shot was right or left or being driven overhead at considerable height). The general attitude he noted was that of 'a half turn to the right front' with the chest at 'an angle of about 45 degrees to the line of fire'. There is a slight forward lean in Stanbury's position and the rear (right) heel is slightly lifted. The front leg is kept straight and acts as a pivot so that hips may move right or left with ease (generating the power for the swing). The heels are 6–9-inches apart. If the shooter stands on a clock-face his front foot will be positioned at one and his rear foot at about three o'clock

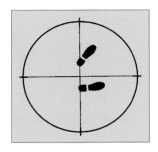

Stanbury foot position.

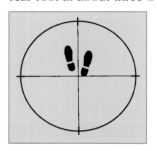

Churchill foot position.

Robert Churchill who was of a stockier build than Stanbury, suggested a quite different way of standing. The Churchill stance is squarer, with the heels even closer ('about three or four inches apart' according to his famous book *Game Shooting*). With Churchill's stance one transfers weight on to the right foot for a shot to the right and on to the left for a shot to the left. Between shots the weight is evenly supported on both legs. On the clock-face the starting position for this stance would have the left foot at about half past eleven, and very slightly forward, and the right foot somewhere near one.

At first glance, there would seem little room for compromise between the two. Stanbury describes standing too square as an error and Churchill, placing the right foot behind the left. He suggests, questionably, that the latter technique prevents the butt sole firmly locating at the shoulder. When, however, one reads between the lines and experiments with both styles, one discovers that they have something in common – the attempt to achieve balance and free movement. Churchill even admits – and I only noted it recently – that when using heavy guns or guns with heavy charges 'a greater proportion of the weight may be thrown on to the front leg'. Both men may have exaggerated their positions for ease of description, and have created stances that suited their body types and shooting style. That is what every Gun must do too, rather than blindly accepting one dogma or another.

Let us add another stance into our discussion now. It has been called 'the Guinness stance' by my friends Peter Croft and Ken Davies. It is a very natural position, standing as if one was standing at the bar in conversation with a pint glass in hand. It is not as square as Churchill, nor as oblique as Stanbury. Both legs are relaxed and straight and, critically, the shoulders are positioned above the heels. If one placed a ruler across the toes and another across the heels, moreover, their lines would be parallel. It is an erect, but relaxed and unstrained position (and consequently a

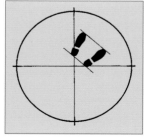

Parallel foot position.

favourite of some of the best competitive clay shots). If it has a flaw, it is that it may not encourage inexperienced Guns to keep their heads down on the stock.

Anyone who wants to improve their shooting style should experiment. Consider the advice of Stanbury and Churchill in the context of your body type. Are you tall and thin or more generously proportioned? I use Stanbury for most of my game shooting. When forced into very hot corners, though, or when standing in difficult, boggy, conditions, where there may be no time or opportunity to move the feet, I revert to Churchill's footwork instinctively. For the right-hander, it is an efficient way of dealing with fast birds appearing suddenly to the right.

Whatever stance you adopt, your feet should not be set in blocks of concrete. You may find that you need to adjust your stance for specific situations (some prefer to be closer-footed for

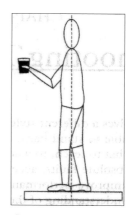

Guinness stance.

high birds than for grouse and partridge where rapid swinging and more stability may be required). If, in any given situation, your stance allows you to be in balance and minimises tension in the swing at the moment you pull the trigger it is probably right. If it feels unstable and/or restricts the swing it is almost certainly wrong.

> British, close-footed, shooting styles have been deeply influenced by driven game shooting in which there was little walking and the arc of presentation of the targets was fairly predictable. Interestingly, if one looks at eighteenth or early nineteenth century British shooting prints – an era before the introduction of driven shooting as we know it – one sees a much wider, edge-on, style. In the United States, where walking is still the norm, this style of standing is still common (the fact that the USA is a nation of riflemen may also be significant). The disadvantage with any wide stance is that swing may be impeded (which is, of course, less significant when flushing birds on a walk-up).

Stance for High Birds

Some right-handers will arch the whole body and keep the weight on the front (left) foot when taking a bird well above (the rear heel will raise or 'unweight' as a result). Some will move onto the back (right) foot for all overhead shots (the front heel will lift as a consequence). Some will transfer the weight right or left as per Churchill's advice, depending on the side the shot is taken. Some will stand erect, and keep their centre of gravity between the feet and keep both feet firmly planted on the ground. It is a question of what allows them to stay in balance best whilst pushing in front of the target.

The Stanbury technique certainly looks most elegant, but there are days when stiff backs may not allow it. Generally, close-footed stances are to be preferred on high birds. This may be contrasted with the situation on a windy moor when keeping the feet a few inches further apart may make sense to maintain balance and provide a good platform for a controlled swing (for more detail on shooting high birds see pages 148-51).

There is no single, right way to stand – what is right is what suits you best in the situation. You must be in balance when the trigger is pulled.

Stance: Simple Advice

If in doubt – stand square.

Take half a pace forward with left foot.

Stand square to the direction where you intend to shoot. Take half a pace forward with your left foot (for right-handers). Allow the rear foot to rotate naturally on its ball, so that it is pointing towards three o'clock and the front foot towards one if you are shooting at twelve. Bring your weight onto the front foot. Front shoulder, front hip and the ball of the front foot should be more or less in a straight line (imagine a fence post going through your body). The rear foot should be at about 90 degrees to your imaginary killing zone. Common errors include arching the back (typically an affliction of beginners who are trying to compensate for the unfamiliar weight of the gun), allowing the weight to be predominantly on the rear foot (which also leads to head lifting), and bending forward with the bottom sticking out (which makes it hard to swing). The weight is kept on the front foot. The back is straight, but *relaxed*. This allows one to pivot easily right and left.

GRIPPING MATTERS

Holding the gun may sound like a simple topic, but it is amazing how many hold their gun in a way that impedes their shooting or is actually unsafe. The hands control the gun; if they do so efficiently purchase is maximised, recoil minimised – the hands absorb far more recoil energy than is generally realised – and the muzzles will be pointed effectively. A well-designed gun in this respect – one with a forend and grip that are well shaped and with effective gripping surfaces – is an important part of the equation. I have picked up some guns that even the most gifted would have difficulty shooting well.

Gunfit must return – briefly – to our narrative. No one can hold a gun properly if the grip causes the hand to slip in recoil because it has been narrowed excessively to its front, or if it is too big, too tightly radiused or if the grip has a poorly positioned palm swell that puts the rear hand in the wrong position. A relatively even grip depth is required to ensure a good hold, and, as previously noted, the shape of the grip in cross-section is important too (a straight grip should not be too round). The forend and grip must not be greatly different in size, a thin grip is not well complemented by a thick forend and *vice versa*, nor should the front and rear hand be made to take up positions that are excessively distant from the barrel axis. If they are, natural pointing will be disrupted.

My preference is for straight grips that are fuller than average and diamond in cross-section (as on Holland & Holland guns), full pistol grips conforming to the classic British rifle pattern (which are notably even in depth and width throughout their length), and the elegant and practical Prince of Wales Grip as often seen on Woodward guns (and copied, not always well, by other makers). Half-pistol grips – those with rounded knobs – deserve to be more popular on over and unders. They are an excellent pattern for game shooting and provide control without cramping.

As far as forends are concerned, some favour a well-shaped *Schnabel* (from the German for a duck's bill) as both Browning and Beretta have perfected. I like a style with more constant width and depth (though Beretta has recently come up with something of a compromise, the 'American' forend which appears to be very similar to its *Schnabel* but with the front lip removed). I do not like Tulip forends on over and unders – because their pronounced belly forces the front hand into a single position – or those grips that are very wide, narrow or deep (the first and last impede natural pointing, whilst the narrow grip impedes purchase and requires too much muscular effort to hold well). For side by sides there is little to beat the deeper splinter of a Purdey game gun, or, on heavier guns, a subtle beaver-tail (as also made beautifully by James Purdey).

What about hand position? Both hands should work together. It is especially important that the rear hand does not dominate the mount. It should maintain a comfortable but efficient position with the bottom joint of the thumb just to the right

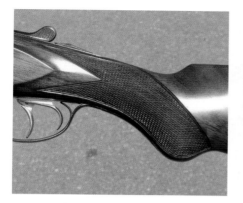
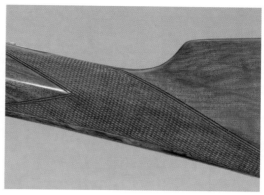

ABOVE LEFT:
This old Beretta has a semi-pistol grip and double triggers. Over and unders with double triggers are rare today.

ABOVE RIGHT:
A Holland & Holland style straight grip – on a Spanish gun – note the central ridge, typical of genuine H & H guns.

LEFT:
A subtle and well-shaped full pistol grip from a 1929 Purdey. Some pistol grips are too tightly radiused for game shooting. They can make it hard to hold a gun comfortably with muzzles up, and some argue that they can impede the swing too.

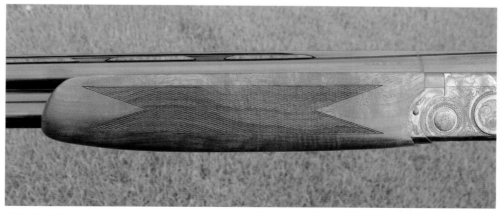

Schnabel forends have been fashionable for some time on over and under sporting guns. Several makers are now offering alternatives which do not have the lip at the front. This is the 'American' style on a new Beretta Silver Pigeon – it is an excellent design, probably my favourite, on a mass-made stack-barrelled, gun.

WRONG. The elbows should be in a natural, unstrained position – the rear arm should not be raised as this can impede the swing.

Both elbows want to be in a natural, unstrained position, usually at about 45 degrees.

of the comb nose/centre line of the rib (assuming a right-hander). Many adopt a rear grip with the web of the hand positioned too high. This creates tension and hinders the mount. Correct positioning of the rear hand also ensures that the elbow falls into a comfortable position. Viewed from the front both arms should appear to be at about 45 degrees but with the elbow of the rear arm just a little higher than the front. The trigger finger should be extended without strain or twisting. The rear elbow should not be raised as it may cause an impediment to swing. Where should the trigger finger make contact with the trigger? Most good shots prefer to use the pad of the trigger finger, rather than the first joint as sometimes advocated (although the latter technique may be adopted if trigger pulls are too heavy or a grip too short). The pad is the most sensitive part of the finger and its use encourages a consistent pull rearwards without lateral stresses. Another important point worth making with regard to the rear hand is the position of the thumb pad; it must not 'ride' the safety catch (which invites a painful injury and reduces purchase and hence muzzle control). The thumb should normally be wrapped around the grip unless actually in the process of operating the safety (an action that take places a moment *before* the mount begins not during it).

Some position the trigger blade near the first joint, others use the pad of the trigger finger for increased 'feel'.

Front Hand Position

If the hand comes too far back, speed of swing may be increased but control diminished (a technique deliberately adopted on occasion by George Digweed on fast crossing shots). The opposite is true if the hand is extended forward in the manner of George V. Control is increased, but the swing may be checked. Try it. Pick up a gun, prove it empty, and engage an imaginary overhead bird with the front hand variously positioned. Do the same for crossing targets. An exaggerated forward hold – as once favoured by many game shots – makes both types of target more difficult (and may lead to misses behind). It also restricts the ability of the front arm to keep the barrels up on line on quartering and crossing shots. A far better position is a naturally comfortable one with the front hand positioned at the tip of the forend of side by sides or *about* halfway up the forend of over and unders.

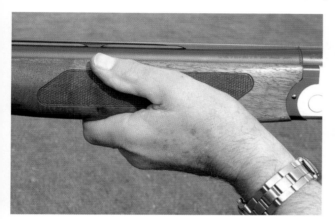

Usually, the front hand should be about midway on the forend of an over and under.

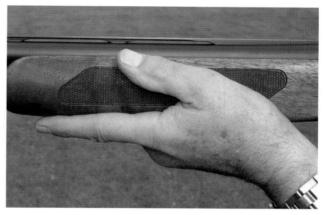

Whether or not you extend the first finger is a matter of preference.

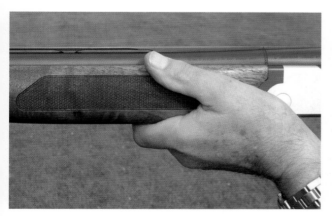

If you bring the front hand back, you will increase your speed of swing but lose some control.

I call this the 'claw grip'. It is frequently seen but not efficient or elegant.

Some choose to extend the index finger of the front hand as an aid to pointing; for others this is uncomfortable. One often sees the index finger running along the bottom rib of side by sides and along the side of the forend of over and unders. My preference is to half-extend the index finger, as full extension requires tension. What is certainly wrong, is to allow any of the fingers of the front hand to obscure the view down the rib (unavoidable, to a degree, in some small-bore side by sides with poorly designed, excessively shallow, forends).

Another bad habit, but not as significant, is what might be called the 'claw' grip (as illustrated on the previous page) on an over and under. In this, the hand is brought to the side of the forend (reducing support) with the index finger in splayed position pointing above the axis of the barrels and second digit below. One sees similar idiosyncrasies in some side by side users. In both cases the function of the front hand and arm is being impeded.

Often, poor hand positions are adopted to compensate for other flaws in technique, for example, the failure to use the body well to generate power for the swing (it should rotate like a tank turret for crossers or bend like a bow for driven birds). Although one should not use the arms and hands too much to achieve *primary* gun movement, the front hand has an important part to play in pushing the barrels in front of the bird and in the follow-through once the shot is taken. The front hand also needs to push up diagonally as the body rotates or bends during the swing on a crossing bird to keep the gun up and on line. A good, relaxed and efficient, front-hand position, moreover, encourages the front elbow to fall into a natural unstrained position.

What about grip pressure? Neither hand should have a white-knuckle grip. Opinions vary beyond that. The late D. Lee Braun, a fabulous shot and one of the USA's most respected old-school instructors, used to say that one should grip the forend 'as if holding a handful of eggs'. Many might say that was not hard enough, at least as far as game or sporting shooting is concerned (although it may suit competitive trap shooting). But, it makes the point that if there is too much tension movement may be restricted. First-class shots, even those who are very powerfully built, always seem to hold their guns with a certain delicacy, facilitating fine control.

Over-extending the front hand may check your swing.

Front hand looks fine – index finger pointed with barrels. Head is down. Stock length is good.

Holding the Gun: Simple Advice

The rear hand should have a comfortable grip on the gun with the thumb wrapped around the grip and not left extended riding the safety catch. The thumb should almost touch the second finger. The rear hand must not be rolled over the grip, moreover, the bottom joint of the thumb should be just to the right of the centre line of the grip (for a right-hander). The base of the thumb should be in comfortable contact with the nose area of the comb (but not pushed forward uncomfortably by it).

If you pat the right side of the stock with the flat of the right hand (assuming you are a right-handed shooter again) and extend the hand forward keeping contact with wood so that the forearm lies along the side of the stock, the hand will fall into the correct gripping position as it comes to the grip. It should require no rotation of arm or wrist when it takes up its final postion.

To get the rear hand in the correct position pat side of the butt with open palm and simply slide it forward onto grip.

Using the front hand well – it is much more than just a lifting lever – is one of the secrets of good shooting. It controls the muzzles and has a vital role to play in finishing the shot.

Any shot is well advised to go for an annual 'check-up' with a qualified instructor. The weight is well forward here and the head nicely down. But, is the front arm too straight? Perhaps the stock is too long.

Front Hand: Simple Advice

Extend the front arm forward without straining, and rotate the hand so that the palm faces up. Make a clenched fist, then relax the hand so that your fingers open without tension. Holding the proven empty gun with the rear hand allows the forend to fall into the relaxed half-open hand. If you are shooting an over and under, the hand should, roughly speaking, be in a mid-position on the forend. If you are shooting a side by side, you should end up gripping half wood and half metal. In other words some of the hand should be in contact with the forward part of the forend. Do not extend the front hand too far up the barrels (because it will impede your swing) or bring it right back to the action (unless this is a deliberate attempt to increase the spread of swing or compensate for too long a stock).

Developing a good gun mount is one of the key skills of shooting.

THE MOUNT AND SWING

A good gun mount is the hallmark of a first-class shot. The mount should be an unhurried but positive action, elegantly executed to three beats at a relatively slow tempo. Economy of movement must be combined with smooth flow. It will always be difficult to complete a good mount without a good stance and a good hold on the gun. Many, if not most, poor shots rush the mount, losing control of the muzzles in the process. The frequent tendency, seen as often on a pheasant drive as at a sporting clay shoot, is to 'bash and slash', i.e. to slam the gun up to the shoulder at light speed and then slash at the target. Wild shooting is the inevitable result. Those inclined to rush often end up rushing to a dead stop (and so miss the bird behind – often with a puzzled look on their face).

The essential problem of the mount and swing – it is important to realise that the two are usually happening together – is that one must achieve fairly precise control without checking gun movement unduly. Economy of movement is required, but flow as well. The stock is *raised to the face* and shoulder (the face should never be brought down onto the gun after the stock has reached the shoulder) with a coordinated movement of *both* hands. If any hand leads this action, it is the forward one.

The front hand fulfils a critical function during the gun mount as noted. It does not just lift the barrels, but it keeps the muzzles on line as mount and swing progress. It also helps to push the gun ahead of the target (though the primary energy for this is body rotation or bending as noted) and it has a vital role in finishing the shot. One often observes that the left arm of clients does insufficient work and the right arm and hand too much. The required balance of action is not achieved.

Unnecessary head movement is also detrimental to a good mount (to find out why, try pointing at a distant object whilst keeping your head still, then try the same thing whilst lifting the head slightly). The head should remain almost still relative to the neck and shoulders as the mount and swing progress (although it will, of course, rotate as the upper body moves). I often find myself advising clients to lower their chins a little before beginning the mount.

As the stock comes to the face it locates comfortably under the cheekbone. There is some variation in technique, and, generally, game shots may prefer to position the comb of their stocks a fraction lower than the more deliberate clay busters. The head is not forced down onto the comb of the stock, but the cheek should be in *positive contact* with wood when the mount is completed. Many fire their guns with their heads well off the stocks, or lift it prematurely as the shot is taken. Both habits may be considered absolute errors (and are typically combined with bringing the weight back) and can result in inexplicable misses behind and above.

Advice on the starting position for the muzzles and butt varies. Stanbury advised keeping the muzzles well up – touching the line of sight – and the butt well down. This might be described as a classic position and keeps the muzzles safely raised.

*Practice should begin with mounting a **proven empty** gun at a static or imaginary mark.*

One should also practise the mount and swing combined as a means of developing good upper body rotation.

Churchill advocated an unusual starting position with the butt tucked in under the armpit and the muzzles lower, as we have already explored. His concept, a useful one provided one considers the safety implications was that the barrels should be kept *parallel to the line of sight* during the mount.

In the case of a Stanbury-style mount, the barrels will pivot about the axis of the muzzles as the mount progresses (an effort must be made so that they do not rise above the line of sight). There is some slight forward movement of the gun. The shoulder comes forward to meet the butt sole as the mount is completed. In the case of the Churchill mount, the gun is pushed out more obviously as the mount commences and the movement of the shoulder to the gun at the end is less apparent (although Churchill might have argued the point). With the Stanbury system, it is almost as if the gun has a sliding hinge at the muzzles. With the Churchill mount, one might imagine that there are wires attached to the front and rear of the gun. These are both lifted simultaneously by a celestial puppet master as the mount proceeds.

These two methods are not the only mounting options. Experiment has led me to a 'third way' where the muzzles are kept fairly high (just below the line of sight) and the stock, in a natural position just below and forward of the shoulder, is held gently between tummy and forearm. This gets the best of both worlds. If you were to argue the merits of the classic approaches, you might note that the Stanbury technique is more generally useful and keeps the muzzles safely up, but the Churchill method is

Chris Bird, Chief Instructor at the Holland & Holland Shooting School demonstrates Churchill-style mount. Wisely, he holds his muzzles higher than Robert Churchill, though.

excellent for anyone having problems with consistent gun mounting. It ensures that the gun is properly positioned at the shoulder as the mount is completed and makes it easier to bring the gun to the face well.

I often use the Churchill mount as a teaching aid. I also use it when walking up sometimes. If one does adopt the Churchill mount, one must always make an effort to hold the muzzles well up. In its purest form as demonstrated by Robert Churchill, it would seem to encourage a low ready position (and hence create a potential threat to advancing beaters or working dogs). This is easily remedied, however.

Where Should the Gun Come to at the Shoulder?

It is often said that the sole of the butt must come to the so-called 'shoulder pocket', that is the natural hollow between shoulder joint and collar bone. For many people, this is good advice, but some very good shots mount their guns on or partially on the shoulder joint because they have a narrow shoulder pocket. Frequently this works perfectly well. Mounting the gun on the arm, as will happen if the stock is too long, may be considered an absolute error, as discussed. In all cases, the gun mount should be an unhurried, fluid and rhythmic movement. A particular effort should be made to control the tip of the gun – the first few inches of the barrels – throughout the process.

The latter, subtle but important, point of refined technique was first brought to my attention by an old and much missed Norfolk gunmaker, Paddy Woods. Paddy asked me to mount a gun in his shop one day, and noted 'You're, a good shot boy'. I smiled prematurely. 'But, you don't shoot with the tip of the gun, do you?' I had

I like to see the heel of the stock just below the shoulder line in most circumstances.

not thought about it before, but he was quite right: my muzzle control was not what it might be. The muzzles were rising above the line of sight as I raised the gun to his mark (as I remember, a ping-pong bat with a hole drilled in its centre). This necessitates a downwards correction as the mount is completed. The expert, by means of front-hand control and disciplined focus on the target, mounts the gun perfectly to the mark and maintains the line with the minimum of movement.

Speed of Mount

Many game shots rush, completing the mount far too early in their swing. This reduces visibility, impedes timing and may lead to a 'mount and slash' style of shooting as criticised earlier. 'Windmilling' is a common malady too, where one allows the gun to pivot about the axis of the front hand, moving the muzzles messily below and above the line of sight to the target (similar to, but more extreme than my bad habit as described above). A mount dominated by the rear hand nearly always leads to this sort of unnecessary and inelegant extra movement (the solution, of course, is for both hands to work together).

Practice

You should practise the mount as often as possible, as you might a golf swing or batting stroke. Many of the best shots pick up a gun for this purpose every day. If you

As already noted, practise your gun mount whenever the opportunity arises. Many good shots practise 'dry' (with a proven unloaded gun) every day.

do this be careful to prove the weapon empty first and do not just practise the simple forward mount at a static target, but work on perfecting the combined swing and mount. Do not bring the gun to face and shoulder too early. Place a new emphasis on using the hands well – using the front hand to control the tip of the gun. Generate the power for the swing from *body rotation* or body bending (for driven shots). Bring the gun to the face smoothly. Keep the shoulders *level* (unless you are deliberately inclining them to match the line of the bird). Keep the head in contact with the stock as you follow through. Don't unlock the face from the gun too early. Don't forget your rhythm: One: Two: Three. And, all the time, keep your eyes glued to an imaginary bird. Don't focus on the gun.

The Mount: Simple Advice

If you have any doubts about your mount, try the Churchill method first where the gun butt begins under the armpit gently squeezed against the rib cage and the barrels are kept parallel to the line of sight. Practise with a proven empty gun at a fixed mark above the horizontal. Don't be in a hurry. When you feel confident that the gun is coming up to the face and shoulder without a glitch, you may try mounting the gun with the stock in a more conventional starting position. In classic Stanbury style, the comb should be roughly parallel with the top of the forearm, and the muzzles just under your line of sight. Be aware of the muscles of the front arm and hand, and make sure by their good use that the gun does not windmill. The front hand controls the tip of the gun throughout the mount. Keep your head still and your eyes focused forward on the mark.

The Churchill-style mount performed with higher muzzles can be a great aid to improved gun mounting.

When one swings, the shoulders should usually stay level (with certain exceptions relating to advanced technique). This is a simple exercise to demonstrate the point.

With the Stanbury system the weight stays on the front foot for a shot to right or left.

Mount and Swing: Simple Advice

As well as mounting at a static mark (which has the advantage that one may focus upon it too), you should practise the swing and mount combined (I say swing and mount because the swing should begin before the mount is completed, not after). If you are using a Stanbury style of stance, pivot on the front foot and swing the hips right and left as you hold the proven empty gun in a ready position (about 45 degrees up) keeping the shoulder level.

When you feel comfortable with this movement, and you will note the body and the gun moving as a unit, you can introduce the mount into your training scheme. Rotating right and left, shoulders level, bring the stock to the face and shoulder slowly and smoothly – controlling the muzzles with the front hand. Now, try swinging along an imaginary or actual line (for example, the line created where the wall meets the ceiling if you are indoors). Call out the three-beat time – You: Will: Win!

ADDRESSING THE TARGET

When shooting artificial targets one has the great advantage – if one takes it – of knowing from where the bird is coming and to where it is going (at least in the case of skeet and sporting clays). One can, and should, select a killing point so that one can swing on and through the bird without tension; a point where the gun will be held (so that unnecessary gun movement is avoided) and a point where the eyes will look in anticipation of the target (so that they will lock onto it without delay). In the field, one does not have the benefit of the same pre-shot intelligence. The great challenge of game shooting is that it is, essentially, an unpredictable business. But, you can still stack the odds in your favour.

If you hold a gun in the ready position, butt down, muzzles up, and rotate the upper body right and left, the arc within which you will be able to shoot *without moving the feet and without too much tension or discomfort* will be immediately apparent. One of the first stages in preparing your address position when driven shooting, therefore, is to make sure that this arc matches, or nearly matches, the zone in which the birds are likely to fly. Simple? Maybe. But it is amazing how many people have never bothered to test precisely their ability to move right and left in this way and considered their stance and address in the light of the result. If you hold the gun as a right-hander, you will discover your movement to the left is significantly easier than to the right.

Before progressing further, let us get something else out of the way: the position of the muzzles when at the ready. Arguments about the relative merits of Mr Stanbury's and Mr Churchill's styles not withstanding, most of us like to see the muzzles held well up when waiting (or walking) for game. The most efficient position will not be too high, however. Barrels should point safely above the horizon, but not so high as to hinder movement of the muzzles to the bird. Something in the region of 60 degrees (with variation depending on the ground and conditions) is usually about right. This is an ideal 'orange' alert stage – the position adopted when birds are imminent and when all requirements of safety have been met.

On occasion, however, safety or convenience will dictate a near vertical or vertical hold – you must learn to judge when it is appropriate (it should, for example, be routinely adopted as beaters come in ear-shot or view). The vertical hold is a slightly less efficient position from which to get the gun into action, but safety overrides all other considerations. With the gun butt comfortably rested against the hip, it may also be seen as an 'amber state' waiting for the whistle or early in a drive.

The body should be relaxed in so far as it is possible when waiting for birds (though it is always good practice to have two hands on the gun). The eyes should be scanning the area to one's front looking *just above* or through the muzzles. You

My normal ready position.

As the beaters approach, I believe it is good manners to raise the barrels nearer the vertical – <u>safe and seen to be safe</u>.

This sort of lazy ready position may result in you not being asked back – you have to raise the barrels through the beating line.

are not just looking for quarry birds, of course, but anything out of the ordinary (escaped vultures, courting couples, bolshie ramblers etc.). Too many have been accidentally shot because the gunner *assumed* there was no one there. If the first rule of gun safety is never point your gun at something you do not wish to shoot, the second is never assume. Those who point their barrels low on a driven game shoot, let alone those who shoot low, take an unacceptable and foolish risk.

The trigger finger should be extended along the trigger guard in the address, the safety catch must be engaged, and the thumb should be wrapped around the grip rather than riding the thumb-piece as previously discussed. The safety is only removed *once a safe target is identified, just before the gun is raised to face and shoulder*. The trigger finger should only be brought on to the trigger towards the end of the mount. Far too many Guns wait either with the safety off and/or with their finger on the trigger. Some fiddle with the safety nervously. All are horrible and potentially fatal habits.

Once we have determined *what it is, where it is going and approximately where we may want to shoot it* most us will want to take the barrels to and through the bird (though other options will be considered shortly). If there is no opportunity to move the feet, one must rely on body rotation and good use of the front arm as discussed, or one may adopt a Churchillian weight transference technique (as is natural when one is surprised by a bird on one's strong-handed side – a right-hander naturally brings the weight onto the right foot to take a quick shot to the right).

The Churchillian syle is especially useful when movement is restricted or when early movement may give away your position. One of my regular shooting companions, Dig Hadoke, wrote on an early manuscript of this work:

I remember shooting pigeons over stubble one October. I was standing, back to a large oak tree as the birds came directly towards me into the decoy pattern, wings set, like driven grouse, visible from 100 yards away. I had to take a conscious decision to stand close-footed, fairly square, in Churchill fashion and remain motionless until the critical moment to mount and shoot arrived. I killed 97 birds that afternoon. The Churchill style – more instinctive than Stanbury – may also be useful when driven pheasants may rocket out from tall trees in front and be in shot at very close range as they traverse a ride, then disappear into trees behind you. There is no time to change foot position. See the bird, lean onto right or left foot – mount gun, swing and fire.

Taking a bird to the right with a Churchill-style technique – note the weight coming on to the right foot for this shot to the right. The feet are a little wider than Robert Churchill might have advised, but I find this a comfortable and effective technique for taking sudden shots to the right.

Usually, however, there is time to move the feet. Most of us in fact do not move them nearly enough (and consequently end up wrong-footed and running out of swing more often than we should). Moving the feet needs to become a habit, our SOP (Standard Operating Procedure). The stance and address position needs to be considered in this light as well – a means to the end of facilitating good movement of body and gun whenever possible. A good address provides a compromise position for dealing with unpredictable targets to one's front, but it also provides a firm, balanced, position from which one may step right or left *into the line of the bird* for ideal style as one takes the shot.

We will consider turning to shoot behind the line in a later section, but here, we can note that the good shot, who adopts a Stanbury style or a variation of it (which accounts for the majority) should move the muzzles and the front foot together. The Churchillian does too (the end result, however, is more of a controlled poke because body rotation is reduced). The modified Stanbury sequence goes something like this:

See the bird.
Assess it.
Quartering high right or left?
Yes.
Decide: Shall I move?
Yes.
Where do I want to kill it?
The front foot and barrels move in unison right or left as required. The rear foot stays put and acts as a pivot.
The new foot position is completed. The weight is transferred to the front foot.
Upper body rotation continues and the shot is finished with good use of the front arm, head on the stock, and eyes on the bird.

Complicated? Not really. Try it. Pick up a gun. Prove it empty and unobstructed. Take up an address position for driven birds to your front. Imagine a bird breaking right or left of centre. Let's take one to the right. 'Touch' the muzzles to it. Keep the muzzles on line and up by good use of the front hand. Take a small step into the line of the bird with the front foot. Complete the shot keeping the gun moving and well up on line.

Addressing the Target: Simple Advice for Driven Shooting

As you see distant birds approaching, mark one, read its line of flight and likely deviation as it nears your peg. You should be in balance, relaxed but alert, with the gun held up at 'the ready'. Move your feet – if time permits – as your body and mind react to the path of the bird and the approximate spot where you intend to kill it. A good address position keeps the muzzles safely up and puts you in an efficient position to deal with any presentation. The eyes should be looking just above, or, sometimes, through the muzzles if they are being held especially high.

An alert but relaxed ready position – waiting for imminent action – note front shoulder is over ball of front foot.

A slightly higher address. Weight will transfer to front foot as soon as things hot up.

Whenever the opportunity arises, as noted, you should step into the line of the bird. You must judge when this will help you and when it will not. The goal is to minimise tension at the moment the shot is taken. As an exercise, take up a proven empty gun and practise taking a driven shot right and left of centre without moving the feet, and then with very small steps right and left into the imaginary line. You will quickly discover that the stepping technique once mastered is much to be preferred.

FORWARD ALLOWANCE — A LEADING STORY

The subject of forward allowance is one of the most interesting, and certainly one of the most controversial, in shooting. Everyone has an opinion. Let us jump straight in. If you want to hit a moving target you must shoot where it is going rather than where it was. That is the simple truth. Yet, it never ceases to amaze me, even after forty years of wingshooting, how much lead some birds need.

A friend and I were once shooting at a midi-type clay pigeon (smaller and faster than the standard target). It was fully 60 yards away, a true crosser and still very fast. A lot of people had trouble with it. Having watched them miss behind (typically two or three yards) again and again, I determined not to do the same. Nevertheless, it still took me a couple of shots before I had the courage to get sufficiently in front. Something in the region of 20–25 feet ahead (as I saw it) was required to break the bird. It was hard to believe that it needed so much. The reasoning mind was just reluctant to accept it.

My disbelief of the lead required in that situation reminded me, however, of similar comments from clients when I am trying to stretch their limits on live quarry or clays. Once the bird is more than 30 yards away, whether it is a clay or a rocketing pheasant, many people do not appreciate just how far forward they need to be to kill it cleanly. They simply do not understand the extent of the lead required. Birds are missed in front (and we shall discuss this error shortly) but – as far as average shooters are concerned – most misses are undoubtedly behind when shooting at medium range and beyond. There is a psychological reluctance to shoot into blue sky (particularly apparent in those who started their shooting life with a rifle).

Birds are also missed behind more frequently than they are in front because it is all too easy to stop the gun even when one fully realises the need for lead (initial rushing, poor body movement, anxiety, poor visual contact, distraction and poor footwork are amongst many potential culprits for misses behind). Sticking to the KISS philosophy, if everyone increased their lead pictures by 10–20 per cent they would gain more birds than they'd lose. On longer birds – not that I would advocate shooting birds much beyond 40 yards – the average estimation of lead is often wrong by a factor of 50 per cent or more. One has to become comfortable with lead. Once birds move out, you need to take something of a risk.

9ft

Practice on a clay range with a good tower will make a big difference to your shooting. Here, I am taking on a long 40 yd crosser and seeing about three yards of forward allowance.

We all see lead in different ways. Some claim not to see it at all. Most of us are aware of seeing a gap however. Some look for a specific distance. With this in mind, let us consider a few of the many ways – conscious and unconscious – that one might shoot a moving bird.

1) One can *swing through* a target from some distance behind and fire as one passes through the bird or a moment later (a long-favoured method with British game shots).

2) One can mount onto the *tail feathers* of the bird and push through in front of it.

3) One can sustain a precise *measured lead* (a popular method for both wildfowling and clay pigeon shooting in the USA and used by some high bird specialists here).

4) One can maintain a lead in front of the target by means of natural hand-to-eye coordination without measuring as in John Bidwell's *Move: Mount: Shoot*.

5) One can *snap shoot* at a spot in front of the bird (an instinctive method used by a significant number of game shots but which cuts gun movement to a minimum with certain consequent risks).

6) One can *ambush* the bird with a more or less stationary gun (not to be generally recommended).

7) One can move the muzzles onto the bird, track it and *Pull Away* (better suited to clays than game).

8) One can 'touch' the bird momentarily (but deliberately) with the muzzles and move ahead smoothly without any tracking phase (which I now call *Point and Push*).

9) One can bring the barrels up to the bird instinctively and push through, relying on good timing, balance and sustained visual contact rather than any deliberate measuring. I call this *Positive Shooting*.

Which method is best? They can all work in some circumstances. For game shooting, I would advise methods 2 and 8 as starting points. This is not an absolute diktat. As I have said concerning other aspects of techniques – experiment (on clay birds, initially, of course – preferably with someone who can read the shot behind you). Find out what works for you and when it works for you. Understand forward allowance and develop control of your gun (when holding clinics for shooters, I usually asked them to try half a dozen of the above methods as a means to this). Swing through is good for establishing line and keeps the barrels moving well. It works best in my experience when the 'point of insertion' of the muzzles is not too far behind the bird (hence method 2, a refinement of the older form). **Positive Shooting** – a constant speed technique – offers economy of movement and, hence, elegance. Deliberate sustained lead ensures you stay ahead – and can be useful for very long shots (though it may cause those with eye-dominance issues to get into a muddle). Instinctive maintained lead is quick, like spot shooting, but has more gun movement and is therefore likely to give more consistent results (though with the caveat concerning eye dominance still applying).

Conscious or Unconscious Forward Allowance?

Some (for example, Robert Churchill, Major Ruffer and John Bidwell) have suggested that you should not look for a deliberate picture, others suggest applying a mental tape measure to every shot. Both positions are too extreme in my experience. Many shooters *after training and practice* will not need to look for a deliberate lead picture inside 30 yards or thereabouts (see below). Once you have taken on board the need to shoot in front of a moving target, the correct lead will often be applied automatically *provided one shoots with good timing, good balance, and sustained visual contact.* You simply cannot overemphasise the importance of looking at the bird well (just as one might stress looking at the ball in tennis or cricket). Think of it like this: In the shooting context, vision is most definitely *a skill.*

One has to learn to keep/lock fine focus on the bird throughout the shooting process. It is hard to do, both mind and eye muscles need to be *trained.* Within this context, you also need to develop a visual strategy. If engaging a game bird, look for the head or the beak. If facing a clay, make an effort to look for the precise shape. Look for the ridges; note if there is any reflected light on the surface. Sustained visual contact is *the* great secret of good shooting. Keep looking at the bird and you will keep swinging. And, nine times out of ten, you will apply the correct lead too. If, on the other hand, you let the focus wander back to the bead or barrels, the gun will slow down, judder, and a miss behind will almost certainly ensue.

Some have suggested that one need *never* do more than look at the bird; the subconscious mind will do the rest in all circumstances. After much trial in the field I think this advice only holds true to a certain point. I have chosen 30 yards as an arbitrary limit for unconscious shooting (but it might be 25 or 35 depending on the individual). As far as most people are concerned, though, it is advisable to act a little more deliberately at longer ranges. This applies *whatever specific method you may have used to get in front of the bird.* You may simply say 'I am going to give this bird a bit extra', or, you may be more deliberate, 'This one needs three yards'. If you take either approach, you should, of course, look for the lead *at the target.* The muzzles are seen, but only in peripheral vision as a blur.

Good Advice for *Most* Experienced Shots

When you are bringing a gun up to a bird that you have decided to shoot, you should have (in normal circumstances and at normal range) only one conscious thought once you have identified it as a safe shot – locking your vision on to the bird's head or beak. This is not to deny the need for preparation and set-up prior to the shot, nor that a regimen of training is required to consistently achieve good results. But, at this *committed stage* in the shooting process all your energies and efforts should be focused on the bird and nothing but the bird. There is simply not the opportunity to think consciously about much if anything else and shoot well.

Of course, you should have *trained* to move the feet so the shot is taken at the point of minimum tension. You must keep the weight forward and the head

A pheasant typically flies at 35-40 mph, a partridge 30-35 mph, and a pigeon at about 50 mph (but sometimes significantly more). Theoretically, a 40 mph bird requires a lead of 5-6 feet at 30 yards. If you sustain focus on the bird, though, and unlock your hand-to-eye coordination, you may not need to look for lead consciously.

on the gun. You must use the front hand well too – keeping the gun up on the bird's line with delicacy and precision – and you must follow through completing the shot with the gun moving and head down. You should have learned to shoot with good rhythm (always three beats as noted with the tempo changing depending on speed, range and angle). But, once committed to the shot – assuming that it is a shot within normal range – you only have that one *conscious* task: to maintain visual contact and thus unlock your extraordinary subconscious abilities.

Watch the bird. Watch the bird. Keep watching the bird! It sounds so simple, but it is incredibly difficult to do *every time* that you shoot. It is insufficiently understood, moreover, that vision is an active process in the context of shooting, a skill to be practised and refined, not just a 'natural ability' to be taken for granted. The optic muscles need to be trained in the shooter just as the biceps and triceps of the weightlifter. One needs a visual plan and you need to learn that any external distraction or mental clutter will have the effect of disrupting vision and may bring the focus back to the gun (and thus cause the gun to stop and rise with a miss behind and above ensuing).

You will have noted that I have made the qualification 'within normal ranges'. My sustained visual contact system is not the same as Mr Churchill's (or Major Ruffer's). I believe that most of us need to be a little more deliberate at longer ranges. I am not dogmatic about the way forward allowance is applied (although the method described has implications for forward allowance which will be discussed later). Different things suit different people. You should experiment with 'swing through', 'maintained lead' and 'point and push' as well as the more instinctive techniques.

Explaining forward allowance is always hard. You have to shoot where the bird is going and not where it was.

One Man's Inch is Another Man's Yard

People see lead differently. This is frequently given as a reason for not being specific about leads. I do not buy this entirely. If someone tells you that he sees only a couple of inches of lead it is a sure sign that he (or she) is looking at the muzzles, rather than the bird. And, there are, practically speaking, many occasions when it is useful to tell someone to increase their lead by a more-or-less specific amount: 'try a yard extra on that', or 'go on, give me four yards in front'. It can also be useful to give an instruction based on comparison with the distance between fence posts, the width of a gate – whatever is convenient and may make the individual apply the correct forward allowance. Provided that you have established a bridge of communication and can read the shot reasonably well, specific instruction can be a real help to some shooters.

Ballistic Lead

Most targets have a theoretical or as it might be called 'ballistic' or 'mathematical' lead. If facing a very high bird, it may be useful to start saying to yourself: 'well, that pheasant is about 40 yards away, so I want to be at least 8 feet ahead'. One of the skills of learning to apply forward allowance, is learning to appreciate distance and discovering the specific leads that might work at different distances on standard targets (time to dig out your Eley diary which includes much interesting data on theoretical leads at different ranges).

It is a useful exercise to attempt to shoot artificial birds with slightly different deliberate leads. Most find they can extend their normal forward allowance and achieve better kills. They also discover that there is usually some margin for error ahead but none behind. Another point to be discovered on the road to increased awareness, is the huge variation in leads required by different birds. The range that most shots operate within is far too limited. One must be brave in applying lead. You need to get into the habit of making fairly dramatic variations. As noted, you must be willing to take a risk sometimes. Better a miss in front than a bird shot in the tail.

The Perception of Lead

A number of factors affect our perception of lead. Some are quite surprising. Most people need to see *less* lead with long barrels (especially when they shoot deliberately). When I shoot a 25-inch gun compared with my usual 30-inch one, I am aware of a need to increase apparent forward allowance substantially. Well-balanced guns, moreover, seem to reduce the perceived lead (no surprise here – they swing more easily).

Another important consideration is the speed of swing. Many game shots have developed into what might be called 'slashers' or 'flickers' because it is the only way they can achieve sufficient barrel acceleration. They have never really learnt how far in front they need to be to achieve the same thing in a calmer more controlled manner. The slashers begin the mount and swing with the gun too far behind the bird. Then, they move the barrels wildly ahead. It looks awful, but it can work *some* of the time. The flickers have an exaggerated flick of the muzzles at the end of the swing. It looks untidy but can work.

Timing

Try to become more aware of your timing. Elegant shooting is always performed to three beats. We have already noted:

> One: Two: Three
> Bum: Belly: Beak
> You: Are: Dead

And, tongue in cheek,

> You: Will: Win

This three-beat time – One: Two: Threeeeee – remains constant in all circumstances, but the tempo changes depending on the speed and distance of the shot. *One* as you see the bird and take the gun towards it: *Two* as mount and swing progress and lead is developed: *Three* as the trigger is pulled and the shot completed and followed through. It is another useful exercise for the game shot to shoot simulated birds (as one might find on a skeet field or middle height tower) with different tempos. To do this, one should change the killing point for the target. If it is beyond your 'sweet spot' the tempo will be slowed. If it is before the sweet spot for the particular bird, the tempo must be raised. Try it.

Forward Allowance: Simple Advice

Relax. Pick the bird up. Focus on its beak. Take the muzzles of the as yet unmounted gun towards the bird, controlling the barrels with the front hand (the swing should always begin before the gun is mounted). Mount the gun 'onto' the tail feathers and smoothly push through. Don't dwell on the bird. Keep your head down. Keep pushing. Power for the swing comes from core body movement, fine control from your hands. Pull the trigger as you see a bit of daylight. (If in doubt, or if you think this instruction is a bit imprecise, try about a yard in front for birds at medium range – 25-30 yards. If that does not work try experimenting with more and less lead. You should always complete the shot with the eyes locked on the bird, your head still on the stock, and the barrels *moving*. Don't rush but do brush – i.e. 'sweep' the birds out of the air with a smooth, flowing, action.

Missing in Front

Having gone to considerable length to explain the dangers of missing behind up to this point, it is time to come clean and admit that many misses in the field are in front, most notably when an experienced shot is shooting *under pressure at close birds*. There is a tendency to misjudge distance and to over-swing in this circumstance. At what range is the average pheasant shot? Probably 25 yards. It may even be less if we are honest. At such ranges minimal lead is required provided the gun keeps *moving*. The key to success is to sustain this movement without rushing. It might also be noted that the use of maintained lead techniques on such close birds is inadvisable (as they can aggravate the tendency to miss in front).

Feeling The Lead

The problems of forward allowance may be summed up thus: many shots have not developed sufficient understanding of lead nor have they developed sufficient *feel* for it. It is not just a question of knowing how many feet in front, but of having a *muscle memory* for it. The range of leads required by different birds is much wider than most people realise. One must introduce flexibility into one's shooting and not attempt to engage everything the same way. Leading a bird often demands that you are a bit adventurous; you have to risk it on occasion. By a similar token, lack of confidence will invariably cause the gun to stop (as will distraction).

Try shooting driven clay birds by different methods. Try birds at different ranges and elect to kill them in different places as discussed. Experiment with subconscious and deliberate systems for applying forward allowance (try the 30-yard rule).

Whatever method you use, always try to shoot smoothly with control and good rhythm. Fine focus locked on every bird. Keep the barrels moving. Keep your head on the stock as you follow through. Don't prematurely unlock the head from the stock (repetition, I know, but it is such a common problem amongst game shots).

The Unconscious Approach: Simple Advice for More Experienced Shots

If you adopt an unconscious approach to forward allowance – and there is much to recommend it at close and medium ranges – you should have only one conscious thought once you have identified a bird as a safe shot – locking your vision on to the bird's head or beak. If you are disciplined about this, it will unlock phenomenal natural abilities with regard to hand and eye coordination.

You should have trained to keep the weight forward and the head on the gun, and, when the opportunity arises, to move the feet. The goal is always to take the shot in balance and at the point of minimum tension. You must use the front hand well too – keeping the gun on the bird's line with delicacy and precision. You must follow through still keeping the eyes on the bird and the head down. You should have learned to shoot with good rhythm too. Once committed to the shot, the primary task is to sustain visual contact. Watch the bird. Watch the bird. Keep watching the bird! Pin sharp focus before and after pulling the trigger. Keep the gun moving.

Line As Well as Lead

One often hears about the 'badness' of 'canting' barrels, but many seem to misunderstand the nature of the problem. Disrupted visual contact and stopping apart, failing to follow the line of the bird smoothly is one of the commonest errors game shooters make. It causes visual confusion and poor gun movement. The problem is not canting the barrels *per se*, rather, it is not matching them to the bird's line. At the moment the shot is taken, the barrels of a side by side should, ideally, be parallel to the flight-line of the bird, and those of an over and under, perpendicular to it.

There is a particular danger on driven shots of quartering slightly to one side. Lazy Guns often attempt to take them as if they were straight driven birds. This shortcutting of proper process does not usually bring good results (though some people get away with it – especially if the gun is open choked and the shot in question has no eye-dominance issue). Typically, firing occurs with the barrels canted relative to the line. The back over-arches. The centre of gravity shifts back. Balance is lost and the barrels lose their proper relationship with the bird and its line.

Rather than consider bad style in any more detail, let us consider the technique for shooting well. If a bird is going high, half right or left, anticipate where you want to kill it (moving the feet if possible) and *deliberately (but slightly)* twist the barrels relative to the line of the bird. This controlled canting – accomplished by both hands working together – is clockwise if the bird goes to the left, anti-clockwise if it goes to the right. The quartering bird ends up being treated more like a crosser.

If a side by side is being used, a line drawn through the centres of the muzzles must remain parallel with the line of the bird during the swing, shot and follow-through. In the case of an over and under, a vertical line drawn through the muzzle centres would be perpendicular to the line thoughout. You can cant the barrels – but you must not cant them *relative to the line of the bird at the moment of firing*. If you adopt this refined technique, the shoulders may not remain level relative to the horizon, but they do remain level, or more-or-less level, relative to the line of the bird.

The shot that catches many right-handers out, is the mid-range or high bird that is only slightly right of centre. This is one of the toughest of all birds to hit consistently (particularly if you have any sort of eye-dominance issue). It's difficult to get a perfect line by any method in this situation. The solution – or the fudge – is to take it as an incomer but to twist the comb very slightly anti-clockwise into your cheek as you take the shot.

SPECIALIST TECHNIQUE

Grouse/Walking Up

In the British context, there are two forms of walk-up to consider: walking up in line with other Guns, and walking up individually or paired with another Gun. In all cases safety is the paramount issue. Guns should only be loaded when one is level with the other Gun or Guns. Muzzles must be kept forward at all times. One walks with muzzles well up. It is a safe, alert, position and minimises gun movement when the shot is taken. *Two* hands should be kept on the gun when walking (if one trips, one has a better chance of controlling the weapon). The safety must be applied and the finger off the trigger.

Walking up grouse in Scotland.

It may be considered bad form to walk with an open gun when one is in the vicinity or probable vicinity of grouse – one might lose opportunities to shoot birds – so one must really stay on the ball with regard to muzzle control. The particular danger is to let one's muzzles drift to one side through laziness and lack of muscular effort by the front hand/arm. Good safety in this context requires constant mental and physical effort. Keep looking sideways to your companion(s) as you control the gun forwards.

Another particular issue is to keep up with the line – falling back or moving in front is potentially dangerous. One should not only pay careful attention to the other Guns but to canine companions as well. Note that Labradors and spaniels with the shooting party may pick up the scent of birds, as well as the pointers dedicated to the task. Watch *all* the dogs, they may forewarn you of opportunity. Another thing to bear in mind when walking up is to keep your ears as well as your eyes open: you may hear a bird before you see it.

Lead with the left and don't get caught wrong-footed or rush the shot when walking up.

When you see a bird rise, assess it as safe before anything else. Remove the safety catch a moment just before the mount begins – not during it. The Churchill style of gun mount – with the butt beginning under the armpit gently squeezed against the ribcage – also works very well in this context. It ensures clean mounting and good gun control (but you must make an effort to keep the muzzles up when appropriate).

As noted in the picture sequence above. Don't be caught *wrong-footed*. When walking you must (if right-handed) become left-foot conscious. Lead with the left, lead with the left – that's the rule. You will find it a little unnatural to be so left-foot led initially. But, it will soon become a habit. When you stop, always do so with the left foot forward. You do not want to get into a position where you are forced to take a shot off the right foot with the weight back (you will almost certainly miss over the top and behind if you do).

If two Guns are shooting over dogs, it is important to have a plan concerning who will do what when birds are scented. This should prevent cross-firing and other adrenalin-related error. Grouse shooting is a fast, sometimes frantic, business. To avoid panic and over-reaction, one must practise. Some shoot captains may think a line rehearsal worthwhile when novice Guns are present.

Although walked-up birds are generally missed underneath, it is also easy to miss over them (especially when the birds are driven – hence the old adage 'grouse wear spats'), or to one side. The birds appear to move very quickly because one is close to them. It is all too easy to over-react. Grouse contour as well, keeping much lower than other species. Pay particular attention to the good use of your front hand – it is especially important in grouse, woodcock and quail shooting because of the speed at which the action happens. One must control the movement of the gun. There is an ever present risk of over-swinging and/or moving the gun wildly. As with all game shooting, don't rush and do keep your eyes on the bird. It is also especially important to keep the head down on the stock. When action is fast simple things may be forgotten.

The gun that is suitable for driven shooting is not the necessarily the most suitable for walking up. The ideal tool would be a fairly lightweight 12 or 20 bore.

A Beretta Silver Pigeon 28 bore – an ideal lightweight gun for walking up early in the season. Note the bed of heather!

A 28 bore may also be used (especially in the early season when birds are less aware and tend to get up closer). It is essential that the gun can be mounted quickly without any glitches (so the stock should not be too long or equipped with a sticky pad). It must fit for cast as well – this is more critical in this context because there are so many going-away shots – as well as for drop. Margins of error are reduced when most shots are taken quickly.

On the cartridge front, as many birds are shot with their rear end facing the muzzles, a relatively heavy charge is to be preferred. An 1¹⁄₁₆ ounce or an 1⅛ ounce of 5 shot or 6 shot would be a good choice in a 12 bore, and 1 ounce of 5 shot or 6 shot in a 20 or 28. Not that many shots are likely to be taken in a day, so a load that might be a bit punchy when fired a hundred or more times in a driven situation is unlikely to be noticed in these circumstances. My own preference in a 12 bore is 1¹⁄₁₆ ounce of 6 shot early season and 1⅛ ounce of 5 shot once the birds become cannier. I use 1 ounce of 5s in my 28 bore.

Finally, consider your footwear. Walking up grouse can be hard physical work and the terrain can be tough (don't contemplate walking up grouse unless you are reasonably fit). I prefer a modern, lightweight, Gore-tex lined, boot such as the Brasher Supalite or Musto Arncliffe. These weigh little more than shoes, but provide a lot more support to the ankles and cushion the heels (and spine) as you walk. I have also had good success with the high Dubarry boots (which are great for boggy ground). Many similar products are available.

High and Mighty

High birds are one of the great challenges of game shooting They should, however, only be tackled by competent shots who have made the effort to prepare. There are three fundamentals required to shoot high birds well: a practised, comfortable stance and experience with the extended lead pictures required, and suitable equipment.

Various opinions have been expressed concerning footwork. I am not pedantic. There are various options and I suggest that you try them and select the most comfortable. Essentially there are three ways to go as shown in the picture sequence: off the back foot [1], with a central, or, near central, weight distribution [2], and with the weight over the front foot as made famous by Percy Stanbury [3]. The Churchill technique, where the weight is transferred right or left depending on the side to which the shot is taken, has also been mentioned but is not, in my opinion, well suited to high bird work as far as most people are concerned – it is harder to adjust for subtle variations of line overhead.

Ultimately, it does not matter which method you choose provided the chosen one allows you to stay balanced and keep the gun moving. Whenever the opportunity arises, moreover, move the feet to facilitate the shot. Step into the line of the bird, the tip of the gun and the front foot (assuming a Stanbury style) moving together. Keep the foot movements small, and keep the feet fairly close together.

The Marquis of Ripon's famous advice 'Hold high and do not check your swing' is true in most game shooting, but it is of particular importance when facing high birds when continuing the swing and holding up on line takes real effort. Avoid

Off the back foot (as may sometimes be kinder to your back).

With a central weight distribution.

Taking a high bird with classic Stanbury stance – weight on the front foot.

extending the hand too far forward as noted – it may look elegant, but it will impede your swing and may pull you under on some shots as well. I favour three techniques for applying lead with high birds – controlled swing through, point and push, and deliberate maintained lead. The former two ensure that you fire with an accelerating gun, the latter is a simple way to glue a five bar gate or two on an orbiting pheasant. You should, of course, experiment on clay birds before you consider applying any technique to live quarry.

Finally, though lead is all important, consider the *line* of the bird just as much and as already discussed. For right-handers, the bird breaking slightly to the right can cause real problems, as noted, especially when it is misread as straight. Good advice on this shot is to cant the gun (slightly) anti-clockwise as you complete the mount. This will lock it into the face and keep you on line. Yes, I know I am repeating myself again.

Another good tip is not to shoot at birds which are beyond your ability (see box). Practise at a shooting school with a decent 100 foot plus high tower – discover the limit of your own ability. Keep the barrels moving as the trigger is pulled. Don't lift your head. Don't be afraid to experiment with your lead pictures. My favoured chokes for high bird work are three-quarters and three-quarters, but this is more a matter of confidence than anything else; improved cylinder and quarter will still bring 'em down. Cartridge selection is more important when shooting high birds than in less challenging situations. It is sensible to increase the pellet payload and individual pellet size when shooting high birds. My usual choice would be 1⅛ ounce of 5 shot, some prefer 1¼ ounce of 5s or 4s.

When partridge shooting mark your bird cafefully in any covey. Don't be tempted to 'brown'.
Keep your cool. The feet are quite widely positioned here but the stance looks stable.

When Does High Become Extreme?

Sir Ralph Payne-Gallwey once noted: 'The height of a pheasant above ground is …invariably over-estimated'. Not much has changed in 100 years! My simple rule is to subtract 10 yards from general guestimates of altitude. Most pheasants are, in fact, shot at 20–25 yards (and I have many times heard birds described as 'high' at the upper end of that range). Some are shot at 30, a few at 35 and a very small number at 40 and beyond.

What are the real limits? I have shot a carrion crow crossing at a measured 76 paces (a fluke), Texas dove at 60 yards on occasion (because temptation got the better of me), a crossing quail (once) at 55 yards (I had thought it closer) and a battue clay at 94 yards in a shoot-off by distance (witnessed and measured). I have never shot a pheasant *overhead* much beyond 45 yards (nor would I want to). Indeed, all this talk of 'extreme birds' concerns me. For the sake of argument, let us say extreme means over 40 yards. With modern cartridges a kill *overhead* on a pheasant is ballistically possible to about 60 yards. But, there is the question of marksmanship to be considered too. It is a big and troubling question.

Most shooters cannot hit pheasants *consistently* much beyond 30 yards. Good shots stretch themselves over 35 yards. Yet, the so-called 'extreme' bird has become something of a fetish in some circles. Granted, many birds described as such are, in truth, only high. But, there are some genuinely stratospheric birds on offer today, and, sadly, I have heard people bragging that they have been on shoots where they could only connect with one in ten. They would be better advised to spend their money on shooting lessons. Bringing down one in eight or ten almost certainly means some birds are flying on wounded.

It seems that the trendy 'extreme' tag now justifies exorbitant prices and, essentially, unsporting conduct. I know of several cases, moreover, where those talking of extreme birds have the greatest difficulty in consistently connecting with ordinary ones. There is nothing clever in shooting at birds beyond one's ability. The question therefore should not be what is extreme so much as what is *your* extreme? When you can only connect with one in four or five, you have certainly reached it. Indeed, Danish shooters have adopted a one-in-three figure to guide them as to when they need to hone their shooting skills.

Positive Partridge Shooting

Partridge shooting is always sure to provide plenty of action. I think there are two secrets to partridge shooting – over and above the ancient and well-proven advice of not 'browning' i.e. firing into a flock of birds rather than at a specific target. The first is an alert, safe, address position – muzzles well up, feet not too far apart, finger extended along the trigger guard, eyes and suitably protected ears wide open. The second, is a well-honed, and unchecked, mount and swing (this has certain implications for equipment and clothing – your stock must not catch on the way up, it must not be too long, and your clothes should allow free movement).

Birds will explode in front of you and there is not always time to move the feet (though when the opportunity arises, take it). The upper body must move fluidly at all times. When the feet are not ideally placed, the front hand must work harder than normal to keep the barrels up on line. An attacking style may help some people, though you must not be wild. If a bird surprises you to the right, do not be afraid of transferring your weight to that foot. It may not look elegant, but it may well put another bird in the bag.

The front hand should not be extended too far forward. Creeping it forward will hinder the swing. When the gun is brought to the face and shoulder, the front arm does as much or more work as the rear. It is more than just a lifting lever. It controls the tip of the gun and plays a vital role in completing the shot as we have already considered.

Shooting Behind the Line

We have noted many times the importance of moving the feet when the opportunity arises in the normal shooting context. Good footwork is one of the hallmarks of a good shot. Most Guns do not move their feet nearly enough. They get caught wrong-footed, and, as a consequence, attempt to shoot when they are out of balance (typically with so much tension in the body that they cannot swing the gun or keep it on line). Good footwork actually begins with good thinking. One must mark one's bird well, focus upon it and anticipate where it is going. Concentration creates order out of the chaos and has the apparent effect of slowing everything down. It buys you time to move.

Once the bird is marked, one steps into its line – right or left – whilst keeping the barrels with the bird. The essence of the skill is doing *both things at once*. Assuming a classic left foot forward, oblique style, the front foot and muzzles move together as if connected by a puppet master's wire. The ball of the rear (right) foot acts as pivot and bears all the weight until the leading foot is replanted on *terra firma*. It is an elegant, unhurried action in which the front foot is lifted only slightly and then moves a few inches to either side dependent upon the bird's direction of travel. Balance is maintained throughout the process. It is a very natural movement. If properly executed, you should end up with the rear foot positioned at about 90 degrees to the point where you plan to kill the bird.

When a shot is taken behind the line, the basics of the turn are similar but the extent of it is increased. It should remain a graceful manoeuvre. The bird is marked. The muzzles and front foot move together (in the case of the turn to the right, a small rearwards step may need to be taken with the right foot first). Special care must be taken to keep the barrels well up when passing through the line. And, as the shot is taken, one must also make a special effort to finish well with a good follow-through. It is all too easy (especially if one has not turned quite far enough) to stop the gun because one has run out of swing. The secret to performing the full turn well – like so many other things in shooting – is plenty of practice. I am not a believer in dancing charts to explain the footwork (I am still trying to work out the ones in Churchill's *Game Shooting*). You must find a way of turning that is comfortable and stable *for you*. It may not be exactly as I have suggested here: experiment. You need to find a way of turning that allows you to exercise fine control of the muzzles at the same time as you keep them moving.

The Gun in this photograph has turned to take the cock bird behind the line.

Safety is always of paramount concern when considering the turn, <u>and you must be seen to be safe</u> as well. Movements must be controlled. Nothing should be rushed or wild. You should never let your muzzles pass within 45 degrees of another person. To give yourself some margin of error and to show your neighbour that you are making the effort, I suggest keeping your muzzles near vertical as you complete the turn. The action of the safety catch is also worth consideration; it should not be removed until movement of the feet is completed, i.e. after the muzzles have passed through the line. It is also important to have a gun with a well-designed grip and forend, both of which should be crisply chequered. In cold or wet weather, it is advisable to wear thin leather gloves to improve grip. Another good tip is to stamp down the mud around you (when required) to create a more level, and therefore safer, shooting platform.

When may one take a bird behind the line? The simple answer is only when the shoot captain has told you that it is permissible, and when all normal safety and sporting criteria are met. In most circumstances low birds to the rear will be avoided (just as they should be to the front), but there are occasions on the flanks when they can be safe (provided thay are not too low – always look for some sky before taking a shot). The choice and the responsibility always rests with the Gun. Novices should not take birds behind the line – even when it is theoretically permissible; they have enough to worry about shooting in front without complicating the issue. What about a bird a neighbour may have missed? Again, the choice is yours. You must not rob your neighbour of a second shot, but if he has fired twice or only once but has clearly abandoned the bird, you may decide to fire, especially if the bird has been pricked. Be respectful. If you are with Guns you do not know and have any doubts about the shot, the best advice is to choose another bird. You can only lose your name once!

Double Gunning

Double gunning is another situation that puts extra stress on the Gun (not to mention his loader) and demands a clear head. It increases the things one must think about, and, notably, the number of potential mistakes that one might make on the shooting field. One cannot afford to suffer 'brain fade' in this situation. Here are some basic principles from which a drill might be constructed (assuming a Gun firing off his or her right shoulder with the loader standing behind and slightly right).

1) The fired gun is handed back with the right hand (the loader taking it with his left hand a few inches forward of the action body) over the right shoulder.

2) The fresh gun is taken by the shooter with the left hand – the palm facing upwards to receive the gun. *The shooter's eyes, meantime, keep looking forward towards the birds.*

3) <u>The safety catch must be on when the gun is passed back to the loader</u>; the shooter's trigger finger should be off the trigger and the hand firmly wrapped around the grip behind the bow of the trigger guard.

4) Gun muzzles must be held well up as they pass from hand to hand.

5) When he is opening the returned gun, the loader must make sure that the muzzles are pointed safely. When he loads and closes the gun, the muzzles should be directed towards the ground (noting the potential danger to his own and other Guns). There is never a need for the loader to have his fingers near the trigger or touching the trigger guard.

6) The shooter should pass his gun back when a single shot has been fired if no other shot is immediately anticipated (safety reapplied, of course).

Double gunning, like turning, requires practice under realistic conditions. Even if you never intend to shoot with two guns in the field, it is an enjoyable and interesting experience to have a go with a reasonably matched pair of guns on a suitable driven stand on a clay layout. You'll be surprised how difficult it is to maintain good timing

until you get the knack. If you are not shooting with a true pair, the fit, trigger pulls, weight and handling qualities of the guns want to be similar, and the barrel lengths the same. Don't forget to apply the safety catch before you hand the gun back to your loader. It is all too easy to forget in the heat of the moment. If you have access to a video camera ask someone to film you and the loader working as a team (it may show up more faults than you think). One tip for loaders: give the cartridge bag a good shake – it will bring the cartridge rims up, which will make it easier to pick up shells.

The Gun must keep looking forward at all times and remember to apply the safety catch before handing his gun back. Gun and loader are a team and both must trust each other.

Pigeon and Duck: Train Hard, Flight Easy

I have never been a great fan of shooting from a sitting position, but it is sometimes required when pigeon shooting or wildfowling. It is, at best, awkward, potentially uncomfortable, and, well...plain difficult. The best place to improve your sitting technique is on a skeet range (though any clay range will do at a pinch) equipped with a suitable chair or stool.

Having obtained suitable permissions, start on station 4 (the middle position). This is the spot that requires the longest leads. Behaving as if you were in a hide – muzzles up – try the crossing birds from right and left. Once you have mastered these, try a round of singles. Do not worry about pairs, yet. Two birds per station – high and low house – will be quite enough to keep you fully occupied.

It is really tough to keep the gun moving in these circumstances. Upper body rotation – vital to all good shooting – is drastically impeded when sitting. Nevertheless, persevere. A skeet range is ideal because it was designed by Messrs Foster and Davies to simulate all the angles one might meet in the field – incoming birds, quartering birds, crossing shots and overhead shots. They are all there.

Do not extend the hand too far forward. Indeed, bring your hand back an inch or two from your normal position. Put extra effort into the front arm – pushing up as required to keep on line. Keep your head well down, meantime, and, as ever, always shoot with an accelerating gun keeping your eye or eyes on the bird.

Any other advice? The sitting position ensures that felt recoil is substantially increased; you cannot roll with the punches as when standing. If you intend shooting from a sitting position on a regular basis, consider a lighter payload cartridge, a

You can practise shooting sitting or kneeling on a clay range (with permission). This is an excellent means of improving your shooting from these potentially awkward positions.

SPECIALIST TECHNIQUE   157

slightly shorter stock (to help you swing), a gas-operated semi-automatic, and or, the fitting of a modern, polymer, recoil pad to your existing gun. As well as shooting sitting you may wish to practise the movements required from a sitting *ready* position – i.e. starting from sitting position and standing to take the shot.

With regard to forward allowance I think that pigeon shooting should usually be instinctive business. For wildfowling, however, deliberate maintained lead may be useful in some challenging situations, though controlled swing-through or point and push remain my preference.

Clay Shooting for Game Shots

I have often referred to clay shooting as practice for game shooting in this work. Clays tend to be predictable, whereas the great joy of game shooting is that it is not. Most modern game shots, however, learn on clays. The old prejudice against clay shooting held by some gameshots has largely vanished. It remains true, though, that game birds tend to be speeding up and rising and clays tend to drop and quickly lose speed and consequently are more often missed over the top than live quarry when driven.

Clays are without doubt great practice for game shooting *provided their limitations are recognised.* Shooting schools have long used clay birds to teach game shooting (the origins of sporting clays may be traced directly to British shooting schools). Skeet was devised by Messrs Foster and Davies (American gameshots) for off-season practice in the First World War era, and became an Olympic sport.

One can still recognise the charm in the old English method of introducing a boy to shooting via live birds and .410, 28, 20 and 12 bore (the 16, traditionally, was favoured by older shooters), but the modern method of thorough, intense, instruction at a shooting school has much to recommend it too. Visual issues are picked up at an early stage, safety is constantly stressed and marksmanship ability develops quickly in most cases. Skeet shot (gun-down) and sporting clays are also an excellent means of off-season practice for the experienced shot (I shoot most of my game with a 28 bore these days, and I enjoy using the same gun for skeet and sporting practice in the spring and summer).

The techniques of clay and game shooting are significantly different. As most game shooters shoot clays today, and as many do not always do quite as well as they might, I am going to include here details of a very simple technique – based on my Positive Shooting System – well suited to skeet and sporting clays. Before I spell it out more precisely, let me note first that many game shooters hold their muzzles too high when clay shooting (they should be just under the line of the bird). And, typically, they stand towards the trap rather than the spot where they intend to shoot the clay (and hence run out of swing). They also tend to rush.

Bearing those three points in mind, here is a shortened version of the Positive Shooting System (as set out in some detail in my book and DVD *Positive Shooting*):

1) Always stand to where you want to break the bird – rear foot at about 90 degrees to the intended breaking point (assuming a Stanbury or modified Stanbury stance).

My son Jamie learnt on clays, but is now a keen game shot too.

2) Wind back to the point where you first see the bird clearly – where you first see it as a *solid object*. The muzzles should remain just under the line of anticipated flight.

3) Look back to the area where you first see the clay as a blur (not to the trap).

4) Call for the target, lock your eyes on to it and begin moving without delay, but without rushing either.

If you maintain visual contact, the muzzles will naturally move in front of the clay as your body unwinds. If you keep the gun moving and keep the eyes locked onto the bird (look for the ridges of the disc rather than a black mass), there is every chance that you will break it. This is an instinctive method based on conscious preparation. Deliberate Point and Push also works well.

I will end with a few specific tips. When shooting clay bunnies, always shoot at the bottom edge (if you make a slight error the pellets will bounce up and into the target). If you have persistent problems, try shooting at them. When shooting teal and going-away birds consider starting with a premounted gun though it may look inelegant. Vertical teal are typically missed under (as the real thing), those angling away, tend to be missed over the top. When shooting long crossers, be brave with your forward allowance. Remember that midi and battue targets are probably going faster than you think and may need more lead too. Minis on the other hand (the ones that look like aspirins!) are travelling at about the same speed as a standard clay. As far as looping standard birds and battues are concerned be more concerned with the lead they require than any apparent need for compensation under the line. Dropping targets, on the other hand, should not be tracked for too long and may need a considerable allowance underneath. Driven clays at good height are often missed behind (like the real thing) and also off line (again, like the real thing). My most important tip though – and I confess a vested interest – is do not begrudge a few pounds on proper instruction at a shooting school if you are having persistent problems.

Shooting – The Mental Game

The best foundation for 'getting your head right' on a shoot day is relaxed (but safe) attitude and a sound basic technique. This is not just about maintaining visual focus, putting your feet in the right place and mounting the gun well (important though these things are). It is also concerned with having the right thoughts at the right time. Most of us are far too sloppy in our approach, some are easily distracted or panicked, moreover. As a first stage in improving the mental game, I advise my clients to build a routine of thoughts and actions based on increased awareness of what they ought to be doing. If you have read this far this process has already begun!

Vic Chapman is a first-class game shot. He loves his shooting and has a very relaxed style based on plenty of practice. He also gets a bundle of invitations because he keeps everyone laughing. Many would be well advised to smile a bit more when they shoot.

To take an example from clay pigeon shooting (as discussed in the previous section), I know that if I spend time assessing the target (what it is, where it is coming from and to where it is going), and that if I then make decisions that lead to actions (setting my body up towards the spot where I want to kill the target, taking the muzzles to the spot where I first see it as a solid object, and, directing the eyes to the area where it is first seen as a blur) my chances of success will be greatly increased. If I positively *visualise* a kill before calling for the bird, my success rate rises further (because mental rehearsal make a positive outcome more likely). And, if I make a *conscious* effort to lock my eyes on to the target and keep the gun moving once I have called for the target, success is even more certain. What I do in the preparation and performance stages is pre-considered and specific. My objectives are limited. My routine is clearly defined.

When game shooting, you should also run a mental programme as part of the shooting process. It functions both as a safety checklist and as a means of monitoring performance. It also blocks out negative thinking and anxiety by occupying the mind productively. In the preparation phase – which begins on arrival at the peg – the quarry and ground are considered. Where are the birds likely to fly? Is the ground deceptive? What cover is there? What is the wind doing? The position of other Guns (and anyone else on the shooting field) is noted, as is the direction in which the beaters are moving. Decisions about arcs of fire are made. Movements of the feet are anticipated (and practised discreetly). A positive attitude is maintained (including the visualisation in the mind's eye of the shots about to be taken). Cartridges and equipment are re-checked. All these things are done *consciously and methodically*. A simple routine is followed to make sure that nothing is forgotten.

With the preparation completed, you should relax for a few moments and enjoy your surroundings before moving on to the more intense performance phase. With birds in the air, stress levels rise dramatically and adrenalin starts pumping. One must remain steady – quiet and focused. *You must retain a positive frame of mind.* Visual contact is established on a particular bird. The critical shoot/no shoot decision is made. The upper body begins to turn towards the quarry. The feet move simultaneously if there is opportunity. The safety is removed a moment before the mount begins. The front hand takes the muzzles to the bird. The swing and mount progress without rushing or hesitation. Fine focus is sustained on head or beak. The muzzles move through the bird (assuming a smoke-trail method or variant). The gun comes into the face and shoulder. The shot is completed with a good follow-through. Flow is maintained. The apparent paradox of relaxed concentration is achieved.

Unlike the preparation stage, only a few things in the performance stage should be the subject of conscious thought (for the rest we are dependent on good training). Limit your inner dialogue to: 'watch the bird', keep the barrels moving 'stay safe'. You might mouth the words: 'You: Are: Dead' on occasion to ensure good rhythm. And, when you need a metaphorical kick up the posterior, you might tell yourself to 'move the feet' or 'keep the head down on the gun'. This brings up an interesting point; experts find it easier to 'concentrate' because they have learnt exactly what to concentrate upon. They have isolated those points of technique that

This shooter seems to have everything right. The gun is well mounted with head and hands nicely positioned. Relaxed control is evident. He'll account for his share of the bag.

Two shooters who are ready for action – note muzzles well up, alert demeanour, and well-balanced positions. The Young Gun looks serious but this is appropriate as he is new to driven shooting.

must be attended to in particular phases of the shooting process and cut out all the clutter. You can do the same. Think about what you need to do to shoot really well in both the preparation and performance phases. Visualise your actions in your mind's eye. Write a short list for each stage. Put the items in order of importance. Can anything go? What is vital? Now you are developing the right mind-set.

Let us move on to some other points of the mental game. Confidence grows from applying basic technique consistently well and *expecting* success. Stretching yourself in training is also part of the equation. If you have phobias, face them (bogey birds or problem situations are easily simulated at a shooting school). In a competitve context winners expect (and need) to win. Losers expect to fail. The same applies to first-class game shots. They expect to drop the bird (if not every time, more often than not). Believing in yourself is not enough in itself; there must be a sound basis of developed competence. But, once you have acquired the skill, the Gun who has self-confidence will do better than the Gun who has not. Confidence has *physical effects*. It tends to improve gun movement and keep the weight forward. It makes us a little more determined and perhaps a little more aggressive. The head stays on the stock, the eyes on the bird, the gun keeps moving. Anything other than a confident state of mind will impede performance.

You must avoid the paralysing condition of *Ballistic Thrombosis* – a pathological neurosis worrying about details of the gun and ammunition. Check your gun, gunfit and ammunition methodically and then relegate these things to the mental filing cabinet where they belong. Obsessive concern about equipment only serves to distract. Like confidence, it has physical effects – but of the wrong sort. It brings the mental focus back to the gun and causes the gun to move hesitantly to the bird. The mind thinks negatively 'I've got the wrong cartridges – these chokes won't do the job – these barrels are just too long/short/bent'. In all cases the probable result is a miss behind and/or over (as noted, the wrong conscious thought at the wrong moment tends to bring the psychological and physical focus back to the gun, causing the weight to come back, the head to rise, and the barrels to rise and stop).

The intelligent Gun is engaged without being over hyped-up. *He is calm but alert*. He recognises that we can be under or over-stressed when shooting. (The inverted U hypothesis of psychological theory suggests that there is a level of arousal at which we all perform best. If it is exceeded – or we fail to obtain it – performance falls.) He has discovered a *comfort zone* in which he can perform most effectively. When you watch someone and see nothing out of place, and when you see that everything is moving towards the same end, you know the individual is on the right track. He is *connected*, totally engaged. The boundaries between himself and what he is doing have blurred. If he manages to repeat this regularly, he may be able to achieve the state sports psychologists call *flow*. If this is entered, all the conscious effort and discipline that we have discussed thus far become superfluous. They have achieved their goal.

This shooter has a determined gleam in his eyes; he shows good technique, and will almost certainly kill his bird. Some people need to 'gear up' to do well, others benefit from a more relaxed approach. Which are you? Does it depend on the circumstance?

Never forget to enjoy yourself, but always bear in mind the lethal potential of firearms. My friend, Shirley Payne, has an infectious laugh, but she is still in control of her gun.

Many will not manage this shooting *nirvana*, but the intelligent Gun always enjoys and respects his sport and his own performance within it. He is not focused just on the result, but takes as much pride and pleasure in the *process*. He knows that if he puts the effort into shooting well – with good style and a relaxed discipline – he will achieve a satisfaction others miss and will probably be responsible for a fair share of the bag as well.

And, one more thing: I believe that to shoot game well you need to 'go for it' on occasion. There is a bit of a paradox here, but I will leave it unresolved. It is something for you to explore. The first-class shot needs good technique, and a relaxed, but disciplined, frame of mind as noted. But, there are occasions when one must simply get on with the job and allow the hunter within to take charge. Thinking about it *too much* will only get you into a muddle.

General Principles of Good Shooting Psychology

Think through and visualise what you ought to be doing when you shoot.
Cut the clutter: Develop a shooting routine focusing on essentials.
Develop confidence based in a mastery of basic skills.
Expect success.
Don't get neurotic about guns and cartridges.
Explore your comfort zone and extend it.
Anxiety or distraction may cause you to bring focus back to the gun.
Enjoy the process and environment of shooting as much as the result.
Find time to 'stop and smell the flowers'.

Technique – Conclusion

We have considered many issues thus far; this is a chance to try and condense what has been written. Safety first. It boils down to this. Treat your gun as loaded – always. Never point it at something you do not want to kill. There are other rules, but if you remember these, if you live by them, and recognise your fallibility, you are far less likely to fall victim to tragedy. Vision comes next. If you get the eyes right, everything else falls into place. You must ensure that you have no natural impediment to seeing the target well. If you have not done so already, visit an optometrist for a thorough check-up (and return regularly as advised). The sensible Gun will not assume that he knows what his eye dominance is. He will present himself for testing by

All guns are loaded. Don't point them carelessly.

a professional shooting instructor/gunfitter. Most people do not have quite the eye dominance that they think. Typically, they – or those responsible for previous testing – have failed to consider the possibilities that exist between full right and left dominance. Many undergo a change in eye dominance in middle age or in certain specific situations. The probability is high – 50:50 – that you are missing some birds now because your eye dominance is not as you believe it to be. Get it tested.

Once the eyes are properly sorted – and there are no shortcuts to the instructions above – the next thing to be considered is gunfit. You will never do your best work until your gun fits. It must point naturally to where you are looking. It must encourage an unchecked swing and it must control recoil effectively. Again, the probability is high that you have a gun that is not a perfect fit (the problem, as with eye dominance, is that many are unaware of it). A quick test, as noted, is to bring the gun up to the face and shoulder closing the eyes just before the mount is completed. If on opening the eyes you cannot see the rib, if the eye is way off line with the rib, or if the rib appears to be climbing excessively, the chance is high that something is wrong in the gunfit department. Similarly, if your butt sole snags at the shoulder in mounting the gun normally, or if the base of your thumb is very close to, or touching, your nose. But, let me emphasise, these are just quick checks to show up gross errors. To deal with gunfit effectively, you will need professional assistance. It is a subtle business with all sorts of interacting and potentially confusing variables.

A well-fitted gun should be effortless to use and shoot to where you look.

This pattern placement is close to being right but a smidgeon more cast-off is required for perfection.

It is good general advice not to get too obsessed about your equipment, but you cannot afford to ignore it either (unless you abrogate responsibility to your shooting instructor or gunmaker – a course of action that has much to recommend it). The experienced shooter sees his gun as a tool. He regards it with detached interest. It is unlikely (but not impossible) that you will have the good fortune to obtain a gun that is precisely right for you 'off the shelf'. Its fitness for purpose must be checked methodically and modifications made if required. The goal is to have a reliable piece of equipment, well suited to its task and which has no feature that is going to impede you. Trigger pulls and balance are as important as fit practically speaking. So are small things like chequering and the position and size of the safety catch. The barrels must not be too heavy (nor the gun) and their length should suit your style of shooting and the application. Guns should also be checked to make sure that both barrels shoot to the same point of aim. If you come across any gross problems, and they are confirmed by a competent person, the simplest advice is to get rid of the gun and try another.

As for choke, the simple advice is as follows (see also pages 202-3). For medium-range birds – the sort that most of us shoot – many need less choke than they have. For normal walked-up and driven game shooting, I prefer a very open first barrel on a 12 bore. I know it works well. Too many driven birds are missed or damaged because guns are over-choked. We seem to forget that modern cartridges, effectively, increase choke (I do, however, prefer a bit of choke in a small-bore). On the subject of cartridges, ensure that your shells are suited to the weight of your gun and that you have confidence in them. An ounce of shot will do the job in most circumstances, but

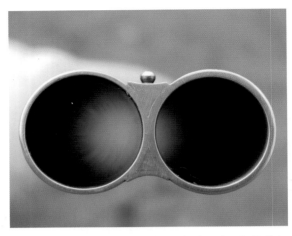

Improved cylinder and half choke is the classic British game gun norm.

if you prefer ¹⁄₁₆ ounce or ⅛ ounce more, fine. Do not get neurotic about pellet size – 5 shot, or 6 shot will both do the job (though current research suggests the larger pellet may be more effective for pheasants). Do not opt for overly heavy payload shells for normal use. Do use a larger pellet and increase payload when the range increases or when birds are especially tough (as they may be at the end of the season or if wild). Make the effort to experiment. When you find a shell you like, buy it in quantity and stick with it.

Now, to issues of technique. Successful, stylish, shooting requires sustained visual contact, balance and good timing on every shot. If you are deficient in any of these areas, it will cost you birds. The importance of keeping your eyes on the bird is critical. Fine-focus on the head or beak. You may read and re-read it here, and you may say to yourself 'of course I watch the bird', but the majority of us do not watch the bird consistently. We are insufficiently *focus aware*. In the context of the

The importance of keeping the eyes on the bird, the body unstrained, and the gun moving cannot be over-emphasised.

WRONG. Bringing the weight back is a common mistake – get your front shoulder over your front foot – the hip should come forward too (assuming a Stanbury or modified Stanbury stance) so that a straight line could be drawn through front shoulder, front hip and the ball of the front foot.

shotgun shooting sports, *vision is a skill.* Locking fine focus on a moving object for more than a few moments is not the way we normally use our eyes. We need to train ourselves to do it. Make no mistake, it is difficult! <u>You must make the effort on every bird you shoot.</u>

The first-class shot works on stance and is not afraid to change it to suit specific situations. He is aware of his centre of gravity. Many lesser shots allow the weight to come rearwards unintentionally as the swing progresses. This frequently results in misses behind and above as the barrel stops and the face comes off the stock. Another very common error is to fail to move the feet when required (and so fail to orientate the stance to the killing point for the bird). A good, stable, stance may allow for shooting within a defined arc of fire without moving the feet on some occasions. But, it is always better to move the feet if the opportunity arises. It vastly reduces body tension and makes the swing much more effortless and graceful.

Timing is important too. The simplest way one can become aware of it is to think in musical terms. Endeavour to shoot to three beats – One: Two: Threeeee – but modify the tempo according to the shot. If you have developed a good, unrushed, mounting style and achieve sustained visual contact with the bird, shooting with a good rhythm becomes much easier. A common fault is to rush the mount, completing it too early in the swing. This leads to a 'bash and slash' style of shooting, which looks awful and is unlikely to produce consistent results. Another stylistic error is to develop a flick at the end of the swing. The expert is calm, rhythmic and finishes his shot well with a smooth follow-through. Birds are brushed out of the air with unhurried elegance. Do not be afraid of calling out the time as you shoot on occasion to develop your sense of rhythm.

Use your body fluidly. Don't extend the front hand too far. Keep the weight forward and the head on the stock.

Concentration is vital, but the competent shot has learnt exactly what to concentrate upon.

With regard to forward allowance, the best advice is to experiment (and the only sensible place to do this is at a shooting school). When shooting close-driven birds, misses in front are more common than most people think, but once beyond 25 yards or so, misses behind and off line are the norm. Many experienced guns have never really understood the amount of lead needed on some targets. The range of leads that they apply is often too limited. They may, moreover, try and apply lead with insufficient body movement. Foward allowance should be felt as well as seen. It should be applied by use of the whole body not just the arms.

Power for the swing should always be generated from *body bending (driven shots) or rotation (crossing shots)*; the strength of these core body movements prevents the barrels stopping prematurely (as they often do if the arms are used too much). The first-class shot does, however, use the arms and hands to elevate and point the muzzles. Indeed, he makes a special effort to use the front arm well – pushing up as the body rotates or bends and developing fine control of the muzzles.

Finally, on the subject of mental attitude: a good shot learns to concentrate by paying attention to

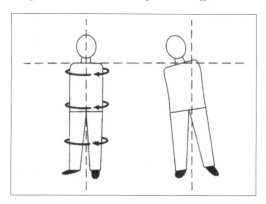

A good swing requires core body movement.

specifics. He prioritises what is important and creates a personal shooting routine. His confidence grows as he sees the results of following the routine and applying basic skills with care. He learns that confidence itself is important to keep the gun moving. He operates in a *comfort zone* where he remains calm but alert. He is disciplined, but no control freak. He shoots because he loves it and takes as much pleasure in his style as in his tally. He knows that if he applies a methodical approach, puts the time and effort into practice, and pays attention to the fine points of technique his performance is likely to be respectable.

KEEP YOUR EYES LOCKED ON THE BIRD

KEEP THE GUN MOVING AND YOUR HEAD ON THE STOCK

MOVE THE FEET WHEN YOU CAN

ENJOY THE DAY

PART IV

DEVELOPMENT OF THE SPORTING GUN

Ancient History

The first hand-held firearms, which appeared in the fourteenth century, were no more than small hand cannon and offered almost as much hazard to the user as the target. They were hard to point effectively and subject to almost uncontrolled recoil. Early in the evolution of the *handgonne*, barrels were attached to poles or planks of wood to make aiming the gun easier and firing more comfortable. Early stocks might be held under the arm, on top of the shoulder, against the chest, or, later, as became common in many Northern European sporting weapons of higher quality, against the cheek without support from the shoulder.

Early gun stocks might be held on top of the shoulder, under the armpit, or rested against the cheek without support from the front of the shoulder or chest.

Ignition was achieved by hot iron or coal, burning ember or slow match in early firearms. The first successful gun lock – the matchlock – appeared in the fifteenth century. It took the basic lever-trigger mechanism from the crossbow and adapted it to use in firearms. This was simple, and successful in military arms (especially in refined sear trigger form) and remained in use for more than two hundred years. However, the matchlock was far from convenient for sporting use and subject to malfunction in inclement weather. Its great disadvantage was that soldiers or sportsmen had to wander around with a burning match made of hemp or tow.

The wheel-lock, wound up with a spanning key and operating on something like the principle of the Zippo lighter, was developed around 1500 for wealthier sportsmen (the matchlock remained the standard military weapon, meanwhile). A complex, and therefore costly, piece of machinery based on a clockwork

Firing a Joseph Harrison 20 bore flintlock gun of 1817 – note the smoke!

mechanism – it was sometimes known as 'the mechanic's delight' – it had a jaw that gripped a piece of iron pyrites. This was brought down on a spinning, serated, wheel creating sparks that were directed into a priming pan of fine gunpowder. This was much more convenient than the matchlock, when it worked, but it was only suitable for use against stationary targets.

In the late sixteenth century the snaphaunce appeared, operating on the much more efficient flint and steel principle. This speeded up ignition significantly and soon evolved into what we now call the flintlock (perfected by French gunsmiths around 1610). The advantage of the latter was that sparking steel and pan cover were combined in one piece. It was more reliable and therefore safe from wind and rain – until the moment the hammer fell upon the frizzen cover. Here was a system that made shooting on the wing much more practical.

As locks were being perfected, barrel-making technology had also become much more sophisticated, allowing for lighter barrels. The Spanish became famous for their light, strong, barrels of twist steel (and any visiting English gentleman would make a point of buying such a barrel to be made up by his gunsmith at home). The stock evolved too. The clumsy fishtail style seen on many military weapons in the late sixteenth/early seventeenth centuries, was replaced by the so-called 'French' or 'club' stock. This was similar in profile to a modern stock, but much wider. Nevertheless, it was a handier, more ergonomically efficient design, much better suited to wingshooting. By about 1700, lock, stock and barrel were all much improved.

During the eighteenth century the sporting gun was refined further. Powder became significantly better, and, as importantly, 'patent breeches' were devised which improved powder combustion. Double-barrelled guns became far more practical as barrel length could be reduced without significant ballistic loss. The first British side by sides were seen *circa* 1750 (made by Griffin of Bond Street). But, they were still considered as little more than expensive novelties until makers like Manton put their genius into them. The side by side would, however, become the dominant shotgun configuration in the second half of the nineteenth century.

By this time, there had been extraordinary progress in lock technology. The Rev. Forsyth, a keen wildfowler, developed the percussion or 'detonating' system of ignition *circa* 1805 and patented it with the help of his friend James Watt of steam engine fame in 1807. It would not only make wingshooting even easier – reducing the delay between pulling the trigger and the moment of discharge – but also allowed, a few years later, for the development of the percussion cap, and shortly after that, a practical self-contained cartridge (and consequently a truly practical breech-loader). The advantages of the percussion system, like those of the patent breech, were immediately recognised and quickly adopted by other makers.

Percussion caps were usually packed in tins like these from the famous maker Joyce.

The Breech-loader

Jean Samuel Pauly, a Swiss-born veteran of Napoleon's army, developed the first self-contained cartridge, centre-fire, breech-loader as early as 1812. His shotgun had a fixed barrel, but he also devised a breech-loading pistol with a hinged barrel into which the cartridge could be inserted in the modern manner. As far as the ammunition for his shotgun was concerned, a tiny amount of fulminate – lacquered-over to hold it in place – was packed into a shallow, central, hollow of a brass

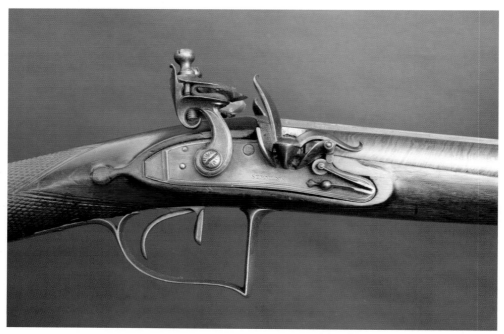

A Thomas Stevens flintlock circa 1814 – note half-cocked hammers. (Knowles collection)

A percussion lock 14 bore Purdey of 1842 – note the caps in place and fully cocked hammers. (Knowles collection)

rosette at the base of a partially consumable paper cartridge. Pauly received some acclaim for this revolutionary invention, but was forced to flee his workshop in Paris in 1814 as the allied armies entered the city. He went to England, formed a partnership with the gunmaker Durs Egg, and became distracted by airships.

The modern breech-loading shotgun emerged onto the British scene via the Great Exhibition at Crystal Palace in 1851. The display of the Parisian gunmaker, Casimir LeFaucheaux, attracted particular attention. His hinged, drop-action, gun, had two barrels side by side and external hammers. Each fell on a thin rod projecting perpendicularly from the base of a self-contained cartridge driving it into the detonating compound.

The early pin-fire breech-loader was not especially efficient ballistically, nor that safe. Indeed, it was not very reliable either, but its quick-loading and quick-firing advantages were immediately apparent. It did most of the right things. The new type of gun achieved significant popularity and rapidly evolved. Pin-fire breech-loaders were soon made in England by the likes of Lang and Purdey (both ex-Manton and Forsyth employees) before they gave way to the now dominant central-fire systems. This all happened within a decade and a half of the pin-fire's British debut at the great expo in Hyde Park.

In the early 1850s, Charles Lancaster presented his 'Base-fire' gun (probably observing further developments in Paris – a hotbed of design activity in the first half of the nineteenth century). His system put the detonating charge on a base disc punctured with flash holes at the rear of a gas-tight case. The disc was covered by copper foil and struck by a blunt firing pin. The 'Base-fire' cartridge looked much like a modern one, and 'system Lancaster' became synonymous with the central-fire breech-loading gun.

In 1861, the British gunsmith, Daw, developing the ideas of Eugene Schneider – from whom he had acquired patent rights for a snap-action gun with cartridge extractors – introduced a centre-fire cartridge of truly modern type with a primer positioned centrally and incorporating an anvil at its rear (a small but vitally important component that ensured reliable ignition). It caught the imagination of both trade and shooting public. Daw tried to establish a monopoly for his clever product, but could not maintain it – his patent was successfully challenged by Eley Brothers in 1865.

The means of locking the barrels to the standing breech was also much improved in the 1850s and 1860s. The Jones rotary under-lever system of 1858 offered strength, but was not especially convenient, requiring the removal of the rear hand from the grip to operate it. The Dougal Lockfast was strong, but odd in that the barrel slid forward for a short distance before hinging open for loading (it achieved an efficient gas seal however, and in this respect was superior to many early breech-loaders). Schneider's action had its sprung, hinged lever under the trigger guard. The key development was the mating of Purdey's underbolt of 1863 with the Scott spindle of 1865. Shooters then had a sprung 'snap-action' fastening operated by means of a thumb-piece on the top-strap. It is still in general use.

Stanton's rebounding hammers (patented in 1867) would replace the potentially more dangerous manual half-cock type. More than one hundred other safety devices were introduced from 1870 to 1890. Damascus barrels – once an innovation – would be replaced by Sir Joseph Whitworth's 'fluid-pressed steel'.

A splendid T. Bland, double 8 bore intended for wildfowling. Note the Jones rotary under-lever.

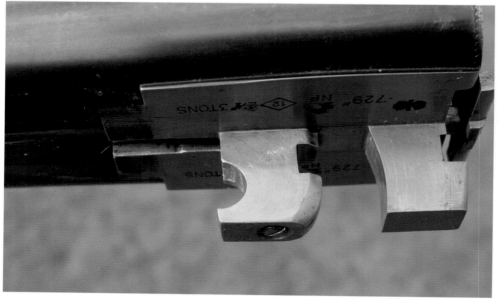

The twin lumps on a Purdey. This feature combined with the 'Scott spindle' and top-lever helped to create the classic English game gun. They are now standard features on the great majority of side by sides (though there are exceptions).

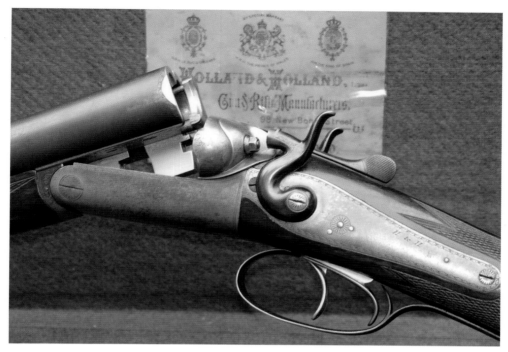

Note the rebounding locks, and the top-lever, on this Holland & Holland. It identifies it as a later type of hammer gun. The 'side clips' are an unusual feature more commonly seen on pigeon guns, rifles, and 'ball and shot' guns.

W.W. Greener was responsible for popularising choke-boring in England during the mid-1870s, having been inspired by certain American gunmakers. (The actual invention of choke-boring is uncertain, and may date to the seventeenth century or earlier.) Choke-boring would become the norm by the 1880s. It was typically accomplished by constriction towards the muzzles or jugging (relieving the bores) just behind them.

Self-cocking, hammerless designs were perfected in the 1870s and 1880s. Ejectors would be refined too, Needham's patent of 1874 setting the pace. The flow of ideas and the pace of invention from 1850 to 1890 was truly remarkable.

Surprisingly, however, the essential form of the British gun established in the late eighteenth century remained relatively unchanged in the nineteenth century despite all the innovation and improvement in its mechanism. In fact, a Manton flintlock double *circa* 1800 still has the recognisable proportions of a modern side by side. The stock dimensions are very similar and the weight at around 6½–7 pounds is also about the same. Even the barrels are of similar length (about 30-inches). Bores, however, tended to be smaller in flintlock sporting guns than the modern 12 bore norm.

Gunmaking Practice

Rather than radically change the outward appearance of the sporting gun, gunmakers tended to develop the component parts to improve efficiency. Because this was usually a subtle process, one may still encounter flintlocks converted to percussion, (less commonly) muzzle-loaders converted to breech-fire, pin-fire guns converted to central-fire ignition (the tell-tale sign of which is a date around 1860 and a barrel ⅛-inch or ¼-inch shorter than the full inch – e.g. 29¾-inches or 30⅞-inches), non-ejectors converted to ejector and cylinder-bored guns converted to choke (typically by swaging or re-boring at the muzzles).

Most British sporting guns in the nineteenth (and, for that matter, twentieth centuries), continued to be made 'on the bench' by a team of artisans – barrel-maker, actioner, lock-maker, stocker and engraver – much as they had in the eighteenth century. Techniques of production were refined in the Victorian era, however. Steam power was widely used by the larger makers, metal quality improved and trades, at least in the gunmaking centres of London and Birmingham, became more specialised.

In Birmingham the interchangeable principle and semi or actual mass production was developed in the sporting as well as the military context by makers like BSA (formed by fourteen Brummie gunmakers in 1861 in reaction to the opening of the Royal Small Arms Factory at Enfield) and Bonehill. The Americans had led the way in this respect; they had used the technique since the first quarter of the nineteenth century. And, in the 1880s, they would adapt it to repeating shotgun designs. W&C Scott (later, Webley & Scott) and Cogswell & Harrison would also become well known for their partially machine-made guns as well as more expensive hand-crafted products.

Shooting, meanwhile, was the dominant national participation sport in mid and late Victorian England (both game and target rifle shooting were extremely popular). The Birmingham makers thrived on volume production (by hand or machine), and the Gun Quarter boomed as did the nearby proof house. The London makers, a more individualistic and socially ambitious lot, targeted the carriage trade of St James's and Piccadilly. They offered, at very significant price, bespoke perfection based on the latest advance as proven at the pigeon traps of Hurlingham or the Gun Club, Notting Hill (or, with little less fanfare, in the coverts of Holkham or Audley End).

The speed of development in this era was extraordinary. Within half a century, propellant ignition by flint and steel had moved to the Forsyth detonator, to the percussion cap and through to pin and and hammer and hammerless central-fire. It is not just a British story – gunmakers and inventors based on the Continent, particularly in Paris, were highly influential as were gunsmiths and mass manufacturers in the United States as noted. But, during the nineteenth century, British gun and ammunition makers established themselves as the world's best.

Gunsmoke

Until the second half of the nineteenth century, the propellant in all these cartridges was, of course, black powder. The traditional sulphurous mix, itself much improved in the eighteenth and nineteenth centuries, would soon be challenged by 'smokeless' or nitro (nitrocellulose) alternatives. Schonbein had invented gun cotton

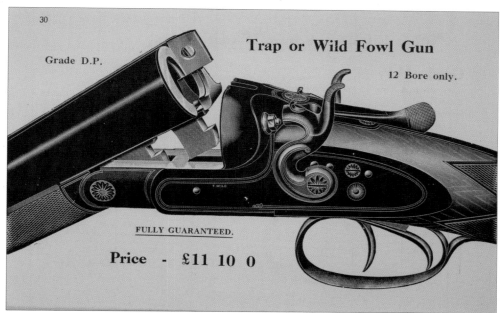

The Birmingham gun trade produced reliable sporting guns in vast quantity at reasonable cost before the Italians began their dominance of the European trade post World War II.

David Sinnerton a modern, master craftsman specialising in building and restoring guns of the highest quality.

Nitro powders as we use today began to replace the sulphurous black variety in the third quarter of the nineteenth century. By the 1890s they had become dominant.

in 1845 by nitrating cotton waste in nitric and sulphuric acids. A Prussian Artillery officer, Colonel Schultze, developed the first commercially successful 'smokeless' propellant in about 1860. He treated wood particles with nitric acid and added barium or potassium nitrate. This created a relatively fast-burning substance, suitable for shotguns – which were the first firearms to use smokeless powders – but not rifles. Advertisements appeared in the British sporting press in the late 1860s, and, a factory was built in England (at Lyndhurst in Hampshire).

Testing and Development 1860–90

Public trials of guns became popular as a means of helping the increasingly bewildered sporting shooter to decide what really was better – muzzle or breech-loader, choke or traditionally bored gun, nitro or black? Live pigeon shooting contests – at their zenith in the 1870s and 80s – and the publication of increasingly sophisticated, but frequently partisan, technical books were also a feature of this age. Sportsmen must have felt much as we do now when the latest digital gizmo is replaced by a significantly better one a few months later.

The famous Field Trial of 1875 popularised the use of choke first patented by William Rochester Pape in 1866, but perfected and popularised by W.W. Greener after his study of American guns in US based trials. It was also in the year of 1875 that Anson & Deeley's boxlock was developed. Messrs Anson & Deeley were employees of Westley Richards and their gun patented in 1876 was the first practical hammerless design to be cocked 'by the fall of the barrels'. Theophilus Murcott of Haymarket is, however, generally credited with the first hammerless gun (patented in 1871 as previously noted). In it, an under-lever was used to open the gun and cock the locks. It was a rather complicated arrangement and became known as 'Murcott's Mousetrap' as a result.

The now classic Anson & Deeley achieved great popularity as a platform for game guns, especially in the medium and lower grades, as, having fewer parts, and requiring less steel, it was less expensive to produce than sidelock designs: it inspired many other gun makers, not least W.W. Greener (who created his *Facile Princips* in a successful attempt to get around the A & D patent). In 1880 Beesley developed his self-opening hammerless sidelock and offered the design to Purdey (who bought the rights for £55). Its brilliant design was brought to near-perfection with the arrival of reliable ejectors in the 1880s.

By 1890 the specification and form of the hammerless game gun we know today – the boxlock or sidelock ejector – was established. This sounded the death knell of the external hammer gun. Hammer actions, however, continued to be used for cheaper grade guns (such as 'keeper' models), and for live pigeon shooting well into the twentieth century. Walsingham continued to use hammer guns throughout his life. George V was another great exponent of the external hammer gun (and had Purdey make his with ejectors). He believed hammers were an aid to effective alignment.

Over and Under History

What about the over and under? The configuration has its roots in antiquity (and pre-dates the side by side by at least two hundred years). Some of the earliest

Anson & Deeley guns were made in all qualities as both ejector and non-ejectors.

George V shooting with his Purdey hammer guns in 1907 – note the straight front arm style which he popularised.

A close-up of a modern Purdey over and under with exceptionally fine engraving. The Purdey OU is based on the Woodward design, bifurcated lumps allow for a low profile action.

double guns were made on the over and under principle (or under and over as some British makers prefer to call it). The Beretta museum in Brescia contains a double flintlock over and under dating from around 1790, and the Kremlin Armoury has a Tula-made gun of similar vintage. Earlier seventeenth century examples may be discovered in the Tojhusmuseet in Copenhagen (one of the world's most extraordinary collections and well worth several visits).

Both Dickson and Greener experimented with side-opening over and unders in the late Victorian era. German makers – who have long retained a special interest in multi-barrelled guns – were also innovators in this field. But the honour for the first really practical over and under design must go to the Robertson & Henderson Boss of 1909. An important feature of this ground-breaking and much copied gun was its 'bifurcated' (split) lumps.

Locking lugs beneath the barrel and a cross pin for hingeing – as seen in nearly all side by sides – were dispensed with. Rather, protrusions on either side of the barrels engaging with rotating bushes located at the knuckle of the action. Under-barrel bolting was replaced by small, square-section, pegs coming out of the breech-face that engaged with bites to either side of the bottom chamber mouth. The action also had 'draws', whereby a concave face on the rear bifurcated barrel lump engaged with a corresponding convex face on the inner action walls.

In 1913, Woodward patented a similar low-profile bifurcated lump action. But the company's design incorporated a tongue and groove system, which locked the barrels to the side of the action walls and used a different hingeing arrangement with trunnion-like stud pins, upon which the barrels could pivot (as adopted by Beretta, Remington, Perazzi, Rizzini and many others in later years).

Although the Boss and Woodward sidelock designs are of the greatest importance, the two most popular modern over and unders are those made by Browning and Beretta. The Browning, 'Superposed' (now known as the B25) was invented by John Moses Browning around 1920 and was first marketed in 1930. The Beretta was brought to the market as the Model 55 in the 1950s (its derivatives include the Models 56, 57 and 58 and the 68 series as sold today). Beretta, however, was making over and unders before this. Its SO sidelock model was clearly inspired by the Boss gun (a precise copy of which was made by Beretta in 1933 and rests in the company museum in Brescia to this day).

The Browning and Beretta 55/68 series guns are very different. The Browning has lumps positioned beneath the barrel and a full-width hinge-pin (necessitating a higher-action profile); the Beretta, copying the Boss and Woodward 'bifurcated' principle, has its lumps either side of the chambers, machined into the breech metal. Moreover, like the Woodward, the barrels of the Beretta pivot on stud-pins located in the action walls near the knuckle.

The bolting systems of the Browning and Beretta are very different too. The former has a wide, flat bolt, which engages slot bites beneath the bottom chamber mouth (copied in the Winchester 101 and other simplified versions of the basic B25 design), whilst the Beretta has conical bolts that emerge from the breech-face as the gun is closed and locate in small round socket bites either side of the top chamber mouth. These are a very clever feature of the design, and, like the hinge-pins, may be replaced by over-size parts to allow for wear.

A number of mid-priced over and unders such as those made by Franchi, various members of the Rizzini clan and Caesar Guerini in Italy, combine stud-pin hingeing with a Browning-style flat bolt engaging a bite under the bottom chamber mouth. These guns are a little higher in action profile than those made to the Boss/Woodward/Beretta pattern but are shallower than those designs that combine the full-width hinge-pin with the Browning-style bolting arrangement.

The proponents of the over and under would note the advantages of the single sighting plane and stiffer barrels. There is some truth in this – it is my experience (and that of many shooting instructors)

The open action of a Beretta Silver Pigeon – note the circular recesses either side of the bottom chamber mouth – these, conical locking bolts which locate in them, are a distinctive feature of this popular model.

that for the new shooter, the over and under gun is the easier to master. That is not to say that there is anything wrong with the side by side – far from it. They are great guns, and may be the gun of choice for walking up, or, when rapid loading is an issue. Many of the old hammer and hammerless guns of the 1870s and 1880s, moreover, are still in daily use with modern ammunition. (I use an 1870 Lang hammer gun and a Holland & Holland of 1885 vintage routinely.) Gun making in the last 120 years has involved more refinement than innovation.

My sleeved, non-rebounding lock, 1870 Lang helped me win the British Side by Side Championship in 2004 and has also accounted for much game. It often travels with me to the US where it is not subject to import restrictions because of its age (pre-1898).

Repeating Shotguns

The American inventor, Sylvester Roper, also known for his steam motorbikes, came up with an intriguing four-shot magazine shotgun in the 1860s. The cutting edge of technology in its day, it used self-contained steel cartridges and had screw-in chokes (and probably qualifies as the first mass-produced multi-choke gun). Christopher Spencer's hammerless pump action design patented in 1885 (upon which Roper also collaborated) was one of the first repeating shotguns to achieve real success. It was intended for use with normal cartridges (the development of repeating shotguns in the second half of the nineteenth century was much impeded by lack of standardisation in cartridge manufacture). Annie Oakley used a Spencer, and Charles Lancaster imported them to England, fitting some with his own barrels.

In an age before an anti-repeater prejudice had established itself in Albion, Basil Tozer (who used the pen name 20 Bore) even wrote in his *Hints on Shooting*, a book of 1887:

> *On the whole... a repeating shotgun is preferable when battue shooting or driving, or in what is commonly known as a 'warm corner'... To the Spencer gun we would give the priority; it is light for a repeater, weighing but 7¾ lbs., and in this gun the mechanism of both lock and magazine is remarkably simple... it handles far more pleasantly than any repeating gun we know of. In a hot corner, with a couple of such guns, nothing more could be desired.*

Nevertheless, the Spencer firm ran into some financial difficulties, leaving the way open to Winchester. They had applied their lever system to shotguns in the

The lever-action Winchester Model 1887, one of the first really effective repeating shotguns.

sturdy Model 1887 (and later in the Model 1901) but it was the Winchester Model 1893 pump, designed by John Moses Browning, that really dictated the future of repeating shotguns. The Model 1893 was fast cycling and reasonably well balanced although, unlike the Spencer, it had an external hammer. Thirty thousand were made before the Model 1893 was replaced by the even more successful, some might say legendary, Model 1897. This was a modification of the '93 with a stronger action and side ejection. It was especially intended for use with modern smokeless cartridges which the earlier gun had not been.

Later advances in repeaters put the hammer back inside the receiver (most elegantly in the Winchester Model 12) and harnessed recoil or propellent gas energy to cycle the gun. Again it was John Moses Browning who led the way. His A5 (the A stands for Auto, 5 – for live shot) was the first successful semi-automatic. He fell out with Winchester over the gun – he demanded royalties rather than a one-off payment as he had previously received from the firm for his designs. Browing decided, after negotiations with Remington, to go to Belgium where he came to terms with Fabrique Nationale who were already making his .32 semi-automatic pistol. The Browning arms company was born in this era, and guns bearing that now famous name came out in the early 1900s. It was a so-called 'long-recoil' design where the barrel actually moves back into the receiver as the gun is fired. Browning's son Val came up with an improved 'short-recoil' design – in which barrel movement was significantly reduced but not eliminated – a generation later.

Meanwhile, the gas-operated military rifles of World War II inspired a new generation of gas-operated semi-automatics. The first was brought out by the High Standard company in 1956 as the 'J.C. Higgins Model 60'. It was actually made for Sears Roebuck. The real commercial breakthrough, however, came with the Remington 1100 in 1963. The firm has brought out several gas guns in the late 1950s, but the 1100 was mechanically ingenious and streamlined. It became popular

A Beretta 391 semi-auto – a gas-operated gun and one of the most reliable and popular of its type. Gas-operated designs reduce felt recoil significantly.

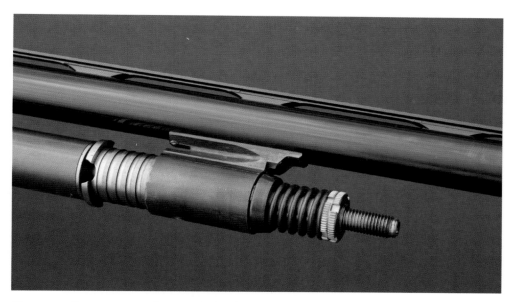

The gas collar, pressure release valve and piston of the Beretta 391.

with both game and clay shooters in the US and established the gas-operated semi-automatic gun. Its notable features were reasonable price and low recoil. Many manufacturers have made gas-operated semi-automatics since.

The Beretta 300 series guns have been especially successful. Unlike the steel-actioned Remington, these employ an aircraft grade aluminium reciever. The latter acts, primarily, as an envelope for all the other parts (and a series of guide surfaces). Stresses upon it are minimised – a steel bolt locks into the rear part of a steel barrel. The mechanism is similar to most gas-operated semis. When the gun is fired, gas is vented off from the barrel and directed – via two small holes forward of the chamber – into a collar that contains a piston. The pressure causes this to move backwards, pushing a sleeve incorporating a cocking-bar. This is attached to a bolt assembly, which moves rearwards extracting and ejecting the spent case. Meantime, a 'rat's tail' attached to the back of the bolt assembly compresses a return spring located in a tube in the stock. This creates the impetus for the forward cycle during which a new cartridge is loaded.

In the Model 391, the latest in the 300 series, you will find a sprung, venting mechanism attached to the front of the gas collar; if a high-pressure cartridge is used excess gas is simply blown out (hence the ability of this gun to handle a wide variety of cartridges). Most modern semi-automatics incorporate this sort of venting feature and may be distinguished from first and second generation gas guns which, generally, did not and tended to be more ammunition sensitive.

Finally, no consideration of the semi-automatic would be complete without some reference to the inertia-operated Benelli gun (a firm now owned by Beretta). The Benelli has been much admired by gun designers. Unusual among modern semi-automatics, it has a fixed barrel and a twin-lug rotary bolt head. The key to the

The Benelli semi-auto is not gas-operated like most modern semi-automatic designs, rather, it uses a clever inertia mechanism.

operating system is the rotary bolt head, which is attached to the main mass of the bolt by means of a short, very strong, spring. When the gun is fired, the rotary bolt head remains stationary relative to the barrel initially, but the breech block accelerates a short distance forward and compresses the spring in proportion to the power of the cartridge. The tension then causes the breech block to accelerate in the opposite direction, an action that also unlocks the bolt head. As the bolt and block accelerate rearward, the cartridge case is extracted and ejected and the assembly of the bolt head and bolt are re-energized in conventional fashion by further spring pressure in the opposite direction caused by a 'rat's tail' acting against a tubed coil spring, as in the case of the Beretta 300 guns (and many others). It will be of interest to wildfowling and pigeon shooting southpaws to learn that the Benelli is one of the few repeaters available in left-handed form (Remington also offers some left-handed models and their new 105CTi is a bottom ejecting semi-auto design also notable for its titanium receiver and anti-recoil features).

GUNS, CHOKE AND CARTRIDGES

We have considered the history and development of the sporting gun in some detail. It is an absorbing subject in itself – especially to the author – but it would be a grave mistake to worry too much about equipment when trying to improve your shooting. It should never be forgotten that a shotgun is only a tool. It may be mechanically ingenious, beautifully engraved and stocked with wonderfully figured wood, but its primary function is as a hunting *weapon*.

Most people, moreover, do not miss because they have the wrong gun or cartridge. They miss because they have failed to apply simple principles. They stop the gun. They shoot with their feet in the wrong place. They fail to keep their eyes on the bird. Sorting out equipment methodically and with a base of sound knowledge is important. The purpose of the history presented and what follows below is to help you do that. But, do not become bogged down. Have fun with this stuff – 'gunology' is a subject in itself – but get on with the primary job!

As we have already considered in some detail, any gun should fit the user, have good trigger pulls (not too heavy nor too light and without creep), and be reasonably balanced. These are things that are of almost equal importance from a practical shooting point of view. The overall weight of a game gun is also an important issue. Too heavy, or too light, a gun will be a significant handicap in the field. Greener's old rule was that a gun should weigh 96 times the weight of its shot charge. Thus a gun firing an ounce of shot should weigh 6 pounds, one firing an 1⅛ ounce, 6 pounds 12 ounces. This applied quite well to side by sides (though 6 pounds is extremely light for any 12 bore). Most would say that a modern, bench-made, 12 bore side by side should weigh something in the range 6 pounds 4 ounces to 7 pounds (long barrels, long chambers, long stocks and self-opening mechanisms all tending to make a gun heavier).

This young man already has all the basics in place – good stance, weight on the front foot, head well down, and eye on his mark.

Mike Ladd (left), one of the UK's premier dealers advises a client in his shop at Crediton, Devon.

Gun Weight: Simple Advice

For someone of average build, using lighter loads, I would usually advise a side by side gun of about 6½-6¾ pounds (assuming 28-inch barrels). Much will depend on the gun in question, however. A well-balanced gun of 7 pounds is always to be preferred to an ill-balanced one of 6½. A 20 bore should usually weigh about half a pound less than a 12 bore, with 6 pounds to 6 pounds 6 ounces, being the norm for a modern 2¾-inch chamber side by side.

The Browning Cynergy is a radical new design. In 20 bore form, I found it to be an outstanding game gun with lively handling and weight similar to a best London side by side 12.

As for over and unders, they tend to be made significantly heavier (a consequence of their more complex mechansim). Somewhere just over 7 pounds is the norm for most of the better factory-made 12 bore game guns (although alloy-actioned, ribless and bespoke guns may be significantly lighter). Practically speaking, 7 to 7¼ pounds is usually about right for a 12 bore over under game gun. Twenty bore over and unders tend to feel too light if made under 6 pounds and feel heavy as they approach 7 pounds. My ideal for a 28-inch barrel 20 bore over and under gun would be about 6¼ pounds, and about 6½ pounds in a 30-inch gun.

Balance

Often, a shotgun is picked up by some sage who immediately pronounces: 'That's really well balanced.' What does he mean? Would he know if you asked him? I rather doubt it in most cases. Light guns of good quality seem to be categorised as well balanced more often than others as do guns with barrels relatively light for length. So, trying to remove the bovine scatology, can we be a bit more specific?

There is much talk of hinge-pins in the context of balance. The gun that balances on the hinge-pin is often considered better balanced than the one that does not. There is some truth in this, but one should not be obsessive. First, the

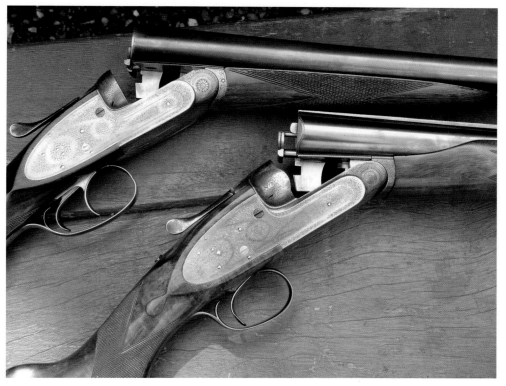

Two Purdeys – one from the 1880s the other (bottom) from the 1920s (a heavy pigeon gun). Both are beautifully balanced, but they are very different guns.

position of the hinge-pin is not constant, the length of actions varies significantly (for example, Greener side by sides have been made with both very short and very long action tables).

Nevertheless, it is fair to say that a well-balanced gun should balance somewhere near the hinge-pin in most cases. Some London makers are very specific about this. I know one firm that builds its 30-inch 12 bore over and unders so that the point of balance is ⅛-inch to the rear of the hinge-pin. It is a formula that works well with that gun. Another very famous maker prefers its 28-inch side by sides to be very slightly muzzle-heavy. There have been few complaints about its products either.

In noting the subtle variations, we might also observe that some mass-produced or poorly modified guns are grossly ill-balanced as far as the hinge-pin index is concerned. Many modern, multi-choked, over and unders are muzzle-heavy in the extreme and will benefit from a little extra weight in the stock (easily accomplished with a lead plug or lead shot in putty). Get these guns to balance near the hinge-pin and they will immediately feel lighter. They will also move better in the hands, helping to promote a good swing.

There is, however, another vitally important component to balance – the way the weight is distributed through the gun. It is a complex variable, though. It is often

Richard Purdey, recently retired, with one of his firm's guns. For over one hundred and fifty years – in many forms – Purdey shotguns have been famous for their balance and superb quality.

said that sidelocks (and Dickson round actions and solid-bar hammer guns) feel better because the weight is concentrated between the hands. Again, there is some truth in this. The way the weight is distributed in the barrels is also critical. For a game gun, it is especially important that the tubes are not too heavy at the front (a particular challenge for makers of multi-choked guns). They must not be too light at the front either (a rarer malady).

I dislike the modern practice of removing the rib under the forend as seen on some mass-produced over and unders. This is done to reduce overall barrel weight, but it is taking weight away at the wrong point in my opinion; better to remove the side ribs and/or the weight of the sighting rib (or, reduce barrel wall thickness). British guns were always famous for their relatively light, thin-walled, barrels. Kemen guns from Spain became popular because they reduced barrel weight in long-barrelled over and unders. Beretta has reduced barrel weight in some models over recent years. The challenge is to create thin, strong, tubes – barrels that are relatively light for length. Modern steels allow for this.

Balance: Keeping it Simple

Any exploration of balance should start with three questions. Does the gun balance near the hinge-pin? Is most of the weight in the middle, i.e. between the hands? Are the barrels dynamically constructed to promote good movement and control?

Barrel Length

Barrel length is a major issue when considering game guns. It is much influenced by fashion. Barrels have tended to get longer in recent years. The 30-inch 20 bore is popular today and 32-inch 12s and 20s are quite frequently used on high bird shoots. I use 32-inch repeaters and over and unders in competition, but have always thought 32-inch too much for a 12 bore game gun – it is too easy to check one's swing. For most people 28-inch is still the best barrel length for an over and under or side by side 12 bore game gun for general use. A 30-inch gun may also be considered if the barrel weight is not excessive, and will especially suit those of large frame and long limb and the over and under user who may shoot clays with the same gun. If you are going to shoot more game than clays, I would still advise the 28-inch over the 30-inch gun in 12 bore. Twenty-nine-inch is also a good all-round length.

As far as 20 and 28 bores are concerned – and there is much to recommend them for most game shooting – I would advise – for those of normal build – 29- or 30-inch barrels on both over and unders and side by sides for the majority of men and 28-inch barrels for women. Longer, slightly heavier, barrels make the smaller bore gun steadier and improve 'pointability' (additional frontal weight may, however, be a handicap to female shots of smaller stature).

What about Churchill's famous XXV (see box)? For someone of average height who shoots infrequently 25- or 26-inch barrelled 12 bore guns can be a good choice. Lead is applied more instinctively with such guns. But, they do not have the

Miroku guns, made in Japan, offer especially good value today. This is the MK60 with fixed chokes and 30" barrels. There is also an MK70 multi-choked model, available like the MK60 with 28" or 30" tubes.

pointing qualities of the Long Toms. In the 1970s 27-inch barrels were in fashion. They are a compromise length – rather like the 29-inch barrels that have recently become fashionable again (a length with many merits).

I do not advise short-barrelled guns to those with eye issues who insist on shooting with both eyes open – they seem to aggravate such problems. Shorter-barrelled guns can, however, be useful when walking in the woods (a point brought home to me on a recent trip quail hunting in Georgia). Does barrel length affect ballistic performance? Robert Churchill might have argued the point, but the ballistic effects of barrel length, though slight, are discernible. There is an increase of about 5 feet per second per inch of barrel length. Thus the difference between 25- and 32-inch tubes, all other things being equal, is in the region of 30 to 40 feet per second – slight but potentially significant.

Barrel Length: Simple Advice

28-inch is the best all-round length for 12 bores (30-inch if you are especially tall or if you want to shoot high birds or clays regularly). For 20 or 28 bores go for 30-inches.

What About Rib Type?

A traditional, subtly tapered, concave rib is as good as any on a side by side, though some may prefer a flat 'pigeon' style. An over and under for game shooting should have a fairly narrow rib (and no mid bead). As far as the former comment is concerned, this is not so much a matter of visual perception, but because there is a weight penalty to wide ribs and no perceptual advantage to the

Most over and unders designated as 'game guns' have a narrow rib.

game shot. I also have a preference for solid ribs on over and under game guns – they are in fact hollowed – because they are less easily dented and therefore more practical in the field.

Regardless of barrel configuration and length, a gun for live quarry shooting must be lively. There should be enough weight to handle recoil and promote muzzle control, but not so much as to suppress the swing. Overall weight is an important consideration, but barrel weight is especially critical as already discussed. Many mass-produced guns have barrels that are too heavy for effortless, elegant game shooting. Fixed-choke game models are usually to be favoured – though there are exceptions – because the barrels tend to be lighter. An additional bonus is that such guns are usually cheaper to buy and easier to clean. Even when a gun is barrel-heavy, all is not lost. A little lead in the stock in compensation can make a big difference.

Changing the sighting rib for a narrower type on over and unders, joining rib modifications, barrel-shortening, and back-boring are all fairly drastic means of reducing barrel weight. I would generally caution against such complex modification – they do not always give the expected results. A simpler option for mass-produced guns is to acquire a lighter set of barrels (for example, replacing multi-choke barrels with fixed-choke ones) or to part-exchange the gun for one of similar type with lighter barrels.

The Kemen KM-4 is an outstanding Spanish gun inspired by the Italian Perazzi.

This most attractive, side-plated, Caesar Guerini, is a typical product of modern Italian high-tech gunmaking. It shows just what can be achieved with the imaginative use of technology.

As far as modern, mid-priced, *factory made* guns are concerned, the handling dynamics of the 20 bore models may be more conducive to good shooting than the 12 bore. The aesthetics of the 20 bore are appealing too. I should come clean and admit a particular bias. My favourite amongst mass-produced game guns is the low-profile Beretta 687 20 or 28 bore. For the price, the gun is hard to beat – it is well made, good looking and great fun to shoot. It is deservedly popular amongst British shooting sportsmen and women.

Browning and Miroku also make excellent 20 bore models. Caesar Guerini now offer some very attractive and well-priced guns as well. In all these cases, one can get a first-class over and under 20 bore for £1,000–£2,000 that handles much like a bespoke 12 bore costing twenty or thirty times as much. Do not let yourself get carried away by my enthusiasm, though. Whether or not a small-bore is right for you can only be determined after you have tried one that fits. (Some people would not be well advised to change. If you tend to rush, for example, a lighter small-bore gun can make your problems worse.)

Over and under or side by side? The modern trend is unquestionably towards over and unders. The single sighting plane has advantages and guns of this type tend to control recoil better. If I was counselling a beginner, I would unhesitatingly advise a stack-barrel rather than a side by side. An excellent gun can be bought new or second-hand at modest cost. One knows it will work well for a very long time (cheaper side by sides tend to give less predictable results).

Existing users of side by sides who do well with them, should stick to their guns (much of my own *clay* shooting is with a Lang gun made around 1870, and wild horses, Texican oil magnates and Russian entrepreneurs would not persuade me to

Buying guns is fun but consider what you really need before you go shopping.

part with it). Side by sides can be made to do 98 per cent of what an over and under can in expert hands. If you need a new gun, however, consider an over and under first.

Do over and unders have any disadvantages? Yes. The gape – the extent to which the gun opens for loading – may not be as wide as on side by sides (so they can be slower to reload). There tends to be a weight penalty as far as mass-produced guns are concerned. Double-trigger models are, sadly, rare today – so, even with a single selective trigger, rapid barrel selection is impeded. And, as far as best bespoke guns are concerned, they are significantly more expensive to buy (in the case of a magnificent new Purdey, the base price of an over and under is £11,000 more than a side by side).

The new Holland & Holland Round Action model. Predominantly machine-made (but hand finished). It is also, unusually, a back action shotgun (like the old H&H Dominion model). This specimen shot superbly. Note the good gape.

This is a most interesting over and under gun – a sound moderated Laporte (based on a Fabarm). It would be ideal for pest control, but sadly is no longer imported into the UK.

28 Bores

There is no doubt that 28 bores have become trendy amongst British game shooters recently (and I hold myself partly responsible, having written so many articles about them). They are lots of fun to use though, and can bring a bit of joy back into jaded shooting lives. I used one – a 30-inch multi-choked Beretta Silver Pigeon – almost exclusively for driven birds in the seasons of 2005/6 and 2006/7 (having previously used a 20). It sounds sad – in the sense that my kids now use the word – but it brings a smile to my face every time I pick it up. It's such a excellent little gun. I seem to shoot it as well or better than my old 20 bore. In fact, and some may argue the point, it seems to shoot as well as a 12 bore in most situations.

The dynamics of my own gun, which weighs just over 6½ pounds – it's not excessively light – are really outstanding. It offers very similar handling to a bespoke gun at a fraction of the price, as noted. I have also found, surprisingly, that it works best at game with a 28-gram (1 ounce) load. If you had asked me a couple of years ago, when I had less practical experience of the 28, I would have said that was too much to stuff through a small-bore routinely. It is certainly a long way away from the ideal 'square' load. Received wisdom also suggests that it would recoil very heavily. I have had no significant problems, though.

With regard to the terminal efficiency of the pattern 28 grams pushed through a 28 bore, seems to work very well. Recoil, oddly, is not excessive (though some brands of cartridge – payload apart – produce more felt recoil than others). What about choke? I use three-quarter choke *in both barrels*. I have always held the prejudice that a little choke helps a small-bore. Three-quarters and three-quarters results in clean – hit or miss – kills. I stick to this choking for sporting clays as well. I do, however, modify the pellet payload for clays, finding 24 or 25 grams is ideal for this sport (and 18- and 21-gram loads are most useful when teaching with a 28).

The XXV Gun

Robert Churchill, one of the best marketing men in the gun trade, popularised the short-barrelled sporting gun with his famous 'XXV' model. Churchill did not, of course, invent the short-barrelled shotgun. Such guns had been seen in the eighteenth century and before. But, they became more practical once nitro cellulose powders came into general use in the late nineteenth century.

Churchill's guns are certainly clever and comparatively undervalued in today's buoyant but focused market. There is more to them than their 25-inch barrels. They have a distinctive narrow, file-cut rib – designed to give the illusion of length and also to lower the point of impact of the short, stiff, barrels. There are other more subtle points. The form of the stock is unusual, inspired by the styles of late eighteenth and nineteenth century muzzle-loaders.

A true Churchill XXV typically has a little more fall in its apparently 'straight' grip than the average English gun. This was intended to minimise cocking of the wrist as the gun was mounted. Another interesting gunfit/stock design feature, is that the comb of the true Churchill XXV is frequently off-set and/or swept. The gunfitting in nearly all the genuine XXV guns that I have come across has been exceptionally sophisticated.

The fad for short barrels – at its height in the 1950s – went into decline in the 1960s (although AyA continued to make a significant number of XXV style guns more recently). (The standard length for game shooting had meantime evolved to 27- or 28-inches.) We are left with a question. Do 25-inch guns work? In refined XXV form, they can be good guns for the those who do not shoot many days a year and who need something that handles instinctively. One might say that they are a good gun for the person who has not learnt to swing well (especially when combined with Robert Churchill's weight transfer shooting technique). I do not advise short barrels for those with significant eye dominance issues.

Checking Regulation

If you are serious about your shooting, you should take your gun to a pattern range and test its barrels for point of impact (by shooting, rifle-like, at a fixed mark). It is my experience that many double shotguns do not have barrels that throw both their charges to the same point of aim (note, though, that many over and unders have a tendency to print the top barrel a little high). This is a complex subject, but sticking to our KISS philosophy: if you and your gunsmith are *sure* that there is a significant problem with the regulation after repeated testing and nothing can be done about it *easily*, get rid of the gun. You will never shoot well with it.

You should also consider the density and quality of your patterns. My earlier comments about choke in small bores notwithstanding, many 12 bore guns are excessively choked for driven shooting – an observation supported by the success of those in the late Victorian era who continued to use guns without choke. For normal use inside 35 yards, anything more than quarter choke in the first barrel is too much (my advice is improved cylinder). The nominal constriction as measured at the muzzles means less, of course, than the pattern actually thrown (which can only be ascertained by the tedious, but important, business of counting pellets at the plates). Whilst I advocate open choke in the first barrel of a 12 bore, my practical experience in the field suggests that small-bores usually work best with tighter chokes in *both* barrels as discussed.

Barrels on quality guns are carefully checked by their makers – nevertheless, it always pays to check regulation for point of impact as well as pattern at the plates. You may be surprised!

Modern crimped cartridge compared to less efficient rolled turn-over type.

Modern cartridges that are crimp closed and have a sophisticated wad are much more efficient than those of a couple of generations back. Typically, they increase the effect of choke. Yesterday's 'half-choke' gun may be throwing three-quarter choke patterns or tighter with modern cartridges. With this in mind, I shot with a Seminole 'spreader' choke – a device that simply trumpets at the muzzles – in the first barrel of a 28-inch 12 bore several seasons back. My hypothesis was that typical ranges of driven pheasant are far less than we like to admit. I had one of my best game shooting seasons ever with regard to kill-to-cartridge ratio (though it was a season without much high bird work). I do not suggest that this device is right for you, but a lot more birds would be shot, and fewer pricked, if we un-choked our first barrels when using 12 bores at typical *modest to medium* ranges. What about the second barrel? For most people quarter- or half-choke would be good advice. If you enjoy picking shots, an even tighter second barrel choke may improve your confidence – though I would rarely advocate more than three-quarter choke in any game gun.*

This is a Seminole spreader choke – a most effective device that is excellent for first barrel use by novices at birds presented at short to medium range.

---

*The bottom line is this: there are many variations in gun and cartridge performance so you should, as a matter of course, pattern test your gun/cartridge combination. Ensure that it delivers a minimum of 100 pellets in a 30-inch circle at your typical shooting range.

Forcing and Back-Boring Cones – Do They Make a Difference?

A fashion for 'chamberless' guns and thin-walled brass cartridges began in Britain in the 1880s. Dr Charles Heath, a surgeon, and later President of WAGBI (Wildfowlers' Association of Great Britain and Ireland), re-awakened interest in chamberless guns in the early twentieth century. His armoury included a 12 bore weighing 8 pounds which fired a 2 ounce pellet payload and a 7¼ pound 12 bore firing 1¾ ounces. Both guns used a relatively modest charge of propellant fired in a wide-bored gun – Heath's 12 bore in fact had a bore size of about 10.

Heath's guns were noted for their lack of recoil. This was sometimes attributed to their lack of forcing cones. Major Burrard did not agree. He stated that 'the true reason [for reduced felt recoil] being the lack of muzzle velocity'. The relatively low velocities at which Heath's guns pushed out their heavy charges must have been significant (velocity is always an important factor in recoil). But, Burrard not-withstanding, long or absent forcing cones and widest bores may also have some odd – and not especially well-understood – effects on pressure over time. They may, indeed, be a contributing factor to lower felt recoil in my experience.

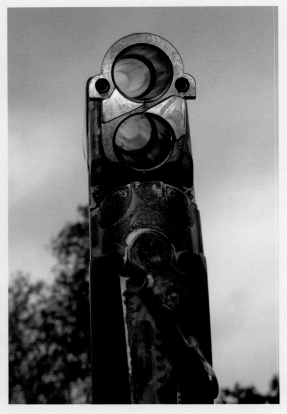

Long cones and widest bores are certainly much in vogue again (the low-velocity cartridge, meanwhile, is waiting to be rediscovered). My own experiments, not very objective I admit, suggest that both modifications can soften *felt* recoil. I have often noted that wider-bore guns seem to kick less when gun testing. I also have considerable experience with a 12 bore modified by Briley in the United States with cones so long that the gun is effectively chamberless now. It feels soft to shoot even though the bore dimensions are *exceedingly tight* (about .715-inch). There needs to be more science in this area to explain this apparent anomaly.

The forcing cones of this gun are clearly visible as a dark crescent just forward of the chamber area.

I do not suggest that any of this is definitive. Some years back, Browning made some serious experiments concerning forcing cones and recoil. It was concluded that there was no advantage to longer cones. Holland & Holland and Beretta equally experienced firms have, however, both moved towards longer forcing cones in recent years. It is also notable that the rolled turnover cartridge – which was the standard until after World War II – needed a more abrupt cone to maintain optimum pressures.

Long forcing cones and large bores certainly make sense for steel shot. Both features reduce the disrupting forces operating against pellets. Anyone considering forcing cone enlargement should, however, seek the advice of a specialist gunsmith. I know from experience that combining forcing cone elongation with back-boring is a bad idea in game guns that are to be used with lightly loaded, felt, wadded cartridges in cold conditions. The gas seal is not efficient. I suspect, meanwhile, that subjective improvement relating to bore and forcing cone modification may relate to subtle changes in operating pressure over time, as noted.

Simple Advice: Recoil

If your gun kicks you consider your technique first – then, consider if the cartridge payload is suitable to the weight of the gun. The angle of the comb may be too steep or, the stock may be too short. The bores may be too tight. The simple advice, however, is try a lower payload, or lower velocity, shell and, if that does not solve the problem fit a polymer recoil pad such as a Kick Eez (which may also be a means to lenghten a short stock) before considering more complex solutions.

Recoil pads come in all sorts of forms. Many believe a leather covered pad is the ultimate for game shooting – because they do not snag. This may be so provided a modern polymer pad lurks beneath the covering.

Cartridges

First and foremost, you must have confidence in your cartridge (just as you must in your gun). It is all important when game shooting. It may make sense to pay a little extra for a premium load if it builds this confidence. A game cartridge wants to be quick (but not at the cost of excess recoil). It wants to be clean burning even in very cold weather. It must suit the gun (e.g. do not put a heavy load in a light-weight gun). And, it must deliver sufficient kinetic energy to kill the quarry efficiently. The traditional British load for a 12 bore being used for driven or walked-up game is 1¹⁄₁₆ ounce (30 grams) of 6 shot. One ounce (28 grams) of 6 shot can work well too, as will 1⅛ ounces (32 grams). The modern trend seems to be towards slightly heavier payloads (especially in small-bores) and bigger pellets.

We are spoilt for choice with good cartridges today. Crimp closure and improved wadding have made cartridges much more efficient.

Brian Jackson of Lyalvale-Express, the UK's largest cartridge maker, notes: 'We are always trying to convince people to use a bit more shot rather than a bit less... the objective is to kill the bird not wound it.' Brian also notes that the sale of 5 shot loaded cartridges has increased in the last couple of years: 'You need something that maintains its energy... No.9 shot fired at optimum angle drops at about 210 yards, but No. 4 shot will drop well past 300... this says it all... if in doubt, use the bigger pellet – it retains its energy better.'

This is sensible advice, and supported by BASC's latest research (though some, the late Sir Ralph Payne-Gallwey amongst them, will argue that smaller pellets produce better patterns. I shot wild guinea fowl in Namibia a few years ago – and

All the standard bore sizes represented here 12, 16, 20, 28 and .410.

they were particularly tough. There appeared to be a really signifcant difference between 6 shot and 4 shot (the latter being much more efficient). I have used 1¼ ounce (36 grams) loads for driven pheasant abroad – the cartridges in question were of only medium velocity – and I found them to be particularly effective. I have also found 1 ounce (28 grams) loads to be much more effective on game than more traditional, lighter, ones when using a 20 or 28 bore at home (though there were differences in felt recoil between brands).

What is the bottom line for UK conditions? For a 12 bore over and under, or modern, 2¾-inch/70-mm chambered, side by side, no-one is going to go far wrong with 1¹⁄₁₆ ounces (30 grams) of 5 or 6 shot in most situations. For snipe, woodcock, partridge and smaller, 7 shot may be considered; 5 shot would certainly be my choice for rabbit and 4 shot for really high birds and hares. In older 2½-inch/65–67.5-mm chambered side by sides, my general preference would still be for 1 ounce (28 or 29 grams) moderate pressure loads of 5 or 6 shot.

An ideal load for high pheasants in a modern gun would be 1⅛ ounces (32 grams) of 4 shot or 5 shot. If pushed at moderate velocities, 1¼ ounce (36 grams) loads can also be relatively comfortable to shoot and may offer a real world benefit in some testing situations. However, 1½ ounce (42 grams) loads, not to mention 3-inch/76-mm 1¾ ounce (50 grams) loads increase felt recoil very signfcantly. The unusable ballistic gain is not worth the extra pain in most circumstances. Much the same may be said of mighty 3½-inch roman candle loads as developed by Federal.

As far as the smaller bores are concerned – 28, 20 and 16 bore – the modern trend seems to be towards the heavier 1 ounce/28 grams loads. My experience certainly supports this as discussed. For a 28 gauge, ¾ ounce, ⅞ ounce or 1 ounce (24, 25 or 28 grams) will all do the job, but 1 ounce will do it most decisively. For a 20 or a 16 bore, do not lose any sleep over it; use 1 ounce (28 grams) and stop worrying. Heavier payloads are available for the 20 and 16 bore, but offer few real benefits. Really heavy loads, especially when used in light guns, can lead to flinching and may disrupt marksmanship.

It is important to realise in this context that it is not just pellet payload and velocity that affect recoil. The way the cartridge is made is also important. Some case and wad types may reduce felt recoil (for example, paper cases and wads with a significantly compressible middle section). The type of powder, primer, and the assembly routine of the components (e.g. the seating pressure of the wad and the type of crimping employed to seal the case), can all make profound differences with regard to felt recoil. The variables are multiple and complex, the best advice is to experiment and find what suits your gun and you.

An ounce (28 grams) of shot will kill most driven birds but some prefer a slightly heavier payload to boost confidence.

As far as the .410 is concerned – and it is not much of a game gun in my opinion, the standard 2½-inch/65-mm loads these days is 14 grams of 5 or 6 shot. In 3-inch/76-mm (actually 73-mm in the case of most .410s) form the standard British load is 16 grams, and the diminutive 2-inch cartridges – required in some old guns – is normally loaded with only 9 grams of shot (yet, I have still seen high clay birds shot with this tiny load). In all bore sizes, save perhaps for .410 and 28 bore, fibre wads are becoming more popular.* As many shoots now insist on fibre or felt, it simplifies things if you opt for them routinely. Not only are you being 'green and friendly' but you are ensuring that you will not be embarassed by turning up to shoot with unsuitable cartridges.

Choke and Cartridges: Simple Advice for 12 bores

Improved cylinder and half choke used with 1¹⁄₁₆ oz (30 grams) of No. 5 or 6 shot.

Non-Lead Shot

It is now generally illegal to use lead shot for shooting wildfowl and over wetlands but the regulations vary in each of the UK countries.

England and Wales. It is illegal to use lead shot on the foreshore for any purpose, or for shooting ducks and geese anywhere, even if they are on an inland flight pond or farmland. It is also illegal to use lead on certain sites of scientific interest which are listed by Defra.

---

*Recent research by BASC has shown that for most cartridges they produce a pattern that often matches and sometimes surpasses that of plastic cups. This is an interesting result and, no doubt, more work will done to confirm it.

Scotland. It is illegal to use lead shot over most wetlands. These are defined by the Ramsar Convention and, briefly, include areas of fen, marsh, peatland, water and foreshore. You can shoot ducks and geese with lead shot over dry land.

Northern Ireland. Legislation is expected but at the time of going to press no proposals have been published.

Detailed information on all the UK restrictions can be found on the BASC website www.basc.org.uk

The main alternatives to lead are steel (actually iron), bismuth, tungsten matrix (tungsten polymer), tungsten iron and Hevi-shot (a tungsten-tin-iron-nickel alloy). Other substances have been tried, such as copper, tin, zinc and various alloys, but the ones mentioned are most popular. Steel is the cheapest, but because of its light density, possibly the least effective at extended range (especially in the loads available in the UK, which in simple terms are of lower velocity because of International Proof Commission (CIP) proof regulations than those available in the United States).

Steel is hard, not especially kind to guns, and requires that plastic cup wads are used and moderate choke constrictions (otherwise barrels may bulge at the muzzles). Because it does not retain energy as well as lead, it is good advice when using steel shot to opt for a pellet size two increments larger than one would traditionally use for lead. It is also sensible to limit range to 35 yards. Bismuth is similar to lead with regard to weight (though slightly lighter) and therefore its ballistic performance is similar though a size one shot larger may be advised. Early bismuth cartridges had a tendency to shatter. This has largely been overcome by alloying bismuth with tin. Some would still argue that it is not as terminally efficient as lead because not quite as much of the pellet may reach the target (the advocates of bismuth might counter that for any given payload bismuth offers about 10 per cent more pellets). Bismuth has the significant advantage, however, that normal choke and wads may be used. It is probably the most widely used non-lead shot and most reports of its use are favourable.

The tungsten cartridges are all pretty efficient and expensive (as bismuth is). Eley was instrumental in developing tungsten-based polymers with their 'Black Feather' cartridge some years ago but gave up on this to develop bismuth loads instead. Hevi-shot, loaded in the UK by Lyalvale-Express, actually exceeds the ballistic performance of lead (being marginally heavier). The use of tungsten loads in older guns, however, may not be advisable and you should treat it as steel and use plastic wads. If in any doubt check with the cartridge manufacturer.

Cartridges – Relatively Simple Advice for Lead

- For modern over and under 12 bores for general game shooting: 1 1/16 ounce (30 grams), felt or fibre wad, 5 or 6 shot.

- For 2½-inch chambered 12 bore guns: 1 ounce (28 grams) or 1 1/16 ounce (30 grams), 5 or 6 shot.

- For 20 and 16 bores: 1 ounce (28 grams) of 5 or 6 shot.

- For 28 bores: (of medium weight and above) 1 ounce (24-28 grams) of 5 or 6 shot.

- For high, large or especially tough birds, or hares: 4 or 5 shot in any of the above in a *slightly* increased payload – not exceeding 1¼ ounces (36 grams).

Non-lead

Steel: 1⅛ ounce (32 grams) 3 shot for duck on foreshore; 4 shot for flighting; 4 or 5 shot for general game shooting where non-toxic shot is required (i.e. copy the load for lead but increase payload slightly and consider increasing two pellet sizes).

Bismuth: 1⅛ ounce (32 grams) 4 shot on foreshore; 5 shot for flighting duck; 5 or 6 shot for general game shooting (i.e. copy the load for lead but consider going up a pellet size as bismuth is slightly lighter than lead).

Tungsten types: 1⅛ ounce (32 grams) of 4 or 5 shot for duck. For geese, 1³⁄₁₆ ounce (34 grams) 3 shot in 3-inch/76-mm chambered guns only (3½-inch guns and cartridges have also been developed but I have yet to be convinced of their benefits for shooting under British conditions).

Relative Densities

Lead 11.3 • Steel 7.8 • Tungsten matrix 10.8 • Bismuth 9.3 • Tin 7.3

Checklist For Guns, Choke and Cartridges

Does your gun fit?
Is it practically finished?
Are the trigger pulls set between 3 to 5 pounds each, with the second pull a little heavier than the first?
Do top-lever and safety function well?
Does the gun balance somewhere near the hinge-pin?
Do both barrels shoot to the same point of aim?
Is the gun over-choked?
Is the gun 'tight' and in proof?
Are you confident in your cartridges?
Do they suit you and the gun?
Does the pellet size and payload suit the quarry?

BUYING GUNS

Many of us muse over buying a really special gun, or perhaps, pair of guns. Assuming funds are in place, how should one proceed? Old or new, British or Continental, side by side or over and under, 12, 20 or 28 bore? What about the weight, chokes, style of stock, and barrel length? There are, potentially, so many questions. As with shooting, one needs to apply a little method to control the potential chaos. Far too many people end up with the wrong gun whether they are spending £500 or £50,000. Why? We tend to be impulsive. We fail to shop around. We fall victim to fashion. We do not seek out the right advice. This is all to be cautioned against. Buying a gun, especially if one is spending capital sums, is a serious business (it should, of course, be fun as well – but you must not let your heart rule your head entirely).

First, develop a clear plan. It should start with three simple questions:

What sort of shooting am I going to do?
What sort of gun has worked for me in the past?
What is my budget?

Be practical. A special gun must delight your heart and eye, but it should also help you to shoot well. Do not buy something that will handicap you on your average day. You may dream of Devon pheasant or Spanish partridge, but what sort of birds do you normally encounter? Be honest with yourself.

A Holland & Holland Sporter Model with extra finish – modern and magnificent – and it shoots beautifully too.

Double triggers, as seen on another Holland & Holland – in this case the new Round Action side by side – offer instant, fumble-free, choke selection. They are my preference for game shooting, regardless of barrel configuration.

Now we could get very complicated. Let's not. As discussed, if you are buying a side by side, the chances are that a conventional 28-inch, 12 bore, barrelled gun will still serve you best (however, it may be embellished). Weight should be in the range of 6½ pounds to 7 pounds (assuming average stock measurements). On 12 bore over and unders, 28-inch barrels are also to be generally favoured. Weight for the 28-inch stack-barrelled gun should be about 7 to 7½ pounds. Lightweight guns feel fine when being dry mounted, but they recoil significantly more than a medium weight gun in the field. The only people who really have need for 'ultra-lights' are those who do a great deal of walked-up shooting.

If you are especially tall, or intend to specialise in bringing down high birds, or have an interest in using one gun for game and clays, 30-inch barrels may be considered or longer in some circumstances. Long barrels tend to appeal to experienced shots and also to beginners (who will usually be handicapped by them). Twenty-nine- or 30-inch barrels are also just the ticket on 20 and 28 bore over and unders because they improve control. Long barrels on any gun can help those with eye-dominance problems and make a gun feel steadier, but they can also impede swing (especially on heavier 12 bores).

I will not elaborate further on the relative merits of the over and under and side by side, save to note that the stack-barrelled gun with its single sighting plane is an easier gun to point consistently and controls recoil better. The side by side tends to be less complex. It also has a special character. All things being equal, it is a little harder to shoot, but faster to reload.

Wherever your fancy takes you, it is always good advice to try the gun that you intend to buy (or something very similar) before purchase. If you go to a professional shooting ground to do this you will also get good advice on fit and other relevant issues. <u>Never assume that a gun that looks attractive in a magazine illustration or that appears to handle well in a shop will work in the field. Only shooting a gun will tell if it really works for you.</u>

Single or double trigger? With game shooting it does not much matter in most circumstances, although I favour the instant selection of choke available with a double trigger. Avoid old English guns with single triggers. Even the best are prone to breakdown. As far as choke is concerned, after much experiment my advice is this. For general shooting, go for an open first barrel, but a fairly tightly choked second. No one ever went wrong by choosing improved and half, though my own, slightly eccentric, preference in a 12 bore is cylinder and three-quarters and three-quarters and three-quarters in a small-bore.

Now, let us consider the bottom line. Are you buying for investment as well as pleasure? How important is it that you can get your money back? Those buying for investment should always have resale in mind and buy the best London names second-hand but in excellent, original, condition. The guns should be appraised independently if possible. Never forget that buying second-hand guns has all the pitfalls of buying second-hand cars.

The side-plated Beretta EELL – this one a 20 bore – is a desirable gun that holds its value well and offers reliability and good looks.

There are bargains to be had (e.g. non-ejector and ejector boxlocks, and shorter barrelled guns) but be careful and seek advice. Money spent on expert help is well spent. If you are considering a new London gun, a single side by side is not going to cost you much less than £30,000 and is more likely to be in the region of £50,000. Over and unders are even more expensive. In London, it would be hard to find a best gun for much less than £40,000 and the norm amongst the great makers would be about £60,000. Continental guns of good quality begin from about £5k, with best guns costing about half their UK near-equivalent. A new Fabbri over and under – which some judge to be the finest gun in the world – will set you back no less than $150,000 *un-engraved*, however. There are other exclusive Italian makers catching up or exceeding London's finest.

If you are in any doubt go for a plain grade over and under from one of the famous makers in new or near-new second-hand condition. You simply can't go wrong with a 12 or 20 bore Beretta Silver Pigeon, a Browning 4 or 525 or a Miroku Mk 60 or 70. If you want to spend a little more, the Beretta EELL 20 bore offers great looks and excellent function. Perazzi and Kemen 12 and 20 bores also make good game guns – their trigger pulls and well-regulated barrels are appreciated by many experienced shots. AyA guns have a fine reputation for reliability (and the No. 2 sidelock side by side model is especially popular with British game shots). I also like the basic grade sidelock made by Arrieta of Spain. The English-finished AyA No. 1 is a very attractive gun. At a significantly higher price point, I have been impressed by Bosis over and under and side by side guns. Caesar Guerini is a new kid on the block and offers style and value, as does B. Rizzini, Franchi and Rottweil. At the budget end of the market, David Nickerson's Lincoln guns made by FAIR (the arms factory of Isadoro Rizzini – one of several firms owned by members of the Rizzini family making mechanically similar guns) are hard to beat. Bettinsoli also offers some good budget over and under guns, as do Lanber, Laurona and Fabarm.

CLOTHES

I have no intention of being a style guru: wear canary yellow stockings and an emu feather in your hat if you like. But, make sure your clothes are comfortable and offer free movement. I prefer to shoot in a traditional tweed or quillted synthetic vest whenever the opportunity arises; I find vests less restrictive. A thin fleece, or an Army-surplus 'Norwegian' winter-warfare shirt may be worn underneath instead of a pull-over. Jackets for shooting should never be too heavy, and, in both vests and jackets, pockets should be large. If you need to keep really warm, build up layers (i.e. an extra sleeveless vest) rather than bulk. As far as shirts are concerned, natural fibres are to be preferred. But, with outer garments, both man-made and natural fibres can work.

Footwear also warrants special consideration if you want to stay comfortable and shoot well. The high-tech leather and Gore-tex boots coming into fashion (such as those made by Dubarry) are practical and attractive. I also like Brasher Supalite boots for shooting and those in the Musto range. Modern boots like the Supalites and Musto Arncliffe do not require too much breaking in, they have good soles, and their Gore-tex lining ensures that they remain waterproof. I am not a great fan of traditional, large and heavy, boots and brogues with hobnails. I have nothing against better quality, unlined, green wellies though (provided they are worn with decent socks or stockings and are a reasonable fit). Leather-lined wellies are expensive, but comfortable.

This shooter looks well prepared, note cap, muffs, shooting jacket, gun-slip, good sized cartridge bag, decent boots and gaiters.

Other Accessories

Cartridge bags should be practical, with a good mouth, a hinge that will last, and a decent strap. Buy the best you can – the cheap ones are a false economy. I have had one of mine for forty years (bought from the old Harrods gun department for the princely sum of five pounds). Gloves for shooting should be of the highest quality leather. They should be as thin as possible. Hats and caps are a means of personal expression; I have always favoured the out-of-fashion trilby as it looks smart and keeps the rain off one's face and neck. I have an irrational prejudice, however, against some of the wide-brimmed leather hats that seem to have become popular recently. They are functional but ugly. Tweed caps have become the modern tradition – they need to be quite deep at the rear to be practical, however.

When you buy a cartridge bag, buy the best you can. I bought the one on the left from Harrods forty years ago when they had their own gun department. I keep it solely for 20 bore shells.

Much the same applies to gloves, buy the very best; anything else will impede your shooting. These are from David Nickerson.

CLEANING GUNS

All guns should be cleaned after shooting to ensure that they continue to function safely. I observe, nevertheless, that those who shoot fall into two categories. No, I am not talking about *thinkers* and *feelers* again – but those who obsessively clean their guns (and who thus delight gunshop owners as the margin on cleaning accessories materials is much higher than on new guns) and those who neglect the tools of their sport more than they should. I certainly fall into the latter, lazy, category. Gun cleaning has never been an especially exciting prospect for me. No blazing fire, glass of malt and comfortable leather chair as I contentedly polish my barrels. I am always in a hurry to get the chore over with as quickly as possible. Happily, modern mass-produced guns are less prone to corrosion than those of yesteryear. If you have a fine English side by side however, you simply can't neglect it at all – it will rust up in no time. Even modern mass-market guns can rust. Some are notably more prone than others. Browning over and unders, for example – great guns in most respects – were prone to chamber rusting until the introduction of chromed bores and chambers in the latest models.

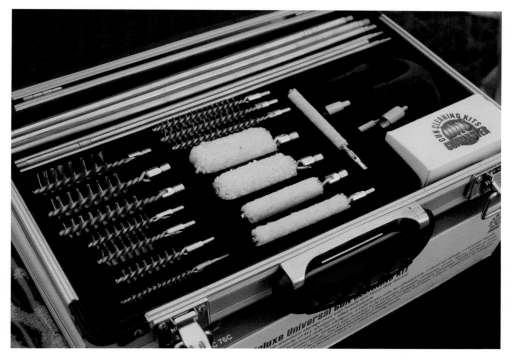

The owner of this cleaning kit will have few excuses. Though my preference is to keep kit simple.

Phosphor bronze chamber and bore brushes. Add another rod with mop and a piece of dowelling for pushing loo paper through the barrels and you have everything that you need to keep your barrels in good condition except for oil.

All guns need regular attention to function well and to increase longevity. As guns become increasingly expensive, it has prompted me to take rather better care of my collection. I have not become a born-again cleaning nut, but I am a little more careful than in years past.

OK where to start? The first (and last) thing to do when cleaning is **to prove the gun unloaded and unobstructed**. It is amazing how many accidents have occurred at home with allegedly unloaded guns. Next, wipe the gun over. Inspect the surfaces before disassembly. The cleaning process may reveal such things as loose screws, barrel dents or missing foresights. In other words, it should not just be considered a cleaning process, but an equipment check too.

For speed and convenience, I suggest having several rods to hand: a conventional rod with a jag attached (if you use patches – I don't); another with a phosphor bronze brush; another with a woollen mop; and a piece of wood dowelling about three and a half feet long (an alternative to a rod with a jag). This may sound excessive but it makes the job much easier. Start the process by pushing plugs of kitchen towel, loo paper or newspaper down and through the barrels (this is where the dowelling comes in useful).

If the gun has multi-chokes, remove them *after* the worst of the muck has been removed – if you take them out earlier you are making work for yourself. Once the choke tubes are removed, wipe them off with loo paper and also use this invaluable material to clean off the threads inside the barrels. In cases of severe fouling you may need to use a brush (did I really mean to say that). Expect to get your hands dirty when mucking around with choke tubes (if it bothers you, wear disposable or plastic gloves).

With the barrel bores and choke tubes more or less clean, address the outer surface of the barrels and the ejector/extractor work. If you are giving the gun a really thorough going over and know how to remove them, take out the extractors. Only do this if you feel confident and have a perfectly fitting turnscrew (assuming one is required). Don't go further – many guns are damaged because over-enthusiastic owners strip them down without the skills required.

The outside of the barrels need as much care as the bores. Special attention is required where the ribs and barrel meet. These areas are especially prone to rusting (ribs on older guns frequently detach or partially detach themselves from the barrels). If you are dealing with a ventilated rib, you may find a feather useful for cleaning under the rib bridges. Pipe cleaners and cotton buds can also be useful for this purpose. If there is rust in the joint between rib and barrel use the sharp end of a pin or needle to get rid of it and spray some aerosol oil into the joint.

Once the barrels are clean on the outside, examine them for dents, bulges and other flaws.* Assuming they pass muster, return to working on the bores. You should continue cleaning until the patch, tow, or paper in use can pass through clean and the interior appears bright. With bores in this pristine state inspect for lingering traces of fouling around the forcing cones and chokes. If they are in evidence you may decide to go back a stage or two. This may entail bringing the phosphor bronze brush into play (which I do not normally use for quick cleaning) and a cleaning agent (for example Youngs '303' or Hoppes No. 9). In really severe cases of fouling you can cork up one end of the barrels and fill them up (carefully) with boiling water. Pour the water out and use a patch soaked with the chosen solvent. Solvents operate much more effectively in heated barrels. Eventually, the barrels should be left dry and bright. Small-bore guns are especially prone to fouling from plastic wads, but a wire brush and some elbow grease will get rid of it eventually.

Cleaning the Action

Do not just wipe the action body over and think that is enough. Get into all the nooks and crannies, e.g. under the top-lever and safety catch slide. Any debris in the visible parts of the action may be removed with the aid of an old toothbrush. As with the barrels particular care should be taken on any bearing surface such as the hinge-pin and knuckle. Several over and under guns of recent manufacture are prone to galling on the knuckle. This is an odd

As well as cleaning inside your action with a toothbrush or similar, make sure you clean (and lubricate) the bearing surfaces of forend iron and action knuckle. Note scraping evident here.

---

*If you see any signs of these <u>do not use the gun</u>: they could cause barrel failure with the risk of serious injury. As soon as possible take the gun to a qualified gunsmith for attention.

A traditional oil finish is the most beautiful and practical of all. It is easily maintained – with an occasional dab of linseed oil mixed with a little turps – and easily repaired (unlike varnish or synthetic finishes).

problem when encountered, one surface seems to drag upon and damage the other. It is tedious to fix and relatively difficult to stop permanently. It is aggravated by dirt and insufficient lubrication. Do not forget to give the forend a thorough cleaning and pay special attention to the bearing surfaces the forend iron that meet the action knuckle.

Finish off the inner surface of the barrels with a very lightly oiled wool mop (or a squirt of aerosol oil followed by a wipe with a mop), and wipe over the actions with a lightly oiled cloth (in either case the smear of oil applied should be so thin as to be just about invisible). A dab of Vaseline or grease may be placed on the knuckle and the hinge-pin or trunnions. The stock may be preserved by rubbing in a dab of boiled linseed. Use all oils sparingly. Excess oil in the action can drip back into the head of the stock, weakening the wood. Excessive oiling may also cause the wood to swell, causing mechanical problems with the lock work.

Condensation is a problem in many centrally heated houses today (and airliner baggage holds) and can lead to severe rusting. A light film of oil on metal surfaces will offer some protection, as will specialist products that can be left in cases or cabinets. Guns should not be stored in hard cases for long periods as these inhibit air circulation. And, always be careful when bringing guns in from the cold to a heated room; the effects of condensation are not always noticed until it is too late.

Final Inspection

Cleaning should always end with a final wipe over with a very lightly oiled cloth and a final check that the gun is unloaded and unobstructed.

Always check your gun for obstructions before loading or when putting it away after shooting.

Simple Advice: Quick Clean

Prove the gun empty. Wipe off the action face, action knuckle and forend iron with loo paper. Remove and wipe off multi-chokes (paying attention to the threads). Tear off a double sheet of loo paper. Crumple it up. Push it through the bore with a cleaning rod or suitable stick. Repeat the process for the second barrel if appropriate. Prove the barrel/s are empty and unobstructed. Assemble the gun. Prove the gun is unloaded and unobstructed. Rub over with lightly oiled cloth. You may find that a 'Bore Snake' a useful accessory to have in the boot of your car or when travelling, it dispenses with the need for rods and patches or paper. If you use one for quick cleaning, don't forget to wipe off the action face as well.

GUN CONTROL

The right to keep and bear arms is enshrined in the Bill of Rights of 1689 (and this is the model for the much more frequently quoted second article of the American Bill of Rights of 1791). The interesting point is that the right to keep and bear arms without impediment, enshrined in English common law until the late Victorian era, is not a colonial invention as many mistakenly believe. In 1870 the requirement for a gun licence was introduced (annual cost 10 shillings) for all those who did not have a licence to kill game. Available from post offices, these licences were no more than a revenue-producing exercise for the Exchequer. The Pistols Act in 1903 restricted handgun sales to those over eighteen. However, serious firearms legislation for rifled weapons did not appear until after World War I, when Revolutionary Socialism and terrorism led to the Firearms Act 1920. This created a nationwide system of controls with Chief Constables given the authority to vet applicants for the new Firearm Certificates (the draconian measures were presented to the public as a simple anti-crime measure, the true reason for their introduction remaining hidden in Cabinet Office documents for many years).

The shooting community have not felt well treated by recent changes to firearms legislation but the issues have been considered for many years.

Part V of the Criminal Justice Act of 1967 created the requirement for a police-issued Shotgun Certificate; this legislation was consolidated in the 1968 Firearms Act (which remains the primary legal instrument for firearms control in Britain). The 1988 Firearms Amendments Act banned revolving shotguns (save muzzle-loaders and 9-mm guns) and shotguns with detachable box magazines. It placed new restrictions on repeating shotguns, limiting their magazine capacity to 2+1 if the owner wished to hold them on a shotgun certificate, required that shotguns be listed individually on the certificate, and increased Chief Constables' powers of refusal.

The 1990s saw the banning of large- and small-calibre handguns after the Dunblane killings in Scotland and saw widespread demonstrations by shooting sportsmen who felt that they had become scapegoats for the ills of society. These demonstrations, which proved sportsmen and their supporters could come onto the streets in great numbers without incident, led directly to the Countryside Rally and later, the even larger, Countryside March and March for Liberty and Livelihood on 18 March 2001. All those who took part in these great events look back upon them with pride and some hope that we may yet stem the tide of anti-shooting prejudice.

APPENDIX 1

Proof

Proof, which involves test firing guns with an especially powerful proof load, was introduced both as means of ensuring public safety and as a form of gun trade protectionism. In the early days of the gun trade, many people who were not gunmakers attempted to make guns. The Gunmakers Company of London was first granted a Royal Charter in 1637 and the Birmingham Proof House was established in 1813 (although there were private proof houses in Birmingham before this date).

The idea of the proof test is to show up any material weakness in the steel. There is an argument that the process of proof testing might weaken a gun, but centuries of experience have proven the efficacy of the present system. The law on proof is extensive. There are Gun Barrel Proof Acts of 1868, 1950 and 1970, and there are also Rules of Proof which supplement the Acts. Examples of recent Rules are those of 1925, 1954, 1986, 1989 and 2006. The 2006 Rules cancelled and replaced those of 1989 and introduced a simplified marking system to avoid confusion over pressure figures.

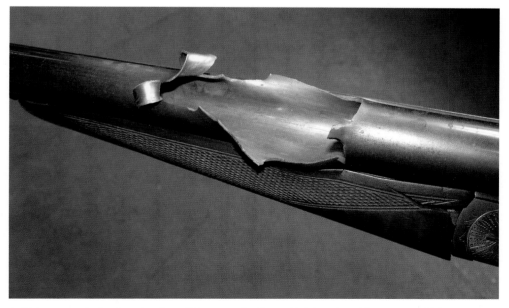

A 12 bore gun in the London Proof House collection which has burst because a 20 bore cartridge was accidentally loaded into the left barrel.

A hammer gun about to undergo proof – note the wheeled cradle. (Photographed at the London Proof House).

The Proof Authorities note: 'The provision of the [Proof] Acts apply to all small arms, whether of present use or future invention, within certain fixed limits of bore size and projectile weight (with the exception of some military arms made for the use of H.M. Forces). Air guns, not being firearms, are specifically excluded... The Proof Acts lay down no small arm may be sold, exchanged or exported, exposed or kept for sale unless and until it has been fully proved and duly marked. The maximum penalty is £5,000 for each offence, but with provision for higher penalties... Arms previously proved and bearing apparently valid proof marks are deemed unproved if the barrels have been enlarged in the bore beyond certain defined limits or if the barrel or action has been materially weakened...'

All new guns sold in Britain have either been proofed here by one of the two proof houses, or by a recognised International Proof Commission (CIP) proof house in another country. (In Britain we recognise the proof marks of: Austria, Belgium, Chile, the Czech Republic, Finland, France, Germany, Hungary, Italy, Russia, Slovakia, and Spain.)

United States and Japan

There is no equivalent of national proof for sporting guns in the United States or Japan, where manufacturers test their own products, thus guns coming into the UK from these countries and others which are not members of CIP must, routinely, be proved in the UK or another CIP country before retail sale. Hence you will note English proof marks on some Japanese-made Browning weapons sold in the UK (although the majority will have Belgian marks instead, as Belgium is generally used as Browning's European distribution centre).

Types of proof

There are basically two types of proof: voluntary Provisional proof, which applies only to shotgun barrels at early stage in their manufacture and compulsory Definitive proof, which covers any arm. There are, however, a number of categories of Definitive proof, namely: Standard Definitive Proof (for standard pressure cartridges), Superior Definitive Proof (for high performance cartridges) and Special Definitive Proof (for special hybrid loads).

Small arms can also be proofed for black powder and high performance steel shot and marked accordingly. We may also note the existence of re-proof which might be applied in any of the above categories (save Provisional proof) and which applies to any gun which falls out of proof (see below).

Standard Definitive Proof is seen on most guns. The information given by definitive and other proof marks will vary depending under which set of rules the gun was proofed. For example, under the old 1925 Rules of Proof a shotgun would not be marked for pressure, but with a maximum shot load in ounces (for example: 1⅛, 1¼ or 1½). Nominal chamber length would be given in inches, the bore size as measured 9-inch from the breech would be given as 12/1 (.740-inch), 12 (.729-inch), 13/1 (.719-inch) and 13 (.710-inch), the nominal gauge would be given in a diamond.

The latest Birmingham proof marks – note metric bore size (18.6mm), 76mm chamber, and 'SUP' – Superior Proof and Fleurs de Lys.

Under the 1954 Rules, the pressure would be given in tons per square inch (e.g. 3, 3¼ or 3½), but this pressure would not be the Minimum Proof Pressure, as marked today, but the Highest Mean Service Pressure. Nominal chamber length would be marked in inches (for example 2½-inch), the bore size as measured 9-inches from the breech, would be marked in thou (for example .729 in a 12 bore), the nominal gauge would appear in a diamond.

Under the 1989 Rules, definitive proof marks in the case of a shotgun will note the Minimum Proof Pressure (e.g. 850 BAR), nominal chamber length in millimetres (e.g. 70-mm in the case of 2¾-inch chambers), the nominal gauge (e.g. 12) in a

Before proofing, the chamber lengths are checked...

...and the bore diameters 9" from the standing breech.

Jeff Darbon at the London Proof House examines a set of barrels.

diamond and, the bore size of the gun as measured in millimetres 9-inch from the breech (in the case of a 12 bore anything from 18.9 down to 18.2). There will also be symbols on barrel and action to indicate that the gun is nitro proved.

The latest 2006 Rules represent a major departure from the previous methods of identifying the pressure to which a shotgun barrel has been tested, in that symbols are now used. For example, loads (such as 1⅛ oz, 1¼ oz) and pressure (whether marked as tons per square inch or in Bar) will not be marked as such. These are difficult to correlate and it is considered that the means by which the Proof Authority obtains the necessary pressures and loadings for proof is of limited academic use, and not much help to the average users of shotguns and purchasers of shotgun cartridges. Therefore, the new system of symbolic marking has been introduced, which means that it will only be necessary for the user to compare the markings on the gun with the markings on the cartridge box to ensure compatibility and safety.

Bore size

For proof purposes bore sizes are measured by plugs. Under the 1925 Rules if a plug gauge of .729-inch diameter but not one of .740-inch diameter would enter the bore to a depth of 9-inch from the breech, that barrel would be marked 12. Under the 1955 Rules the same method was used, but the marking would have been a more immediately informative .729. Under previous Rules of Proof, if the bore was enlarged by 10 thou more than the marked size, it was out of proof. Under current Rules it may be enlarged by only 8 thou (0.2mm) before going out of proof.

Magnum Proof (now superceded by Superior Proof)

Magnum proof is designed: 'to cover loads developing pressures in excess of normal service loads, either as voluntary proof to satisfy a particular requirement or as a compulsory proof where the arm is designed for use with unusually heavy loads' (page 4, *Notes on the Proof of Shotguns & Other Small Arms*, issued by the British Proof Authorities, and available from the London and Birmingham Proof Houses). It was introduced in the late 1960s because Eley introduced a range of high performance, magnum shotgun cartridges. Under previous Rules, a magnum proofed gun would be marked 4 tons per square inch. This referred to the highest mean service pressure. Under later Rules it was marked 1200KG or, more recently, 1200BAR. This refers to the minimum proof pressure. Under the 2006 Rules, guns proved for magnum loads will be marked with the symbol for Superior Definitive Proof.

This covers all calibres from 4 bore down to .410 and with the exception of the 73-mm chamber for .410, all chambers will be 76-mm or longer. Only guns marked as above are suitable for magnum cartridges. For older guns it is recommended that only those with chambers of 3-inch or more, and marked 4.0 TONS or more should fire magnum cartridges. <u>This does assume that these guns are in proof and in good condition.</u>

Remember, if you have any doubts about proof seek out an expert. Never assume cartridges are safe to fire in a gun just because they fit in the chamber.

APPENDIX 2

Buying Guns at Auction

There are many ways to buy a gun: from an established retail shop, from a friend or acquaintance, from a dealer at a country fair, or, most riskily and, arguably, most rewardingly, from an auction. This is not a course of action to take lightly, though, buying second-hand guns as already discussed has all the pitfalls of buying second-hand cars. The highly charged atmosphere of the sale rooms, moreover, amplifies the risk. It is all too easy to get carried away in the heat of the moment.

Time spent in reconnaissance is seldom wasted

Even those who go to sales on a regular basis make mistakes. If you put time into research, prepare yourself and exercise a modest degree of self-discipline, though, buying at auction can offer some good deals.

The gun trade gets a significant part of its stock from auction (though, interestingly, it buys most of it in from people who walk through their doors). If you remain flexible and disciplined with regard to budget, there are some good buys to be had in the rooms (though do not underestimate the peace of mind that comes from buying from a well-established dealer).

Auctions, however, are a lot of fun. Some have a very 'clubby' atmosphere and bring together people of similar interest. They are not only good places to buy guns when you have done your homework and have luck on your side (a factor never to be discounted entirely at auction). They also offer a great environment to improve your knowledge of older guns and related sporting impedimenta. Gun auctions have been described as museums where you are encouraged to handle the exhibits!

Developing a realistic plan

Some might say that you should never go to auction without a specific object, or specific objects in mind. You must consider your sporting or collecting needs carefully and your budget, of course. You should have some idea of what you want. You may even have set your heart on a specific gun. BUT, it would be a counsel of perfection to suggest that you should have tunnel vision with regard to everything else at a sale. One of the joys of attending auctions is that one can bump into something unexpectedly.

Here is more realistic advice: select your auction house (some are better suited to first timers than others), study the catalogue carefully (and if possible recent catalogues of the same and other auction houses as well). And, not least important,

Buying guns at auction is interesting and can offer great value but it has all the risks of buying second-hand cars. Caveat Emptor!

When you handle a gun during a view do not just consider its mechanical condition, but also how much you may need to spend upon it to re-finish it or make it fit you.

Be cool when the bidding starts, don't jump in too early, and don't forget the added cost of 'buyer's premiums' and VAT.

The number of guns on offer can be overwhelming – make sure that you set aside enough time for the view. Don't be afraid to ask the auction staff for assistance or more information.

attend the view with *plenty of time to spare*. This does not mean 30 minutes extra but at least a couple of hours.

Another basic rule – and I confess to breaking it on occasion – is never buy a lot unseen. One of the best shooting guns I have ever owned – a W&C Scott sidelock pigeon gun – was bought in haste from a catalogue description alone. It turned out to be sleeved; I did not read the small print as I listened to the very tempting bidding. I was crestfallen when I examined the gun. Shooting it, happily, put a smile back on my face, but it might have been disastrous. You cannot expect to get a good deal without effort, you might get away with it on occasion, but those who do consistently well from auctions do so because they study the form most carefully.

Be cool

Always set yourself a limit on anything you bid for – don't let adrenaline get the better of you (another counsel of perfection). I recently attended a gun auction where I saw an old glass-ball trap (the forerunner of the clay pigeon trap) sell for about five times what it was worth when a bidding war broke out (one bidder appeared to be bidding it up just for devilment). Frequently one sees silly, frenzied, bidding. Ego, the need to win – call it what you will – can cost you a lot of money.

Here is another pragmatic tip, when you go to the view – and it is very foolish not to do so – examine all the lots you can and make sure that you know exactly what they include (this is especially important in the case of mixed or combined lots). If you are searching for an older gun, *open all the gun cases* (although this is laborious). Don't be afraid to ask questions either. Read the catalogue assiduously. Auction catalogues – new and old – are stuffed with valuable information (and should always be kept with a record of prices achieved).

Seek Assistance

As well as what is printed in the catalogue, other information may be available. This may relate to provenance or condition of the lot. In the case of old shotguns bore-diameters and the wall thicknesses are a *big issue* (like cars, guns can be re-bored – but there are limits to this and they affect both safety and value). The proof status of the gun and its legal category (antique, 'section 2' shotgun or 'section 1' firearm – requiring a firearm certificate with suitable variation – will be stated as matter of routine) but the exact condition of a gun, and, in particular its stock and barrels, will be much harder to determine.

You must assess guns dispassionately and remember that repairs to older guns can be extremely expensive today. Re-barrelling a gun with a famous London name may cost £10,000 or so from the original maker or about half that from an independent out-worker (or, about £1,000 if you opt for sleeved tubes). Restocking – and many guns you see at auction have cracks in the stock – begins from about £1,500 and rises exponentially in the case of London's best. You must learn to walk away on occasion. When you assess an old gun in less than perfect condition, moreover, you must always estimate the cost of renovation (never an easy thing to do – add 50 per cent to whatever rough figure you come up with).

Looking for value

For the sake of discussion, let us say that you are interested in a better quality Birmingham boxlock ejector with an estimate of £700 (the sort of gun that can offer great value at auction). It is the type of gun that you may have seen for about double that amount in gun shops. You like the looks, the engraving looks fine, there is still some action colour and the stock has some good figure but is a little bruised (no great problem). But, should you buy it? This is never an easy question.

You definitely should not buy a gun if there is evidence of it being abused by an incompetent person or if it has been dolled up poorly for re-sale. Nor, should you buy it if the barrels are grossly pitted without sufficient meat for lapping and re-proof. Nor, if they are mirror bright but significantly under 20 thou wall thickness at their minimum point if measured with the proper tools. I have bought guns with bright, recently lapped and un-pitted, bores at 18 thou, but it is always a good thing if there is more metal. When assessing barrels, you must consider even the slightest dent and the state of the blacking. Raising dents and re-blacking may both cause more meat to be lost from the barrels (typically a thou or two).

If the stock is cracked, it is usually good advice to walk away – though some cracks may be repaired. If the stock is too short a recoil pad or extension may be added. That is no great problem either, but may affect value. If the screw heads are spoilt or the trigger guard engraving is worn – I am not usually much bothered if the condition is otherwise reasonable: these things are relatively easy to put right. But, there are a lot of ifs, buts and maybes. It takes experience, and if you do not have it, *good advice*, to buy something that suits you and that will give good service.

Proof

As discussed, this is a complex subject (see Appendix 1). When new, guns are marked with a proof size which allows one to determine how worn they are in the future by using a tool called a bore-micrometer. Typically (with many exceptions) English 12 bore guns measure .729-inch at a point 9-inches from the breech when new. The bores may get enlarged by repair. For example when lifting a dent or removing pitting after which process they may be lapped (re-bored). At some point they will go out of proof. Moreover, bore diameter is not the only issue. The barrel walls may become thinner with wear. At some point they may become dangerously thin. And, safety apart, anything under 20 thou usually reduces a gun's value (because re-barrelling is so expensive as already discussed).

I would normally want to see no more than about 5 thou of enlargement from the last proof size (there are exceptions) and a minimum wall thickness around 20 thou. Some auction houses provide a list of barrel bore diameters and wall measurements as matter of routine, others will provide them on specific guns if requested. A £5,000 Holland or Purdey in the rooms that ends up costing you over £25k when re-stocked, re-barrelled and re-finished may not be the bargain it first appeared.

With cheaper guns, the big problem is that artisan work has become so much more expensive in recent years. With care and caution, you can determine barrel

When buying older guns it is essential that you check the wall thickness of the barrels. Peter Jones looks on as dealer John Farrugia inspects a set of Damascus barrels at a Holt's viewing.

Don't be afraid to use a magnifying glass to check for stock cracks or other faults.

condition. Sometimes, however, a hair-line crack lurks unseen under a lock-plate (just waiting to cost you vast sums of money if the stock breaks right through as a result). I take turn-screws, snap-caps, a bore-light, a small nylon or metal block (for testing strikers and mainsprings), a tape measure and a magnifying glass to all views (though, the turn-screw should only be used with the permission of the staff if you have the skill to use it).

A mental (or actual) checklist should be used every time you look at an older gun with a view to purchase. I rarely buy modern shotguns at auction because you usually find the average Beretta or Browning works out a better buy at your local gun shop or purchased privately. My mind is considering the following twenty odd issues when looking at any old gun:

TWENTY IMPORTANT ISSUES

1) Is the gun in original, worn or re-finished condition?
2) How much action colour is there? Has it been renewed?
3) Is the engraving crisp? Is is original?
4) Is the gun in proof? Has it been re-proofed (if so, to what chamber length, and how much meat is left in the barrels before another re-proof is required)?
5) What are the wall thicknesses? Is there sufficient thickness for safety and future repair?
6) Have the barrels been shortened or has choke been removed?
7) Are the ribs attached to the barrels? (Suspend them, carefully, from a finger by one lump and tap them with a pencil - do they ring or is there a tinny, rattly, sound? – the latter indicates the ribs have come away and require relaying, and, possibly, that there is rust damage to the barrels underneath.)
8) Are there any cracks in the action? (Look with particular care at the area where action face and flats meet.)
9) Is the action face in reasonable condition, has it been welded and refaced? Are you sure?
10) Is the gun 'on the face' or does it require tightening/re-joining? Are there signs of poor quality tightening such as peening of the lumps or action squeezing (guns can be tightened, crudely, in a vice)?
11) Are the strikers and main springs in good condition? (Inspect the striker tips visually and dry fire them against a nylon block.)
12) Does the top-lever spring function? Or, does it feel spongy (in which case it probably needs replacing)?
13) Does the gun have a single trigger? (English single trigger guns are notoriously unreliable – they should usually be avoided.)
14) What ejector system is employed? (Southgate is to be preferred because it is the most reliable and cheapest to repair.)
15) Do the ejectors function? Are they well timed – throwing out both snap caps at the same time?
16) Are there any cracks in the stock? Look *very* carefully.
17) Is the chequering original? Is new chequering honest or is it disguising a repair such as a cracked stock? If the chequering is worn – is there enough wood to re-chequer?
18) Is the wood of butt or forend oil soaked? Are there oil stains on the grip from stock bending?
19) Is the forend complete? (It is a surprisingly expensive job to replace the wood in a forend – almost as much as re-stocking.)
20) Is the gun cased (if so, what else is in it)?

This is quite a list (incomplete though it is). We have not finished yet. There are

An old Webley 700 side by side, the sort of gun that can be bought well at auction – but check the measurements of the barrels and the stock for cracks most carefully. Many guns with other makers' names on the rib are built on Webley & Scott barrelled actions.

A new stock being made for an old gun. This is an expensive job – expect to pay anywhere between £1,500 and £10,000 ((the latter figure is what it would cost to restock a best gun by a top London maker). This is a good quality job on a sidelock and will cost in the region of £4,000 to complete when the cost of wood is added.

Nigel Teague, an ex Rolls-Royce engineer, can fit any gun with his Precision Chokes. This can be a useful means to introduce choke into a gun that has had the chokes opened excessively or which has had the barrels shortened.

Nigel's clever new lining process can restore some 'wall hangers' to shootable condition – this is an 1850s Purdey.

some other real-world considerations. Does the gun have quality (more important than the makers name)? Will the lot attract a lot of interest? Is it really worth spending money on? Do you have someone who can fix it if required? Will the completed gun hold its value?

Seeking Value

Looking at today's market, many note that good quality boxlocks are, generally, undervalued. Non-ejector guns can be ludicrously cheap (they are on offer for £100 or less in many cases). Provincial side locks of quality by lesser known makers (which does not necessarily mean less gun) can be excellent buys too in the range £1-2,000. Old guns by the great makers are not cheap, but guns of the era 1885-1910 can offer wonderful quality and good value.

At the upper end of the market, capital guns – those costing £10-20k or more – can be good value too when you compare them to what a new gun costs. I had the chance to buy a Boss recently made round bar side by side for £20,000 a little while back – a fantastic saving on the new price. Although that sounds a great deal of money I regret not buying that beautiful gun. I do not, however, advise buying Continental shotguns of recent manufacture at auction (unless they are very cheap) – too many people use them and will have a go at the £500-£800 mark – they are better bought privately or from a dealer. There are rifle bargains to be had though – not everyone has the necessary Firearm Certificate.

Using an Agent

A useful alternative to bidding yourself at auction is to use the services of an expert third party to handle your sale-room transactions. This can prevent you getting carried away and buying the wrong gun or paying too much for it. Sadly, a quite surprising numbers of punters buy guns at auction only to return them for sale in the next one.

Buying the wrong gun is, of course, a very expensive mistake; you will have to take the buyer's premium and then a seller's premium on the chin: this could amount to 35 per cent of the purchase price just for trying a gun out for a couple of months. It is also possible that you may not re-sell it for what you paid (rather more likely, than getting lucky in the opposite direction).

A splendid, relatively recent, bar-in-wood Stephen Grant side-lever gun. Treasures like this would star in any sale and will be the museum pieces of the future.

APPENDIX 3

Guns for Pigeon Shooting

Almost any gun may be pressed into service for pigeon shooting. I recommend lighter, shorter-barrelled, guns, because they are easier to handle in the confines of a hide. Semi-automatics and 20 bores can make ideal pigeon guns. The 20 bore not only has handling advantages in the confined space of a hide, but the cartridges are less cumbersome. Several pigeon shooting professionals favour 28 bores (small-bores are especially popular in South America where dove are shot in vast number). I would note, however, that two of our most famous pigeon shots, Will Garfit and Phil Beesley, favour 'old-fashioned', long-barrelled, 12 bore side by sides.

As far as cartridges are concerned a lot of nonsense is talked about armour-plated pigeons. An ounce of 5 or 6 shot will do a perfectly adequate job if it is put in the right place and may prevent your teeth rattling on a big day. Some favour open chokes for pigeon shooting; my own preference is half-choke in a repeater or improved and half in a double 12 (but a bit tighter in a small-bore). Much more important than the degree of choke is having a gun that fits well and that is a natural extension of the hands and eye.

Semi-autos are underrated guns. They are fabulous tools for both pigeon shooting and wildfowling. I also use one when walking up alone.

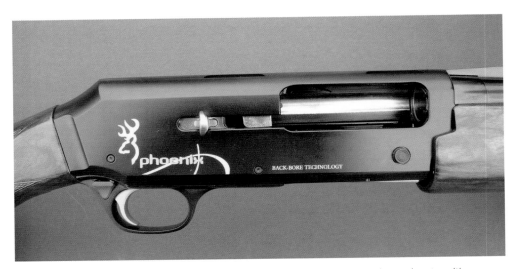

The Browning Phoenix – an excellent, medium-priced, gas-operated, semi-auto with a back-bored barrel.

You must remember to check both chambers and the magazine tube are empty when proving any semi-automatic unloaded. The latter check is often – but most foolishly – forgotten.

Equipment for Pigeon Shooting

Gunshops love pigeon shooters! It seems that hardly a week goes by without some new wonder product for the pigeon-shooting enthusiast. Indeed, it makes one wonder how anyone managed before the days of remote-controlled electronic flappers. Major Coats defiantly refused his publisher a chapter on equipment, supplying only a few paragraphs. His kit included a pocket full of string, secateurs 'to clip off annoying bits in the hide', a billhook 'With a blade man enough for a thickish branch' and an old oil drum 'of a size which fits your particular anatomy comfortably' (which he used as a seat).

We tend to complicate things today, assuming spending is the answer to all problems. Nevertheless, the aspirant pigeon shot needs a bit of advice, or he is likely to fall victim to a silver-tongued salesman. Apart from a decent penknife, a small saw or axe, a seat and a means to carry your cartridges, the most important acquisition will be decoys. There are three main types available: shell; whole body, hard-plastic types (head up and head down); and 'Flexicoys'.

Shell decoys are my favourite because they are easy to pack and light to carry. Moreover, they are good value with twelve (all you will ever need for most purposes) costing around £20. Hard-plastic whole body decoys are strong, but they are bulky. Flexicoys are better; they are a whole body pattern, but made from a rubbery plastic so that they may be compressed for storage. Some decoys tend to become shiny with wear (or wet weather). It is an easy matter to repaint them. Many pigeon shooters add extra (or thicker) white lines to their new decoys to make them more tempting.

Amidst all the gadgets and gizmos on offer today, one really useful device is a cradle attached

A terrifying sight if you happen to be a wood pigeon – Will Garfit. Note the sitting position – Will uses an old office swivel chair by choice.

to a flexible wand. One puts a dead bird in this simple contraption, which appears to hover over the ground as if the bird was just coming in to land. Two or three of these would be a useful addition to any pigeon-shooter's kit. Telescopic hide poles, though quite pricey, are also useful. You can adjust the height of the finished hide so it is just right for you and your gun in that spot. When buying hide poles you will note that most have a clip at the top for securing your camouflage net and a kicker bar on the bottom so that they may easily be pushed into the ground – small but useful features.

Your local army surplus store will be able to supply serviceable nets at a reasonable cost (but make sure they match the ground you are on). If you want to push the boat out, companies like Deben offer a wide range of high-tech camouflage netting (and can also offer the military type at reasonable cost). Anything else? You may feel the urge to acquire lofting poles for placing decoys high in trees. My simple advice is don't bother unless you are roost shooting seriously. They are extra hassle, potentially dangerous as noted, and unlikely to significantly increase the novice's bag.

Much the same may be said of mechanical flappers, which will only scare birds if used improperly. Magnets, however, can be useful.

As for clothes, ex-army camouflage jackets are excellent, practical, attire for pigeon shooting. If you opt for one I do not recommend you buy camouflage bottoms too – it looks too war-like. Jeans or plain green field trousers (also available from surplus stores) look smarter and give a less Rambo-like impression to third parties. A comfortable hat or cap of subdued hue will help shield your face from incomers and a simple gauze mask may be seriously considered – pigeons react instantly to the face of man.

Don't overburden yourself with pigeon-shooting equipment, a few poles and a decent net can create an effective and easily portable hide.

APPENDIX 4
Technical Information
(Reproduced by kind permission of BASC)

Shooting Seasons and Quarry Species
Game[1], Wildfowl – Open Seasons (dates inclusive)

Species	England, Wales & Scotland	Northern Ireland see note[2]
Pheasant	Oct 1st - Feb 1st	Oct 1st - Jan 31st
Partridge	Sept 1st - Feb 1st	Sept 1st - Jan 31st
Grouse	Aug 12th - Dec 10th	Aug 12th - Nov 30th
Ptarmigan (*Only found in Scotland*)	Aug 12th - Dec 10th	----
Blackgame (*Not currently found in NI*)	Aug 20th - Dec 10th	----
Common Snipe	Aug 12th - Jan 31st	Sept 1st - Jan 31st
Jack Snipe	Protected at all times	Sept 1st - Jan 31st
Woodcock	Oct 1st - Jan 31st	Oct 1st - Jan 31st
Woodcock - Scotland	Sept 1st - Jan 31st	----
Duck & Goose - Inland	Sept 1st - Jan 31st	Sept 1st - Jan 31st
Duck & Goose (*below HWM – High Water Mark – of ordinary spring tides*)	Sept 1st - Feb 20th	Sept 1st - Jan 31st
Coot/Moorhen	Sept 1st - Jan 31st	Protected at all times
Golden Plover	Sept 1st - Jan 31st	Sept 1st - Jan 31st
Curlew	Protected at all times	Sept 1st - Jan 31st
Hare (*Cannot be sold Mar 1st - July 31st*)	Moorland & unenclosed land subject to closed season *see next page*	Aug 12th - Jan 31st

Notes for attention
[1] Game licences are still required technically in Scotland, but were abolished in England and Wales on the 1st August 2007.
[2] BASC Northern Ireland can provide further detail on specific isssues relating to Northern Ireland quarry & seasons.

This technical information is for guidance only on laws for taking and killing quarry. If in doubt please always confirm what, where, when and how before pursuing your sport. Approach BASC or consult the BASC members guide for sources of additional information.

Ducks and Geese

Non-lead Shot use for waterfowl in England, Wales and Scotland – See specific technical information from BASC Research Team or Country Offices. Broadly speaking in England and Wales non-lead shot must be used for shooting waterfowl and for use over SSSI (Sites of Special Scientific Interest). In Scotland, non-lead shot must be used over any wetland regardless of quarry.

England, Wales & Scotland: The duck and geese species that can be shot are:

Gadwall	Goldeneye	Pintail	Pochard
Shoveler	Wigeon	Tufted Duck	Mallard
Teal	Canada	Greylag	Pink-footed

White-fronted goose (in England and Wales only).

Northern Ireland: There is no shooting on the foreshore after 31st January, shooting of any wild bird including pest species is prohibited at night. Duck and goose species that can be shot are:

Gadwall	Goldeneye	Pintail	Pochard
Scaup	Shoveler	Wigeon	Tufted Duck
Mallard	Teal	Greylag	Pink-footed
Canada Goose			

The Sale of Dead Wild Birds

The sale of the following dead wild birds is allowed during the period from September 1st - February 28th where present in England, Wales and Scotland:

Pochard	Coot	Shoveler	
Tufted Duck	Mallard	Teal	Pintail
Golden Plover	Woodcock	Common Snipe	Wigeon

The sale of dead wild birds is prohibited in Northern Ireland but the sale of the following species is allowed at all times:

Feral Pigeon	Woodpigeon

The sale of game is subject to the Game Acts, a licence is required to take and/or sell game and is available from main Post Offices.

Bird Pest Species (Note also Appendix 5)

The following fourteen bird pest species may, at the time of writing, be killed or taken by authorised persons at any time under annual open and general licences issued by the respective national government departments. You must ensure compliance with their terms. No individual has to apply for a licence:

Canada Goose[1]	Jackdaw	Magpie	Rook
Carrion Crow	Starling[3]	Woodpigeon	Feral Pigeon
Collared Dove[2]	Jay[2]	Lsr. Black-backed Gull	Gt. Black-Backed Gull
Herring Gull	House Sparrow[3]		

[1]   England only
[2]   Not applicable in Northern Ireland
[3]   Not applicable in England

Mammals Recognised as Pests

The following mammals can be controlled by legally approved methods all year round (see BASC Publication Traps and Snares for more information, for moles see p6 of this booklet):

Fox	Rat	Mice*	Rabbit
Mink	Weasel	Stoat	Feral Cat
Grey Squirrel			

*   All species except Dormouse

Hare Seasons: The Ground Game Act 1880 (Amended 1906) Section 1(3) should be consulted when shooting hares on moorland and unenclosed land in England, Scotland and Wales.

Sunday and Christmas Day Shooting

England & Wales: No game (including hare but not snipe and woodcock) may be shot in any county on any Sunday or on Christmas Day.

No wildfowl may be shot in the following counties on Sunday because orders prohibiting it were made under the Protection of Birds Act 1954: Anglesey, Brecknock, Caernarvon, Carmarthen, Cardigan, Cornwall, Denbigh, Devon, Doncaster, Glamorgan, Great Yarmouth County Borough, Isle of Ely, Leeds County Borough, Merioneth, Norfolk, Pembroke, Somerset, North and West Ridings of Yorkshire.

Northern Ireland (Wildlife Order Northern Ireland): All wild birds are protected on Sunday or on Christmas Day.

Scotland: There are no statutory restrictions on the killing of game on Sunday or on Christmas Day although it is not customary to do so. Wildfowl may not be shot on any Sunday or on Christmas Day.

APPENDIX 5
Bird Pest Species and General Licences 2007
(Reproduced by kind permission of BASC)

History

Many bird species have long been accepted as pests by various government bodies. This was reflected in their inclusion in Schedule 2 of the Protection of Birds Act 1954 and then in Part II, Schedule 2 of the Wildlife and Countryside Act 1981 and the Wildlife (Northern Ireland) Order 1985. This classification allowed authorised persons to kill or take the listed species at any time of the year and by any method other than where prohibited elsewhere in the Act or Order.

Pressure from the European Union to make the UK conform more closely to the 1979 Directive on the Conservation of Wild Birds led to the removal of these 'pest' species from Part II, Schedule 2 of the Wildlife and Countryside Act 1981 and Wildlife (NI) Order 1985.

However, to allow the control of these birds all year round and particularly through the summer period, from January 1993 a system of renewable General Licences has operated. These licences are based on derogation from the 1979 Directive under Article 9. Separate licences were granted for different species and for different reasons, including the protection of crops, livestock and foodstuffs, preservation of public health or air safety, conservation of wild birds, protection of any collection of wild birds and the prevention of the spread of disease.

These licences are issued separately by governmental environment and agriculture departments in England, Wales, Scotland and Northern Ireland and renewed on a regular basis.

The Situation for 2007

Table 1-9 The species that can be controlled under the general licences in England, Scotland, Wales and Northern Ireland

Canada Goose[1]	Jackdaw	Magpie	Rook
Carrion Crow	Starling[3]	Woodpigeon	Feral Pigeon
Collared dove[2]	Jay,[4]	Lsr Black-backed Gull	Gt. Black-backed Gull
Herring gull[5]		House sparrow[3]	

[1] England only
[2] Not applicable in Northern Ireland
[3] Not applicable in England
[4] Removed from the public health/public safety licence in England (WLF 100088) but remains on licence WLF 18 preventing the spread of disease and preventing serious damage to livestock, foodstuffs for livestock, crops, vegetables, fruit, growing timber, fisheries or inland waters; and licence WLF100087 for the purposes of conserving wild birds. No change in Wales or Scotland.
[5] See important note below under England

England

All licences renewed and valid from 1st January until 31st December 2007.

There has been one substantial change to the licences. Jays have been removed from the public health/public safety licence in England (WLF 100088) but remain on licence WLF 18 preventing the spread of disease and preventing serious damage to livestock, foodstuffs for livestock, crops, vegetables, fruit, growing timber, fisheries or inland waters; and also remain on licence WLF100087 for the purposes of conserving wild birds.

There have been a number of changes to the text in the notes sections of the licences. There are two of particular significance.

With respect to the shooting or taking of herring gulls the following note appears: '*The British Ornithologists' Union advises that the Herring Gull (*Larus argentatus*) and the Yellow-legged Gull (*Larus michahellis*) are best treated as seperate species. This licence does not authorise the killing or taking of Yellow-legged Gulls. Yellow-legged Gulls are sometimes confused with Herring Gulls, but are distinct: adult Yellow-legged Gulls have yellow rather than pink legs, a slightly darker grey back than the Herring Gull and a red, rather than yellow, ring around the eye*'.

BASC are fully aware that yellow-legged gulls have been expanding their range from the Mediterranean basin over the last 20 years and that relatively small numbers are now visiting Britain. We are confident that the licensed control of herring gulls does not pose a threat to yellow-legged gulls and the matter will be kept under scrutiny.

With respect to using cage traps the notes have had the following sentence added to the section on rendering cage traps incapable of holding or catching other animals when not in use: *The exact method used will depend on the type of cage trap, but where the door is not fully removed, it must be secured by such means as to prevent accidental operation or unauthorised use.*

Scotland

All licences renewed and valid from 1st January until 31st December 2007.

Northern Ireland

These licences were renewed on 11th September 2006 and are valid until 10th September 2007.

Wales

All licences renewed and valid from 1st January until 31st December 2007.

BASC advise that every person intending to shoot any of the species given in Table 1 read a copy of the licences which relate to the country in which shooting will take place. They must comply with terms and conditions of the licences and their reason why shooting takes place must be supported by the purposes of the licence.

For links to copies of the General licences covering each country go to the BASC website at www.basc.org.uk and click on the 'Shooting' tab and then 'Pest and Predator Control' on the right hand menu.

We would also remind anyone carrying out activities covered by general licences to read the keys points given below.

Key points to remember

1. You are not required to carry copies of the general licence that apply for your activity. However, we advise that you obtain the relevant copies, using the weblink above.

2. You must have the permission of the landowner, preferably in writing, to shoot over their land.

3. In carrying out your activity your prime objective must meet at least one of the criteria for which the relevant licence is issued, such as: the prevention and spread of disease, the prevention of serious damage to livestock, food stuffs, food stuffs for livestock, crops, soft fruits, commercial woodlands and inland fisheries.

4. The terms of the licence state that the 'authorised person' has to be satisfied that non-lethal methods of control such as scaring are either ineffective or impracticable. Here are some points to consider:

    •   When decoying or walking up it is important to realise that pigeons are a highly mobile species and target vulnerable crops as and when they ripen and can vary their flightlines throughout the day. It would be ineffective and impractical to set up any stationary deterrent such as a scarecrow or scaregun as the pigeons would merely move field.

    •   When roost shooting you are targeting birds that routinely damage crops in the area but who are distributed over such a large area that is ineffective and impractical to shoot them on site or employ non-lethal methods.

    •   When controlling corvids for the protection of wild birds you should be aware that the target species are highly intelligent and quickly become used to static or mechanical scaring techniques, which therefore become ineffective and impractical. Because of this shooting, or the use of static or mobile cage traps, is an effective method of control for territorial birds such as magpies, jays, rooks and crow.

5. There is no obligation on you to have tried non-lethal methods before you commence shooting.

6. There is no obligation on you to keep any records of your pest control activities

although it may be to your advantage to maintain records as evidence.

> For links to copies of the General licences covering each country of the United Kingdom go to the BASC website at www.basc.org.uk and click on the 'Shooting' tab and 'Pest and Predator Control' on the right-hand menu.

APPENDIX 6

Useful Contacts

ORGANISATIONS

**British Association For Shooting &
Conservation (BASC)**
Marford Mill
Rossett
Wrexham
LL12 0HL
Tel: 01244 573000
Fax: 01244 573001
www.basc.org.uk

Clay Pigeon Shooting Association (CPSA)
Edmonton House
Bisley Camp
Brookwood
Surrey
GU24 0NP
Tel: 01483 485400
Fax: 01483 485410
www.cpsa.co.uk

Game Conservancy Trust (GCT)
Fordingbridge
Hampshire
SP6 1EF
Tel: 01425 652 381
Fax: 01425 655848
www.gct.org.uk

Guntrade Association Ltd (GTA)
PO BOX 43
Tewkesbury
Gloucestershire
GL20 5ZE
Tel: 01684 291868
Fax: 01684 291864
www.guntradeassociation.com

GUN IMPORTERS

Alan Rhone Ltd (Blaser and Krieghoff)
6 Coed Aben Road
Wrexham Industrial Estate
Wrexham
LL13 9UH
Tel: 01978 660001
www.Alanrhone.com

ASI (AyA)
Alliance House
Snape
Saxmundon
Suffolk
IP17 1SW
Tel: 01728 688555
Fax: 01728 688950
www.a-s-i.co.uk

Guerini UK
Unit 18
Small Heath Trading Estate
Armoury Road
Birmingham
B11 2RJ
Tel: 0121 772 1119
Fax: 0121 772 8118

**BWM Ltd (Browning, Winchester and
Miroku)**
Unit 2 Moorbrook Park
Didcot
Oxfordshire
OX11 7HP
Tel: 01235 514550
E-mail: sales@bwmarmsltd.com

Edgar Bros (CZ and Remington)
Heather Close
Lyme Green Business Park
Macclesfield
Cheshire
SK11 0LR
Tel: 01625 613177
Fax: 01625 315276
www.edgar-brothers.co.uk

Garlands Ltd (Fausti and Weatherby)
Raddle Lane
Edingale
Tamworth
Staffordshire
B79 9JR
Tel: 01827 383300
Fax: 01827 383360
E-mail: info@garlands.uk.com
www.garlands.uk.com

GMK Ltd (Beretta, Benelli, Franchi,
Lanber, and some Arrieta models)
Bear House
Fareham
Hampshire
TO15 5RL
Tel: 01489 579999
www.gmk.co.uk

Mike Meggison (Kemen)
Kelbrook Shooting School
The Shooting Lodge
Foulbridge
Colne
Lancashire
BB8 7QH
Tel: 01282 861632
Mob: 07831 351960
www.kelbrookshootingschool.co.uk

David Nickerson (Tathwell) Ltd
(Lincoln – FAIR – and Ugarfechea)
Bolingbroke Road
Fairfield Industrial Estate
Louth
Lincolnshire

LN11 0WA
Tel: 01507 610084
Fax: 01507 608557
www.ukhunting.com

Ruag Ammotec UK Ltd (Perazzi and
Rottweil)
Upton Cross
Liskeard
Cornwall
PL14 5BQ
Tel: 01579 362319
Fax: 01579 364033
www.ruag.co.uk

Viking Arms Ltd (Ruger, Merkel, and
Fabarm)
Summerbridge
Harrogate
North Yorkshire
HG3 4BW
Tel: 01423 780810
Fax: 01423 781500
www.vikingarms.com

Webley Ltd
Universe House
Key Industrial Park
Planetary Road
Willenhall
West Midlands
WV13 3YA
Tel: 01902 722144
Fax: 01902 722880
www.webleyandscott.co.uk

GUN MANUFACTURERS

E.J. Churchill Ltd
Park Lane
Lane End
High Wycombe
Bucks
HP14 3NS
Tel: 01494 883227
Fax: 01494 883733
www.ejchurchillgunmakers.com

Holland & Holland
31-33 Bruton Street
London
WI5 6HH
Tel: 0207 499 4411
Fax: 0207 408 7962
www.hollandandholland.com

J. Purdey & Sons
Audley House
57-58 South Audley Street
London
WIK 2ED
Tel: 0207 499 1801
Fax: 0207 355 3297
www.purdey.com

J. Roberts & Sons (Gunmakers) Ltd
(also importers of Bosis, Arrizabalaga and
Rizzini guns)
22 Wyvil Road
London
SW8 2TG
Tel: 0207 622 1131
Fax: 0207 627 4442
www.jroberts-gunmakers.co.uk

William Evans
67a St James Street
London
SW1A 1PH
Tel: 0207 493 0415
Fax: 0207 499 1912
www.williamevans.com

RETAIL SHOPS

Avalon Guns
191 High Street
Street
Somerset
BA16 0NE
Tel: 01458 447505
Fax: 01458 840020
www.avalon-guns.com

Chris Potter Guns
2-6 Grover Street
Tunbridge Wells
Kent
TN1 2QB
Tel: 01892 522208
www.gun.co.uk

Elderkin & Sons
Spalding
Lincolnshire
TN11 1TG
Tel: 01775 722919
www.elderkin.co.uk

Kennedy Gunmakers (also importers of
Fabbri, Piotti, Bertuzzi, Desenzani,
Perugini & Visini, and Arrieta)
The Old Armoury
Bisley Camp
Brookwood
Surrey
GU24 0NY
Tel: 01484 486500
Fax: 01483 486580
www.kennedyguns.com

Ladd Guns & Sports
Downes Mill
Exeter Road
Crediton
Devon
EX17 2PW
Tel: 01363 772666
www.laddsguns.com

Litts
Unit 3
Maesglas Retail Estate
Newport
South Wales
NP20 2XF
Tel: 01633 250025
www.litts.co.uk

May of London
21/23 Cherry Tree Rise
Buckhurst Hill
Essex
I99 6EU
Tel: 0208 504 5946
Fax: 0208 505 6664
E-mail: trueshot@btinternet.com

Saddlery & Gunroom (also importers of
Mossberg [sic], and manufacturers of
Hushpower sound-moderated guns)
368 Main Road
Westerham Hill
Westerham
Kent
TN16 2HN
Tel: 01959 573089
Fax: 0195 575590
www.saddleryandgunroom.co.uk

Sportsman Gun Centre
7 Dartmouth Road
Paignton
Devon
TQ4 5AA
Tel: 01803 558142
Fax: 01803 550722
www.sportsmanguncentre.co.uk

York Guns Ltd (also importers of Baikal,
Mossberg, Zabala and Investarms)
Camsey House
Foxoak Park
Common Road
Dunnington
York
YO19 5RZ
Tel: 01904 487180
Fax: 01904 487185
www.yorkguns.co.uk

PROOF HOUSES

Guardians of the Birmingham Proof
House
The Gun Barrel Proof House
Banbury Street
Birmingham
B5 5RH
Tel: 0121 643 3860
Fax: 0121 643 7872
www.gunproof.com

Worshipful Company of Gunmakers
London Proof House
The Proof Master
The Proof House
48 Commercial Road
London
E1 1LP
Tel: 0207 481 2695
www.met.police.uk/firearms-
enquiries/proof1.h+m

CARTRIDGE MANUFACTURERS

Eley Hawk Ltd
Selco Way
First Avenue
Minworth Industrial Estate
Sutton Coldfield
West Midlands
B76 1BA
Tel: 0121 352 3272
Fax: 0121 352 3288
E-mail: sales@eleyhawkltd.com

Gamebore Cartridge Compay
Great Union Street
Hull
HU9 1AR
Tel: 01482 223707
Fax: 01482 325225
www.gamebore.com

Hull Cartridge Company
Buntoft Avenue
National Avenue
Kingston-Upon-Hull
HU5 4HZ
Tel: 01482 342571
Fax: 01482 346103
www.hullcartridge.co.uk

Lyalvale Ltd (Express)
Express Estate
Fisherwick
Nr Whittington
Lichfield
WS13 8XA
Tel: 01543 434400
Fax: 01543 434420
E-mail: sales@lyalvaleexpress.com

CHOKE SPECIALISTS

Teague Precision Chokes
Edinburgh Way
Leafield Industrial Estate
Corsham
Wiltshire
SN13 9XZ
Tel: 01225 811614
Fax: 01255 811 555
www.teaguechokes.co.uk

Briley Manufacturing Inc. (UK Agent: Chris Potter Guns – see retail shops section)
1230 Lumpkin Road
Houston
Texas
77043
USA
Tel: 001 713 932 6995
Fax: 001 713 932 1043
www.briley.com

Seminole Chokes & Gunworks
049 US
1 Mims
Florida
32754
USA
Tel: 001 (800) 980 3344
     001 (321) 383 8556
www.seminolegun.com

SHOOTING SCHOOLS

Braintree Shooting Ground
Fennes Estate
Fennes Road
Bocking
Braintree
Essex
CM7 5PL
Tel: 01376 343900
www.clayhouseshootingschools.com

E.J. Churchill Shooting Ground
Park Lane
Land End
High Wycombe
Bucks
HP14 3NS
Tel: 01494 883227
Fax: 01494 883733
www.wwsg.org.uk

Gleneagles
The Gleneagles Hotel
Auchterarder
Perthshire
Scotland
PH3 1BR
Tel: 0800 389 3737
     01764 662231
Fax: 01764 662134
www.gleaneagles.com

Holland & Holland Shooting Ground
Ducks Hill Road
Northwood
Middlesex
HA6 2SS
Tel: 01923 825349
Fax: 01923 836266
E-mail: shooting.ground@hollandandholland.com
www.hollandandholland.com/shooting

Michael Yardley
c/o Braintree Shooting Ground
Tel: 07860 401068
E-mail: yardleypen@aol.com

The Royal Berkshire Shooting School
Pangbourne
Berkshire
RG8 8SD
Tel: 01491 672900
Fax: 01491 671966
www.rbss.co.uk

West London Shooting Ground
Sharvel Lane
West End Road
Northolt
Middlesex
UB5 6RA
Tel: 0208 845 1377
Fax: 0208 842 1493
www.shootingschool.co.uk

SPORTING AGENTS

E.J. Churchill Sporting
Grindsback House
69 Oxford Road
Banbury
Oxon
OX16 9AJ
Tel: 01295 277197
Fax: 01295 268651
E-mail: sporting@ejchurchill.com
www.ejchurchill.com

Roxtons
25 High Street
Hungerford
Berkshire
RG117 0NF
Tel: 014488 683222
Fax: 01488 682977
www.roxtons.com

MAGAZINES AND PERIODICALS

Shooting Gazette
PO BOX 225
Stamford
Lincolnshire
PE9 2HS
01780 485350

Sporting Gun
IPC Magazines Ltd
Kings Reach Tower
Stamford Street
London
SE1 9LF
Tel: 01780 481077
www.sportinggun.co.uk

Sporting Shooter
The Mill
Bearwardean Business Park
Wendens Amdo
Essex
CB11 4GB
Tel: 01799 544246
www.sportingshooter.co.uk

Shooting Times
IPC Magazines
Kings Reach Tower
Stamford
London
SE1 9LF
Tel: 0207 267 5000
www.shootingtimes.com

The Field
IPC Magazines
Kings Reach Tower
Stamford
London
SE1 9LF
Tel: 0207 261 5000
www.thefield.co.uk

AUCTIONEERS

Holt's Auctioneers
Church Farm Barns
Wolferton
Norfolk PE31 6HA
Tel: 01485 542822
Fax: 01485 544463
E-mail: enquiries@holtandcompany.co.uk
www.holtandcompany.co.uk

Sotheby's
34-35 New Bond Street
London W1A 2AA
Tel: 020 7293 5000
Fax: 020 7293 5989
www.sothebys.com
or www.gavingardiner.com
(Tel: 01798 875300/07831 645551 –
Gavin is an associate of Sotheby's and
acts as their gun expert)

Christie's
8 King Street,
St. James's
London SW1Y 6QT
Tel: 020 7839 9060
Fax: 020 7839 1611
www.christies.com

Bonhams, Knightsbridge
Montpelier Street
London SW7 1HH
United Kingdom
Tel: 0207 393 3900
Fax: 0207 447 7401
www.bonhams.com

Southams
8 Market Place
Oundle
Northamptonshire
PE8 4BQTel: 01832 273565
Fax: 01832 272077
E-mail: sales@southams
www.southams.com

Scotarms Limited
The White House
Primrose Hill
Besthorpe
Newark
NG23 7HR
Tel: 01636 893946
Fax: 01636 893916
www.scotarms.co.uk

SELECTED BIBLIOGRAPHY

Adams, Cyril, and Bradon, Robert, *Lock Stock and Barrel*, Safari Press, Longbeach, CA, 1996.

Arnold, Richard, *The Shooters Handbook*, revised edition, Nicholas Kaye Ltd, London, 1965.
  Pigeon Shooting, Kaye & Ward, London, 1979.

Batley, John, *The Pigeon Shooter: A Complete Guide to Modern Pigeon Shooting*, Swan Hill Press, Shrewsbury, 1996.

Boothroyd, Geoffrey, *The Shotgun: History and Development*, A & C Black, London, 1985.

Brander, Michael, *The Game Shot's Vade Mecum*, Adam & Charles Black, London 1965 (also published as *A Concise Guide to Game Shooting* by the Sportsman's Press in 1988).

Brister, Bob, *Shotgunning: The Art and the Science*, Winchester Press, Tulsa OK, 1976.

Brown, Nigel, *London Gunmakers*, Christie, Mason & Woods, Ltd, London, 1998, and updated and published as *British Gunmakers*, Volume One, Quiller Publishing, 2004.

Burrard, Major Sir Gerald, *The Modern Shotgun* facsimile of 3rd Edition, Vols 1, 2 & 3, Ashford Press, Southampton, 1985.

Chevenix Trench, Charles, *A History of Marksmanship*, Longman, London, 1972.

Churchill, Robert, *How to Shoot: Some Lessons in the Science of Shotgun Shooting*, Geoffrey Bles, London, 1925.
  Game Shooting, Michael Joseph Ltd, London, 1955.

Coats, Archie, *Pigeon Shooting*, 2nd Edition, Andre Deutsch Ltd, London, 1986.

Cox, Nicholas, *The Gentleman's Recreation*, facsimile 1677 edition, E.P. Publishing, Wakefield, Yorks, 1973.

Crudgington, I.M. and D.J. Baker, *The British Shotgun* Vol. 1 1850-1870, Barrie & Jenkins Ltd, London, 1979.

Davies, Ken, *The Better Shot*, Quiller Press, London, 1992.

Downing, Graham, *Shooting for Beginners: an Introduction to the Sport*, Swan Hill Press, Shrewsbury, 1996.

Garfit, Will, *Will's Shoot Revisited*, Sportsman's Press, Shrewsbury, 2005.

'Gough Thomas' (G.T. Garwood), *Gough Thomas's Gun Book*, A & C Black, London, 1969.

Greener, W.W., *The Gun and Its Development*, 9th Edition, Cassell & Company, London, 1910.

Harris, Clive, *The History of the Birmingham Gun Barrel Proof House*, 2nd Edition, Guardians of the Birmingham Proof House, Birmingham, 1949.

Hastings, MacDonald, *The Shotgun*, David & Charles, Newton Abbot, Devon, 1981.

Hawker, Col. Peter, *Instructions to Young Sportsmen in all that Relates to Guns and Shooting*, 8th Edition, Longman, Orme, Green & Longmans, London, 1838 (first printing, 1816).
   The Diary of Col. Peter Hawker 1802-1853, Richmond Publishing Co., 1975 (facsimile of 1893 edition).

Jackson, Anthony, *So You Want to Go Shooting*, Arlington Books Ltd, London, 1974.
   Classic Game Shooting, Ashford, Southampton, 1990.

Lancaster, Charles (H.A. Thorn), *The Art of Shooting*, 1889, 14th facsimile edition, The Field Library, Ashford Press, Shedfield, Hampshire, 1985.

Marchington, John, *The Complete Shot*, 1981.
   The History of Wildfowling, A & C Black, London, 1980.

Markland, George, *Pteryphlegia: or the Art of Shooting Flying*, London and Dublin, 1727.

'Marksman', *The Dead Shot*, 4th edition, Longmans and Green, London, 1896 (1st Edition 1866).

Martin, Brian, *The Great Shoots*, Sportsman's Press, Shrewsbury, 2007.

Page, Thomas, *The Art of Shooting Flying*, fourth edition, Norwich, 1785.

Payne-Gallwey, Sir Ralph, *High Pheasants in Theory and Practice*, Longmans Green & Co., London, 1913 (also available in Richmond Publishing facsimile).

Purdey, T.D.S. and Purdey, Captain J.A., *The Shotgun*, The Sportsman's Library, Adam & Charles Black, London, 1938.

Ruffer, Maj. J.E.M., *The Art of Good Shooting*, David & Charles, Newton Abbot, Devon, 1972.

Ruffer, Jonathan Garnier, *The Big Shots: Edwardian Shooting Parties*, Debrett's Peerage Ltd, Tisbury, Wiltshire, 1977.

Shotgun and Cartridges for Game and Clays, 5th Edition, edited by Nigel Brown, A & C Black, London, 1970.

Shute, Robin, *Shooting Flying, A Bibliography of Shooting Books 1598-1950*, Foxbury Press, Winchester, 2001.

Stanbury, Percy, and Carlisle, G.L., *Shotgun Marksmanship*, 4th Edition, Stanley Paul & Co., London, 1986.

The British Shotgun Vol. 2 (1871-1890) Ashford, Buchan & Enright, Leatherhead, Surrey, 1992.

Trevelyan, G.M., *English Social History*, 2nd edition, Longmans, Green and Co., London, 1946.

Walsingham, Lord and Payne-Gallwey, Sir Ralph, *Shooting Field and Covert*, 2nd Edition, Longmans, Green and Co., London, 1887.
    Shooting (Moor and Marsh), Longmans, London, 1893.

Worshipful Company of Gunmakers, *A Short Account of the Worshipful Company of Gunmakers* 1637-1979, London, 1979.

Yardley, Michael, *Gunfitting the Quest for Perfection*, Sportsman's Press, London, 1993 (re-published in revised form 2007 by Swan Hill Press).
    Positive Shooting, Crowood Press, Marlborough, Wiltshire, 1994.
    The Shotgun: A Shooting Instructor's Handbook, Sportsman's Press, London, 2001.

Others

The Various Rules of Proof and Proof Acts.

Periodicals.

Shooting & Conservation BASC members' magazine).
The Field, Shooting Gazette, Shooting Times, Sporting Gun, Gunmart, Countryman's Weekly and Sporting Shooter.

The very first illustration of wingshooting in an English book – Richard Blome's
Gentleman's Recreation *of 1686.*

INDEX

It's the crack. Shooting is a very social sport. If you don't enjoy the day what's the point?